McGraw-Hill Education

Essential Vocabulary

for the

TOEFL® Test

Also by Diane Engelhardt:

McGraw-Hill Education

Essential Vocabulary

for the
TOEFL® Test

Diane Engelhardt

New York Chicago San Francisco Athens London Madrid
Mexico City Milan New Delhi Singapore Sydney Toronto

1 2 3 4 5 6 7 8 9 10   RHR/RHR   1 0 9 8 7 6 5 4

ISBN   978-0-07-182710-2 (book and CD set)
MHID   0-07-182710-2 (book and CD set)

ISBN   978-0-07-182702-7 (book alone)
MHID   0-07-182702-1 (book alone)

e-ISBN 978-0-07-182703-4
e-MHID   0-07-182703-X

Library of Congress Control Number 2014937221

TOEFL® and TOEFL iBT® are registered trademarks of Educational Testing Service (ETS), which was not involved in the production of, and does not endorse, this product.

McGraw-Hill Education products are available at special quantity discounts to use as premiums and sales promotions or for use in corporate training programs. To contact a representative, please visit the Contact Us pages at www.mhprofessional.com.

This book is printed on acid-free paper.

CONTENTS

INTRODUCTION

Words, words, and more words

The exact number of words in the English language can be estimated at anywhere between 171,476 words in current use (contained in the *Oxford English Dictionary*, Second Edition) and 988,968 words according to Global Language Monitor. Among these are:

- Nouns, adjectives, adverbs, and verbs
- Exclamations, interjections, and prepositions
- Prefixes and suffixes
- Words of foreign origin
- Obsolete and archaic words
- Academic words
- Technical, medical, scientific, legal, business, and other jargon that is specific to a particular field or subject matter
- Slang and colloquial words, and idiomatic expressions

From these numbers you can conclude that learning vocabulary is a daunting task. And it is particularly daunting to learn vocabulary for the TOEFL® test, when vocabulary questions make up only a small part of the whole test. Keep in mind, however, that you need vocabulary not only to answer vocabulary questions but also to understand what you read and hear and to express your ideas in writing.

Vocabulary is directly related to academic performance. A study conducted in 1998 by Douglas Bors and Tonya Stokes concluded that college students with larger vocabularies achieved higher grades, produced better quality writing, and were able to process information more readily and better than those with less advanced vocabulary skills. Clearly, the greater your vocabulary, the higher your chances of succeeding in college and university courses.

So where do you start? Which words do you learn? How do you learn them? And how do you remember all of them?

Acquiring vocabulary is not something you can do overnight. In fact, it is a long-term process that requires dedication and strategy. Therefore, the first thing you should be prepared to do is learn vocabulary for life, not just for the TOEFL® test. Any word that you may learn specifically to pass the TOEFL® test can be used, most likely, anywhere outside the classroom, and anytime besides during the test. So don't think that you are wasting your time learning new words. Remember: a language without a broad vocabulary is like a house without rooms or furniture.

About this book and recordings

McGraw-Hill Education: Essential Vocabulary for the TOEFL® Test has been written to help you learn vocabulary for the TOEFL® test and, more important, for life. How will it do that?

- By helping you recognize words from their function and form
- By helping you use a dictionary and thesaurus
- By helping you figure out the meaning from context, which is the most useful method as you probably don't walk around with a dictionary in your back pocket (You probably have a cell/mobile phone, but that is not necessarily the best substitute for a reputable paper dictionary. I know—I'm old-fashioned!)
- By showing you how to organize the vocabulary you learn so that you can find it quickly and learn faster through associating words in clusters or with images
- By giving you some strategies on how to remember the words you learn
- By letting you hear vocabulary in action with sample texts

This book is divided into three parts:

1. Learning and understanding vocabulary
2. Building and recording vocabulary
3. Using vocabulary

The book contains approximately

- 417 academic words that can be found in the Academic Word List (or AWL, Coxhead 2000)*
- 404 advanced words that are not in the AWL
- 183 words or phrases that are commonly used in a campus context

---

*The Academic Word List, developed by Averil Coxhead, contains English words that occur with high frequency in academic contexts. This list is discussed in more detail in Chapter 4.

These words are contained in Appendix A. Of course, the words indicated by **bold type** throughout the book do not include all the words you may need, but they can be considered indispensable for college and university students. In other words, you will be learning these words for good and practical reasons, not just for the sake of filling your brain. As well, the book contains plenty of useful incidental vocabulary that you will pick up as you work through it.

Each chapter contains a variety of exercises that

- Reinforce what you have learned
- Give you an opportunity to practice using specific words
- Assist you in developing a "feeling" for the English language

Chapters 8 and 9 each contain ten short academic reading texts with vocabulary exercises that demonstrate how vocabulary is realistically used. Whereas readings on the TOEFL® test average 700 words, these texts range from 200 to 350 words. The twenty total texts thus provide a range of vocabulary in different contexts. What you see in this book is what you can expect to encounter in lectures, reading, and assignments. Chapter 10 focuses on campus vocabulary and offers short dialogues featuring idiomatic language relating to life at a North American university. Appendix B gives sample journal pages and entries, which will help you recall and memorize words that are new to you. In Appendix C you will find lists of the most useful prefixes and suffixes.

The audio recordings contain

- Native English speakers reading the sample texts found in Chapters 8–10
- 70 minutes of content

The audio content is tied to the text and is indicated by this graphic: .

A word of caution. As you will discover, this book does not include translations, nor does it suggest relying on translations as a learning strategy. There are good reasons for this.

- To become proficient in a language you have to think in it; translating only encourages a dependency on your native language and will not help you at all in college or university.
- Translating wastes time, and in college you can't afford to waste time on unproductive activities that don't contribute to success.
- Translating, particularly direct translating, can yield inaccuracies and some strange and unintelligible results.

How to use this book

Everyone learns differently, and we all have our own particular weaknesses or problems. Therefore, the best method to use is the one that *works for you*!

Here are a few points to keep in mind.

1. You don't necessarily have to work through the book from front to back, or go through each chapter in chronological order. Start with a chapter that interests you or covers some aspect of vocabulary acquisition that you have a problem with.
2. Skip what you already know and focus on what you don't know.
3. Consider this book a guide, and apply what is useful to you. If you don't like vocabulary journals, don't make one. If flashcards work better for you, then go for it. Again, pick and choose what works for you.

Final word

In the end you must do three things to improve your vocabulary:

1. Practice.
2. Read.
3. Think!

I wish you success on the TOEFL® test and in your studies.

Acknowledgments

I thank my editor, Holly McGuire, for her guidance and resourcefulness, and my husband, Erich, for his constant support.

PART

1

Learning and understanding vocabulary

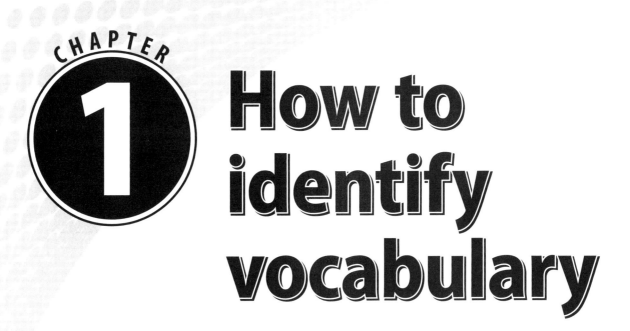

CHAPTER 1
How to identify vocabulary

Objectives

To identify words according to their part of speech and function in a sentence or question

To recognize prefixes and suffixes that form nouns, verbs, and adjectives

Parts of speech

For purposes of building vocabulary, it is necessary to study three main types of words: nouns, verbs, and modifiers—more commonly known as adjectives and adverbs.

Nouns

Nouns are words that refer to a person, place, thing, class, concept, quality, or action. Nouns can be compared to the bricks, stone, and boards with which we construct buildings. Without nouns in a sentence, no one will know what you're talking about.

Verbs

Verbs are the mortar, nails, and screws that hold a sentence together and give it meaning. Some verbs express actions, while others indicate a condition, occurrence, process, or state of being.

Adjectives and adverbs

Adjectives and adverbs are descriptive words. To continue with the comparison, they differentiate one building from another.

Prefixes and suffixes

English words consist of three components: stem, prefix, and suffix.

Understanding prefixes and suffixes can help you figure out the meaning of unfamiliar words. Prefixes change the meaning of the root word—for example, making it negative as in *dis*organization, *ir*regular, *un*tie. Suffixes change the part of speech—for example, work (verb) into work*er* (noun) or work*able* (adjective). Suffixes can indicate negative or positive, size, location, time, and order or number.

(Creating one list of *all* English prefixes and suffixes is difficult, but Appendix C lists the most useful for your purposes in building a vocabulary for the TOEFL® test. The bibliography lists useful websites that discuss prefixes and suffixes.)

Nouns

Nouns can be identified by both their function and their position in a sentence, and by specific prefixes and suffixes that are added to the stem.

Dis + organiz(e) + *ation*

Com + mit + *ment*

Nouns are also frequently preceded by *a* or *the*. Most nouns in English take the plural ending *s* or *es*.

FUNCTION
- To identify the performer of an action—that is, *Who* or *What* the sentence or question is about
- To identify the direct or indirect object of an action—that is, to *Whom* or *What* an action is directed
- To identify the object of a preposition
- To form compound nouns in which one noun describes another—that is, *What kind of* thing or person is referred to in the sentence

    Example: library book, photocopier

- To function as a predicate noun or subjective complement—that is, a noun that refers back to the subject

    Example: John is an excellent student.

POSITION IN A SENTENCE

- Generally, nouns as the subject of a sentence appear at or near the beginning of a sentence.
- Nouns as the object of a sentence immediately follow the verb or preposition.
- Predicate nouns immediately follow the verb.

EXERCISE 1-1

Find the nouns in the following sentences.

1. The report unleashed a controversy concerning the future of the planet.
2. Even identical twins with the same genetic makeup are distinct in their thoughts, feelings, and behavior.
3. The majority of people have always lived simply, and most of humanity still struggles on a daily basis to eke out a meager existence under dire circumstances.
4. Remote-controlled robots are indispensable in space and underwater exploration, military reconnaissance, and search-and-rescue operations.
5. At the Stanford Research Institute in California, a team of researchers programmed a small adult-sized robot named Shakey to sense colored blocks and wedges with an onboard camera, and to push them around a carefully constructed set of rooms.

EXERCISE 1-2

Fill in the blanks with a suitable noun.

1. The _____ read a/an _____ about

    _____.

2. A/an _____ of _____ conducted

    _____ into _____.

3. According to the _____, several _____

of _____ originated in the _____ of

_____ around the _____.

4. Many _____ have made precise _____ designed to

test the _____ of _____ and _____.

5. In _____ one of the most important _____

of _____ was the _____ posed by

_____.

Common prefixes

In addition to being added to nouns, prefixes can also be added to verbs and adjectives to retain or change their meaning.

EXERCISE 1-3

For each prefix, select the correct meaning from the following list. (*Note:* Some prefixes may have the same meaning.) The answers can be found in a dictionary. Then, using a dictionary, find word examples for each prefix. One example for each prefix is provided for you.

extreme, more than normal	one	two
distant	apart, not, opposite	out, previous
against, opposition	between, among	not, in the process of
related to light	twice	small
bad, wrong	before, preceding	around
new	half, partly	many
false	too little, below	across, beyond
under, low, nearly	thousand	exceeding, external
over and above	below normal	self
more than, above	not connected with	million, large, great
	apart, through, across	of the earth

with, jointly, completely   forward, in advance,   outer, too much
three   favoring   the converse of, inside
together with   after   beyond, extreme
again, back, down

	Prefix	Meaning	Examples
1.	an	_____	anarchy, _____
2.	ante	_____	anteroom, _____
3.	anti	_____	antithesis, _____
4.	auto	_____	automation, _____
5.	bi	_____	biculturalism, _____
6.	circum	_____	circumstance, _____
7.	co	_____	coworker, _____
8.	com	_____	communication, _____
9.	con	_____	confidence, _____
10.	counter	_____	counteroffer, _____
11.	di	_____	diameter, _____
12.	dis	_____	disfigurement, _____
13.	ex	_____	exposition, _____
14.	geo	_____	geology, _____
15.	hyper	_____	hyperventilation, _____
16.	hypo	_____	hypoglycemia, _____
17.	in	_____	inability, _____
18.	inter	_____	interference, _____
19.	kilo	_____	kilometer, _____
20.	mal	_____	maltreatment, _____
21.	mega	_____	megacity, _____

Prefix	Meaning	Examples
22. mini	_____	mini-mall, _____
23. mis	_____	misconception, _____
24. mono	_____	monogamy, _____
25. multi	_____	multiculturalism, _____
26. neo	_____	neofascism, _____
27. non	_____	nonconformist, _____
28. out	_____	output, _____
29. over	_____	overachiever, _____
30. photo	_____	photography, _____
31. poly	_____	polygamy, _____
32. post	_____	postdoctorate, _____
33. pro	_____	production, _____
34. pseudo	_____	pseudonym, _____
35. re	_____	reevaluation, _____
36. semi	_____	semicircle, _____
37. sub	_____	subculture, _____
38. super	_____	superpower, _____
39. sur	_____	surname, _____
40. tele	_____	telephone, _____
41. trans	_____	transportation, _____
42. tri	_____	trimester, _____
43. ultra	_____	ultrasound, _____
44. under	_____	undergraduate, _____
45. uni	_____	university, _____

EXERCISE 1-4

Add prefixes to the following roots to make nouns. First try to do this exercise *without* consulting a dictionary.

1. action _____

2. communication _____

3. flation _____

4. function _____

5. gram _____

6. culture _____

7. formation _____

8. cess _____

9. graph _____

10. duction _____

Noun-forming, or nominal, suffixes

Certain suffixes can be added to the end of a verb or an adjective to form a noun, or to the end of a noun to form the title of a person. Some examples:

Verb-to-noun conversion: appear + ance, impress + ion, argu(e) + ment
Adjective-to-noun conversion: dark + ness, negativ(e) + ity, desolat(e) + ion
Noun-to-noun conversion: art + ist, politic(s) + ian, cash + ier

Note: Often spelling problems arise with the use of suffixes. This can be addressed with the use of a good dictionary, a grammar book, or an academic writer's guide.

EXERCISE 1-5

For each suffix, select the correct meaning from the following list. (*Note*: Some suffixes may have the same meaning.) The answers can be found in a dictionary. Then, using a dictionary, find word examples for each suffix. One example for each suffix is provided for you.

state of being, condition	state, quality condition of, belief/practice	having, pertaining to, like
growth (*med.*)		state of being
action, state of being	the act of	action, result
action, condition	place where	pertaining to
domain, condition	study of	agent or performer
person who	quality, result, relating to	inflammation (*med.*)
product, part		

	Suffix	Meaning	Example
1.	age	_____	damage, _____
2.	al	_____	denial, _____
3.	acy / cy	_____	democracy, _____
4.	an	_____	artisan, _____
5.	ance / ence	_____	disturbance, permanence, _____
6.	ant / ent	_____	servant, _____
7.	er / or	_____	worker, auditor, _____
8.	ary / ery / ory / ry	_____	cannery, dormitory, _____
9.	dom	_____	kingdom, _____
10.	ian	_____	electrician, _____
11.	ic / ics	_____	economics, _____
12.	ism	_____	capitalism, _____
13.	ist / yst	_____	catalyst, _____
14.	ite	_____	sulfite, _____

15. itis _____ dermatitis, _____

16. ity / ty / y _____ responsibility, novelty, _____

17. ive _____ sedative, _____

18. ment _____ government, _____

19. ness _____ kindness, _____

20. ology _____ psychology, _____

21. oma _____ carcinoma, _____

22. ship _____ friendship, _____

23. sis _____ osmosis, _____

24. sion / tion /ation _____ erosion, election, naturalization, _____

25. ure _____ exposure, _____

EXERCISE 1-6

Add the correct suffixes to the following root words to make them into nouns.

Note:

- When a root word ends in a vowel, the last letter is omitted.
    Example: inflated / inflation
- Some consonants and vowels will change, so use a dictionary to check your spelling.
    Examples: assume / assumption   specify / specification
                      receive / reception   acquire / acquisition

1. art _____

2. commence _____

3. revolve _____

4. Christian _____

5. restrict _____

6. constitute _____

7. individual _____

8. environmental _____

9. interpret _____

10. illegal _____

11. elect _____

12. occur _____

13. compute _____

14. available _____

15. wise _____

16. appendix _____

17. consequent _____

18. injure _____

19. participate _____

20. slave _____

21. good _____

22. kin _____

23. close (v.) _____

24. obstetrics _____

25. reside _____

26. secure _____

27. emphasize _____

28. publish _____

29. adequate _____

30. commit _____

Practice

Scan any kind of text (textbook, newspaper article, story) and underline all the nouns. Circle the prefixes and suffixes. As you read, be aware of how the nouns function in the sentence. Are they subjects, objects of verbs and prepositions, or predicate nouns?

Verbs

Nouns are either singular or plural, and verbs change to agree with the subject. In English, unlike many other languages, these inflections are minimal. Verbs consist of parts that change in form according to the time the action took place (verb tense) and according to whether they are positive, negative, or interrogative.

In English there are regular and irregular verbs that can be recognized by their principal parts: base form, past tense form, past participle, and present participle.

EXAMPLES

Regular verb   look / looked / looked / looking

Irregular verb   come / came / come / coming

Verbs are either transitive (they take direct objects) or intransitive (they take indirect objects). Transitive verbs can appear in either the active or the passive voice.

EXAMPLES

Active   Shakespeare **wrote** *Hamlet.*

Passive   *Hamlet* **was written** by Shakespeare.

Verbs put ideas into motion. Without verbs, we could not express our thoughts with much clarity, and it would require a considerable amount of guesswork to decipher what it is we mean to say.

FUNCTION

- Verbs indicate **action** or **state of being**. They tell us what the subject is doing / does / did, etc., and what effect one person or thing has on another.
- Verbs **link** the components of a sentence and **establish relationships**.
    Example: This explanation sounds reasonable.

Certain verb forms, such as infinitives, gerunds, and participles are known as *verbals*.

EXAMPLES

Infinitives: to write, to advertise

Gerunds: writing, advertising

Present participles: writing, advertising

Past participles: written, advertised

(Note that gerunds and present participles look the same, but as you will see from the following examples, they function differently.)

Verbals can also function as nouns, adjectives, and adverbs, as in the following examples.

- Verbals functioning as nouns
    Seeing is believing.
    To become rich and famous has always been John's dream.
- Verbals functioning as adjectives
    The panel reviewed the published report.
    Rising interest rates generally lead to falling stock prices.
- Verbals functioning as adverbs
    The team went to the island to study the local flora and fauna.

POSITION IN A SENTENCE

- Verbs always appear after the subject.
- Infinitives and gerunds functioning as nouns appear in the same positions as any other nouns.
- Verbals functioning as adjectives and adverbs appear before or following the word or phrase they modify.

EXERCISE 1-7

Identify the verbs and verbals in the following sentences.

1. The report unleashed a controversy concerning the future of the planet.
2. Even identical twins with the same genetic makeup are distinct in their thoughts, feelings, and behavior.
3. The majority of people have always lived simply, and most of humanity still struggles on a daily basis to eke out a meager existence under dire circumstances.
4. Remote-controlled robots are indispensable in space and underwater exploration, military reconnaissance, and search-and-rescue operations.
5. At the Stanford Research Institute in California, a team of researchers programmed a small adult-sized robot named Shakey to sense colored blocks and wedges with an onboard camera and to push them around a carefully constructed set of rooms.

EXERCISE 1-8

Fill in the blanks with a suitable verb.

1. The professor _____ an interesting lecture.

2. Recently the new students _____ for their classes and _____ with their academic advisors.

3. Wilkins easily _____ a job in his profession because he _____ from Harvard.

4. What _____ you about your time in public school?

5. Further research into restriction enzymes _____ that once an inserted gene _____ by its host organism, it _____ when cells _____.

Verb-changing prefixes

As in the case of their use with nouns, prefixes can change the meaning of verbs and the root forms of verbs. Some examples:

Verb conversion: dis + appear, mis + understand, under + estimate

Root form conversion: sup + press, re + press, com + press

EXERCISE 1-9

For each verb-changing prefix, select the correct meaning from the following list. (*Note*: Some prefixes may have the same meaning.) The answers can be found in a dictionary. Then, using a dictionary, find word examples for each prefix. One example for each prefix is already provided for you.

having, covered with, cause	together with	do the opposite of
reverse, reduce, remove	earlier, before	before
away, out	between, among	bad, wrong
surpassing, exceeding, external	too much	across, beyond
before, forward, for	too little	again, back
under, lower	into, on, near, toward	

Prefix	Meaning	Examples
1. be	_____	befriend, _____
2. co	_____	cooperate, _____
3 con	_____	confide, _____
4. de	_____	decrease, _____
5. dis	_____	disconnect, _____
6. e / ex	_____	eject, exceed, _____
7. fore	_____	forewarn, _____
8. in	_____	ingest, _____

9. inter _____ interfere, _____

10. mis _____ misunderstand, _____

11. out _____ outdo, _____

12. over _____ overpay, _____

13. pre _____ predict, _____

14. pro _____ provide, _____

15. re _____ reread, _____

16. sub _____ subsist, _____

17. trans _____ transport, _____

18. under _____ undersell, _____

EXERCISE 1-10

Add all the correct prefixes to the following stems to form verbs.

1. act _____

2. cur _____

3. duce _____

4. duct _____

5. form _____

6. fer _____

7. fuse _____

8. scribe _____

9. sist _____

10. struct _____

Verb-forming suffixes

Suffixes can be added to the end of a noun or an adjective to make a verb. Since there are only a few of these suffixes, they are easy to learn. Some examples:

Noun-to-verb conversion: beaut(y) + ify, computer + ize, liquid + ate

Adjective-to-verb conversion: pur(e) + ify, equ(al) + ate, dark + en

EXERCISE 1-11

For each verb-forming suffix, select the correct meaning from the following list. (*Note*: Some suffixes may have the same meaning.) The answers can be found in a dictionary. Then, using a dictionary, find word examples for each suffix. One example for each suffix is already provided for you.

cause, make   make

change, become   action

Suffix	Meaning	Examples
1. ate	_____	duplicate, _____
2. en	_____	weaken, _____
3. er / or	_____	wonder, clamor, _____
4. esce	_____	acquiesce, _____
5. ify / fy	_____	purify, _____
6. ise / ize	_____	legalize, _____

EXERCISE 1-12

Add the correct suffix to each of the following nouns and adjectives to form a verb.

1. revolution _____

2. short _____

3. public _____

4. simple _____

5. union _____

6. violence _____

7. minimal _____

8. visual _____

9. anticipation _____

10. moist _____

Practice

Scan any text (textbook, newspaper article, story) and underline all the verbs and verbals. Circle the prefixes and suffixes. As you read, be aware of how the verbs function in the sentence. Do they express an action or a state of being? Do they take direct or indirect objects? Are they in the active or passive voice?

Adjectives and adverbs

Adjectives can be nondescriptive (these, my, some, thirty) or descriptive words that give additional information, such as size, color, shape, nature, quality, and number. Adjectives answer the questions: *Which, What kind of, Whose, How many, How much.*

Adverbs provide information about manner, time, place, direction, cause, purpose, result, and degree. Most adverbs are formed by adding *-ly* to an adjective, although there are a few common and familiar exceptions (fast, hard, etc.). Adverbs answer the questions: *How, When, Where, Why, How often, How long, To what degree.*

Note: Sentences do not necessarily require adjectives and adverbs. In fact, too many descriptive words make writing—and speech—flowery and detract from the essential message.

FUNCTION IN A SENTENCE

- Adjectives describe nouns.
- Adverbs describe verbs, adjectives, and adverbs.

POSITION

- Adjectives precede the noun they modify.
  Examples: an energy-efficient house, enthusiastic drivers
- In the case of nonaction verbs (be, seem, become, etc.), adjectives appear after the verb.
  Example: The candidate was successful in his application for a scholarship.
- Generally, adverbs appear directly before or after the verb they modify, although they can go anywhere in the sentence. Adverbs that modify adjectives and adverbs usually appear before the word they describe.
  Examples: a moderately priced item, a rapidly advancing technology, a very highly recommended publication

EXERCISE 1-13

Identify the adjectives and adverbs in the following sentences.

1. The recent report unleashed a major controversy concerning the future of the planet.
2. Even identical twins with the same genetic makeup are distinct in their thoughts, feelings, and behavior.

3. The vast majority of people have always lived simply, and most of humanity still struggles on a daily basis to eke out a meager existence under dire circumstances.

4. Remote-controlled robots are indispensable in space and underwater exploration, military reconnaissance, and search-and-rescue operations.

5. At the Stanford Research Institute in California, a reputable team of researchers programmed a small adult-sized robot named Shakey to sense colored blocks and wedges with an onboard camera and to push them around a carefully constructed set of rooms.

EXERCISE 1-14

Fill in the blanks with a suitable adjective or adverb.

1. The _____ student _____ reviewed the

   _____ lecture.

2. Combined with an awareness of the _____ consequences of

   _____ consumerism, _____ people sought to

   reduce _____ consumption of _____ goods and

   _____ energy and to minimize their _____ impact

   on the environment.

3. Sunlight is _____, _____, and _____

   to everyone and more _____ in areas _____ to the

   equator, such as the Sahara Desert.

4. _____ pollution control and _____ water and

   waste management have a _____ impact on human health.

5. Hybrid cars are _____, _____, and

   _____, and some shut off _____ when the car is

   stopped at a traffic light.

Adjective-forming suffixes

Nouns and verbs can be converted into adjectives by adding suffixes to the end of the word. Some examples:

Noun-to-adjective conversion: comfort + able, passion + ate, controvers(y) + ial

Verb-to-adjective conversion: persist + ent, attract + ive, expect + ant

---

EXERCISE 1-15

For each adjective-forming suffix, select the correct meaning from the following list. (*Note*: Some suffixes may have the same meaning or no particular meaning at all.) The answers can be found in a dictionary. Then, using a dictionary, find word examples for each suffix. One example for each suffix is already provided for you.

quality, in the style of	worth, ability	marked by, full of, tending to
resembling, related to	state	having the quality of, relating to
made of	marked by, having	
without, missing	comparative	capability, susceptibility, liability, aptitude
having the character of, almost	superlative	
	kind of agent, indication	quality, relation

Suffix	**Meaning**	**Examples**
1. able / ible	_____	capable, edible, _____
2. al / ial / ical	_____	vocal, spatial, theatrical, _____ _____
3. ant / ent / ient	_____	important, latent, transient, _____ _____
4. ar / ary / ory	_____	circular, stationary, auditory, _____ _____

5. ate   _____ inchoate, _____

6. ed   _____ faded, _____

7. en   _____ woolen, _____

8. er   _____ bigger, _____

9. est   _____ cleanest, _____

10. ful   _____ wonderful, _____

11. ic   _____ classic, _____

12. ile   _____ tactile, _____

13. ish   _____ childish, _____

14. ive / ative / itive   _____ passive, tentative, punitive, _____

_____

15. less   _____ worthless, _____

16. ose   _____ verbose, _____

17. ous / eous /   _____ porous, gaseous, verbose, devious,

ose / ious   _____

18. y   _____ pretty, _____

EXERCISE 1-16

Use the correct suffix with each of the following nouns and verbs to form an adjective.

1. horror _____

2. revolution _____

3. illusion _____

4. imagination _____

5. ceremony _____

6. boor _____

7. penny _____

8. contempt _____

9. greed _____

10. fiction _____

11. sense _____

12. comedy _____

13. drama _____

14. create _____

15. space _____

16. identify _____

17. economy _____

18. nausea _____

19. romance _____

20. infant _____

Adverb-forming suffixes

The most common way to convert an adjective into an adverb is by adding the suffix -*ly*. Some examples:

Adjective-to-adverb conversion: quiet + ly, dutiful + ly, happ(y) + ily

EXERCISE 1-17

For each adverb-forming suffix, select the correct meaning(s) from the following two options. The answers can be found in a dictionary. Then, using a dictionary, find word examples for each suffix. One example for each suffix is provided for you.

in the manner of   marked by

Suffix	Meaning	Examples
1. fold	_____	manifold, _____
2. ly	_____	eagerly, _____
3. ward	_____	forward, _____
4. wise	_____	lengthwise, _____

Prefixes and suffixes that form more than one part of speech

It would, of course, be convenient for language learners if specific prefixes and suffixes were restricted to specific nouns, verbs, and adjectives. Unfortunately, language is not that simple. When in doubt, you will have to rely on the word's meaning in the sentence. Take a look at some of the examples.

PREFIX/SUFFIX	NOUN	ADJECTIVE	VERB
ate	triumvirate	inchoate	activate
ary / ory	canary	stationary	—
ic	cleric	semantic	—
ite	graphite	finite	expedite
ive	elective	sedative	—

Some words can function as both a noun and an adjective.

- Examples: elective, romantic, equivalent

Art is an elective.	The patient is going to have elective surgery.
Don't be such a romantic!	This movie is very romantic.
What is the equivalent of 1 kilometer?	You can buy products of equivalent value online.

Practice

Scan any text (textbook, newspaper article, story) and underline all the adjectives and adverbs. Circle the suffixes.

EXERCISE 1-18

Read the following text about ecotourism and identify the words in the list according to their part of speech. Pay attention to the prefixes and suffixes.

Over the past sixty years the world **has shrunk dramatically** because people can travel farther, faster, and **cheaper** than ever before. Distant **destinations** that once took weeks **to travel** to by ship can be reached in hours by airplane. **Exotic** places that people only used **to dream** of or read about in books are as close as the nearest **travel agency** or online booking service. **Luxurious** locations in the Mediterranean are **affordable**. Exciting adventures in the Amazon or Himalayas are **possible**. Cultural **immersion experiences** for sightseers and **globetrotters** are available all because of one of the world's largest and **fastest** growing industries: tourism.

1. luxurious _____

2. destinations _____

3. has shrunk _____

4. exotic _____

5. dramatically _____

6. to travel _____

7. affordable _____

8. immersion _____

9. to dream _____

10. globetrotters _____

11. possible _____

12. experiences _____

13. travel agency _____

14. fastest _____

15. cheaper _____

Word families

Academic words frequently have related noun, verb, and adjective forms, known as "word families." An example would be *achievement* (noun), *achieve* (verb), and *achievable* (adjective). When learning academic vocabulary in particular, you will find it useful to learn all three forms in order to understand and use them. As you will see, not all words have three derivatives: some may have more, and others only one or none. Although you can make an adjective into an adverb by adding *-ly*, not all adjectives can be used as adverbs.

EXERCISE 1-19

Fill in the blanks with a derivative of the given word. Identify the given word's part of speech according to its prefix and/or suffix. First see how many you can work out for yourself before consulting a dictionary.

	Noun	Verb	Adjective/adverb
1. achieve (_____)	_____	_____	_____
2. incorrigible (_____)	_____	_____	_____
3. innovation (_____)	_____	_____	_____
4. acquire (_____)	_____	_____	_____
5. perceive (_____)	_____	_____	_____
6. research (_____)	_____	_____	_____
7. rigid (_____)	_____	_____	_____
8. secure (_____)	_____	_____	_____
9. induce (_____)	_____	_____	_____
10. conversion (_____)	_____	_____	_____
11. consent (_____)	_____	_____	_____
12. utilize (_____)	_____	_____	_____
13. deviate (_____)	_____	_____	_____
14. stimulate (_____)	_____	_____	_____

15. proliferate (_____) _____ _____ _____

16. venerable (_____) _____ _____ _____

17. procrastinate (_____) _____ _____ _____

18. mediocre (_____) _____ _____ _____

19. aggression (_____) _____ _____ _____

20. hypothesis (_____) _____ _____ _____

21. devious (_____) _____ _____ _____

22. arbitrate (_____) _____ _____ _____

23. condolence (_____) _____ _____ _____

24. exploit (_____) _____ _____ _____

25. justifiable (_____) _____ _____ _____

EXERCISE 1-20

For each of the following sentences, fill in the blank with the correct form of
the academic word from the lettered list. As you do this exercise, focus on the
form and function of the word, rather than the meaning. If you do not know
the word, you can always look it up in a dictionary afterward.

1. It is against the law to _____ against people on the basis of their
   skin color, race, religion, sex, age, or sexual orientation.

   Ⓐ discrimination

   Ⓑ discriminatory

   Ⓒ discriminate

2. Olympic athletes are not allowed to compete if they have been taken
   performance- _____ drugs or substances.

   Ⓐ enhancement

   Ⓑ enhancing

   Ⓒ enhance

3. Your _____ of this poem is quite different from the way that I understand it.

   Ⓐ interpretation

   Ⓑ interpretative

   Ⓒ interpret

4. The pharmaceutical company is hoping to come up with a _____ drug for the treatment of breast cancer.

   Ⓐ revolution

   Ⓑ revolutionary

   Ⓒ revolutionize

5. The recipe _____ the ingredients and the exact amount that you are to use.

   Ⓐ specification

   Ⓑ specific

   Ⓒ specifies

6. Gregor Mendel's experiments with peas were a _____ that changed the course of science.

   Ⓐ revelation

   Ⓑ revealing

   Ⓒ reveal

7. Many significant medical benefits have _____ from the research project.

   Ⓐ emergence

   Ⓑ emergent

   Ⓒ emerged

8. The research project was able to go ahead due to a generous _____ of funding from the government.

   Ⓐ allocation

   Ⓑ allocated

   Ⓒ allocate

9. The military government was criticized in the media for its _____ of basic human rights to citizens.

   Ⓐ denial

   Ⓑ denied

   Ⓒ deny

10. What is the _____ number of students who will be attending college in the new year?

   Ⓐ estimation

   Ⓑ estimated

   Ⓒ estimate

11. Currently solar energy _____ less than 0.1 percent of the electricity produced in the United States.

   Ⓐ constitution

   Ⓑ constituent

   Ⓒ constitutes

12. The Internet has contributed to the rapid _____ of information.

   Ⓐ distribution

   Ⓑ distributional

   Ⓒ distributed

13. Sunlight is most _____ at the equator.

   Ⓐ intensity

   Ⓑ intense

   Ⓒ intensify

14. Economists expect to see a _____ in the global economy by the end of the year.

   Ⓐ recovery

   Ⓑ recoverable

   Ⓒ recover

15. _____ flour is not as healthy as whole-wheat flour.

   Ⓐ Refinement

   Ⓑ Refined

   Ⓒ Refinery

16. Tastes and preferences in music _____ greatly with age.

   Ⓐ variation

   Ⓑ variable

   Ⓒ vary

17. One mile is _____ to 1.6 kilometers.

   Ⓐ equivalence

   Ⓑ equivalent

   Ⓒ equate

18. The law _____ smoking in public buildings.

   Ⓐ prohibition

   Ⓑ prohibitive

   Ⓒ prohibits

19. Most of a country's population tends to be _____ in urban areas.

   Ⓐ concentration

   Ⓑ concentrated

   Ⓒ concentrate

20. The rock band is going on tour to _____ their new CD.

(A) promotion

(B) promotional

(C) promote

21. We _____ your help and everything that you have done for us.

(A) appreciation

(B) appreciative

(C) appreciate

22. During the Cold War the United States and the Soviet Union competed for world _____.

(A) dominance

(B) dominant

(C) dominate

23. Athletes who have visual _____ participate in the Paralympics.

(A) impairments

(B) impaired

(C) impair

24. Propaganda uses various techniques to _____ the truth in favor of a particular political agenda.

(A) distortion

(B) distorted

(C) distort

25. Do you feel _____ when you have to speak in front of a large group?

(A) inhibition

(B) inhibited

(C) inhibit

26. I'm sorry, but could you please _____ your last statement?

Ⓐ clarification

Ⓑ clear

Ⓒ clarify

27. His proposal is going to _____ a lot of discussion.

Ⓐ generation

Ⓑ generative

Ⓒ generate

28. Do you think that producing energy without polluting the environment is _____?

Ⓐ attainment

Ⓑ attainable

Ⓒ attain

29. She has come up with an interesting _____, but can she support it with data?

Ⓐ hypothesis

Ⓑ hypothetical

Ⓒ hypothesize

30. Biodiesel is produced when biomass is _____ into fuel.

Ⓐ conversion

Ⓑ convertible

Ⓒ converted

2 How to use a dictionary and thesaurus

Objectives

To determine the meaning of new vocabulary by using a dictionary and thesaurus

To recognize derivatives and word families (the parts of speech—noun, adjective, verb, etc.—related to the head word)

To identify and use synonyms and antonyms

Choosing a dictionary

In order to build vocabulary, you will need a reputable English-only advanced learner's dictionary. Nowadays most students depend on their cell phones to look up words, and although a cell phone is more fashionable and easier to carry than a book, there's still nothing better than an old-fashioned dictionary for learning words. Why?

- Because using a dictionary requires you to use the alphabet to locate the word, and it reinforces spelling.
- Because scanning a page for a word in a dictionary activates your brain. You have to *think* at the same time as you look for a word.
- Because you learn all forms, or derivatives, of the word in the word family.

- Because as you're scanning the pages and columns, you might come across another useful word.
- Because you can rely on a reputable dictionary, whereas some online dictionaries may provide misleading, inaccurate, or false information—particularly if they rely on translation.
- Because English definitions will provide you with additional words that will add to your vocabulary base and help you express yourself in English.
- Because learner's dictionaries provide extra information on capitalization, punctuation, basic grammar, usage, and writing tips.
- Because when you are writing examinations, you may be allowed to take a paper dictionary with you into the examination room, but a cell phone, laptop, or any other electronic device will not be allowed, so you may as well get used to using a conventional dictionary now.

Types of dictionaries

There are many types of dictionaries, ranging from picture dictionaries to general dictionaries to glossaries specializing, for instance, in technical, medical, commercial, literary, and legal language. There are also British English, American English, even Australian or Canadian English and slang dictionaries, and of course bilingual dictionaries, which are to be used only as a very last resort. (Refer back to the Introduction for a word of caution about translation.) Some publishers such as Oxford University Press publish a combined dictionary and thesaurus, which eliminates the need for two separate books. For prospective college and university students whose first language is not English, an advanced learner's dictionary is the most suitable and has the following advantages:

- Learner's dictionaries are compiled with nonnative speakers in mind to take their needs into consideration.
- Learner's dictionaries focus on function and current usage, and the definitions are easier to understand than those found in standard dictionaries.
- They frequently provide sample sentences to illustrate how the word is commonly used.
- Definitions are given in order of frequency; the more obscure, obsolete, or antiquated definitions are not included.
- They often include collocations—words and phrases that accompany the particular word.
  Example: collocations for *impression* are false / misleading / good / bad/ lasting / distinct, as in *a false impression, misleading impression, good impression*, etc.
- They also show if the word is included in the Academic Word List (AWL)*.

---

*The Academic Word List is discussed in detail in Chapter 4.

There are several publishers of dictionaries, and you need to look for a reputable name. Some of the more recognizable publishers of dictionaries are:

- Oxford University Press
- Merriam-Webster
- Longman
- Cambridge University Press
- Collins
- American Heritage

A college or university bookstore will have a good selection of dictionaries, and of course you can always ask your ESL teacher or tutor.

Most dictionaries are now available online as e-books or on CD-ROM, and they provide additional information, such as synonyms, antonyms, and related words in addition to collocations. In the final analysis, the kind of dictionary you choose is a matter of personal preference. The main point is that you learn, and learn effectively.

Using a dictionary

A 1,000-plus-page tome can be unwieldy, but finding your way around is like learning to navigate the streets of any big city. It takes a little time at first to get used to the layout, but once you get the hang of things, you're on your way.

A dictionary entry consists of:

- The headword
- The part of speech
- Phonetic pronunciation
- Alternative spellings (American or British)
- Forms for irregular verbs
- Irregular plural forms
- Numbered definitions, including subject labels (if the word is associated with a specific field, such as sports or music) and register labels indicating whether the level of language is formal, informal, technical, historical, slang, and so on.
- Word origin (Latin, Greek, etc.)

Depending on the type of dictionary and its scope, the entry can include:

- Synonyms and related words
- Antonyms
- Closely related words with prefixes and suffixes
- Words derived from the headword
- Information about the word's grammatical function
- In which English-speaking region the word is used

EXERCISE 2-1

Using a dictionary, locate the following words. (Consider working with a partner or in a group, and time yourselves to see who can find the word first.)

1. explicit

2. perilous

3. repulse

4. ambiguous

5. fascination

6. violate

7. intrinsic

8. widespread

9. coordinate

10. psychology

TIP

Dictionary definitions tend to be written in formal language. Rather than simply copying down a definition, you should think about its meaning and try to rewrite it, if you can, in words that are more meaningful to you and easier to remember.

Read the following two texts and look up the academic words in **bold print**. Give the part of speech, definition, and word family (e.g., noun, verb, adjective) in the space provided. In the case of words that have multiple meanings, record the definition that fits the context.

Text A: Medical technology

Computer technology has **vast**ly improved medical imaging. Three-dimensional X-rays and computer scans produce detailed **reconstruction**s of **anatomical** parts. High-**resolution** CT (computed tomography) and MRI (magnetic resonance imaging) scans can **detect** tumors and steer radiation, biopsy, or microsurgery with **precision**. Stereotactic **intervention**s, which can be compared to GPS navigation systems, are becoming so **sophisticated** that neurological diseases, such as Parkinson's, can be treated without the need for major brain surgery. HUDs (heads-up **display**s), first developed for military, aviation, and auto-racing purposes, can provide surgeons with an integrated picture of X-rays and **monitor**s so that they do not need to look away from the patient on the operating table. As surface computing develops, doctors will be able to drag information onto a work table as they explore and **analyze** various medical data. **Visualization** techniques that **integrate** pictures, graphics, and data will **enable** doctors to react more quickly to **critical** developments in a patient's condition.

	Part of speech	**Definition**
1. vast	_____	_____
Word family:	_____	
2. reconstruction	_____	_____
Word family:	_____	
3. anatomical	_____	_____
Word family:	_____	
4. resolution	_____	_____
Word family:	_____	

	Part of speech	**Definition**
5. detect	_____	_____
Word family:	_____	_____
6. precision	_____	_____
Word family:	_____	_____
7. intervention	_____	_____
Word family:	_____	_____
8. sophisticated	_____	_____
Word family:	_____	_____
9. display	_____	_____
Word family:	_____	_____
10. monitor	_____	_____
Word family:	_____	_____
11. analyze	_____	_____
Word family:	_____	_____
12. visualization	_____	_____
Word family:	_____	_____
13. integrate	_____	_____
Word family:	_____	_____
14. enable	_____	_____
Word family:	_____	_____
15. critical	_____	_____
Word family:	_____	_____

Text B: The Human Genome Project

The Human Genome Project's **ultimate** goal was to provide **fundamental** genetic information that would lead to the treatment and eventually the **eradication** of many of the 4,000 genetic diseases and **defect**s that **afflict** humans. As diagnostic genetic tests become more sophisticated and **available**, doctors will eventually assemble genetic **profile**s for patients, **determine** their risk for disease, and make **diagnoses** before individuals become sick or are even born. With the **focus** on **prevent**ing disease, doctors can begin to provide genetic counseling to families who want to understand their genetic background and to couples who are planning a family. Advances in computer hardware and software will allow doctors to analyze biological **sample**s more quickly and cost-effectively and to **transfer** the information to a patient's computerized file, which they will then carry with them on a computer chip. On the basis of this information, it will be possible to **predict** an individual's susceptibility to drugs and to environmental **factor**s that are responsible for allergies.

	Part of speech	**Definition**
16. ultimate	_____	_____
Word family:	_____	
17. fundamental	_____	_____
Word family:	_____	
18. eradication	_____	_____
Word family:	_____	
19. defect	_____	_____
Word family:	_____	
20. afflict	_____	_____
Word family:	_____	
21. available	_____	_____
Word family:	_____	

	Part of speech	**Definition**
22. profile	_____	_____
Word family:	_____	
23. determine	_____	_____
Word family:	_____	
24. diagnosis	_____	_____
Word family:	_____	
25. focus	_____	_____
Word family:	_____	
26. prevent	_____	_____
Word family:	_____	
27. sample	_____	_____
Word family:	_____	
28. transfer	_____	_____
Word family:	_____	
29. predict	_____	_____
Word family:	_____	
30. factor	_____	_____
Word family:	_____	

Multiple meanings

As you will discover, many words have multiple meanings and can be used in different contexts. This can be quite confusing when you come upon a word for the first time and find four or more different definitions to choose from. Which one do you learn and which is the most useful? Dictionaries list definitions in the order of frequency in which the word is used, but that does not mean that the other definitions are useless or superfluous. In the case of multiple meanings, you will have to rely on the context in which the word appears, but more about that in Chapter 3.

EXERCISE 2-3

Read the following sentences and choose which of the multiple meanings of the word in **bold type** best fits the sentence.

1. _____ After the *Titanic* collided with an iceberg, all passengers and crew were ordered to **abandon** the sinking ship immediately.

    (A) desert or leave permanently

    (B) give up completely

    (C) make no attempt to resist

2. _____ I have to tell the student that he has not been accepted into the degree program, but I don't quite know how to **approach** the subject.

    (A) come near something in the distance

    (B) go to someone with a proposal or request

    (C) start to deal with in a particular way

3. _____ Apple has invested a lot of money in the **promotion** of its new iPad.

    (A) activity that encourages or supports something

    (B) the publicizing of a celebrity or product

    (C) the action of giving someone a higher position

4. _____ Dormitory rules state that students must turn down the **volume** when listening to music after 8:00 p.m.

    (A) the amount of space occupied by a substance or object

    (B) degree of loudness

    (C) a book forming part of a larger work

5. _____ Martin Luther King was awarded the Nobel Peace Prize for his **significant** contribution to the civil rights movement and the struggle for racial equality.

    (A) important or large enough to be noticed

    (B) having a particular meaning

    (C) having a meaning that is not directly stated

6. _____ Before it can be converted into petroleum, crude oil is **refined**.

   (A) remove impurities

   (B) make minor changes to improve

   (C) cultivate or develop good manners or taste

7. _____ The committee will **pursue** the matter until it comes to a satisfactory conclusion.

   (A) follow in order to catch or attack

   (B) try to achieve a goal

   (C) engage in an activity or course of action

   (D) continue to investigate

8. _____ When Stephen returned home after his first year of college, everyone noticed how **mature** he had become.

   (A) fully grown or physically developed

   (B) like an adult in mental or emotional development

   (C) ready for consumption

9. _____ The objective of this course is to examine the effects of human activity on the **environment**.

   (A) the natural world

   (B) the conditions or surroundings in which a person lives or operates

   (C) the overall structure within which a computer, user, or program operates

10. _____ To prove Darwin's theory of evolution as conclusive and irrefutable, scientists have been searching for the missing **link** between homo sapiens and apes.

    (A) relationship or connection between people or things

    (B) a means of contact or support between two places

    (C) a loop in a chain

Using a thesaurus

Synonyms are words that are similar in meaning. They can be very useful for learning vocabulary, particularly if you can link a new word to a familiar one.

To find synonyms you can refer to a **thesaurus**, which contains primarily synonyms but also provides antonyms (opposites) and lists words according to specific topics—for example, the names of human bones and musical instruments. A thesaurus is organized either alphabetically or in large groups of subjects divided into main categories and numbered. To find the word you're looking for, you need to familiarize yourself with the specific thesaurus's categorization system or refer to the alphabetical index.

Synonyms are listed according to part of speech—noun, adjective, verb, adverb, and interjections. Words are also cross-referenced to other categories. Online versions such as thesaurus.com, for example, provide synonyms for each meaning of a word listed in the order of frequency of use and for different parts of speech.

The problem with synonyms is that although they have similar meanings, they cannot always be used interchangeably. Take the simple word *big*, which can refer to size, build, maturity, importance, ambition, generosity, and popularity. If we look at *big* as referring to size, there are about fifty synonyms, some of which are *large, sizeable, huge, immense, gigantic, spacious, voluminous, whopping, monstrous.* In the case of the following sentence—The man has a *big* nose.—it is possible to substitute *large* but not *spacious* or *voluminous* because these words refer to volume or capacity. *Sizeable, immense*, and *huge* would be an exaggeration, and *gigantic, whopping*, and *monstrous* would be ridiculous, if not insulting.

Synonyms also differ in:

- Tone (formal vs. informal, literal vs. ironic, etc.)
- Grammar (how the word fits into the sentence grammatically)
- Collocations (some words are just never used together)

Therefore, you cannot simply plug in one word for another without first cross-checking with a dictionary. Nevertheless, do not be discouraged. Referring to a thesaurus can help you broaden your vocabulary, particularly for writing purposes, so that you do not use the same words all the time.

EXERCISE 2-4

Using a thesaurus, make a list of synonyms for each meaning of the following words. Also note the part of speech. The main meanings are given in **bold type**.

1. accommodate (_____)

    lodge _____

    hold _____

    help _____

2. bias (_____)

    prejudice _____

    diagonal _____

3. mutual (_____)

    reciprocal _____

4. enhance (_____)

    increase _____

5. predominant (_____)

    main _____

    controlling _____

6. voluntary (_____)

    optional _____

    unpaid _____

7. subsidy (_____)

    grant _____

8. offset (_____)

    counterbalance _____

9. discriminate (_____)

differentiate _____

be biased _____

10. radical (_____)

thorough _____

fundamental _____

revolutionary _____

EXERCISE 2-5

Match the word or phrase in the first column with the correct synonyms in the second column. Give the part of speech for each word.

Synonym

1. _____ commodity (_____)   a. brief, momentary

2. _____ suspend (_____)   b. similarity, parallel

3. _____ investigate (_____)   c. item, material

4. _____ liberal (_____)   d. identical, similar

5. _____ respond (_____)   e. interrupt, discontinue

6. _____ temporary (_____)   f. tolerant, open-minded

7. _____ proceed (_____)   g. logical, reasonable

8. _____ equivalent (_____)   h. answer, reply

9. _____ rational (_____)   i. explore, examine

10. _____ analogy (_____)   j. go ahead, continue

11. _____ prestige (_____)   k. feeble, weak

12. _____ decrepit (_____)   l. rigid, inflexible

13. _____ engender (_____)   m. prediction, clairvoyance

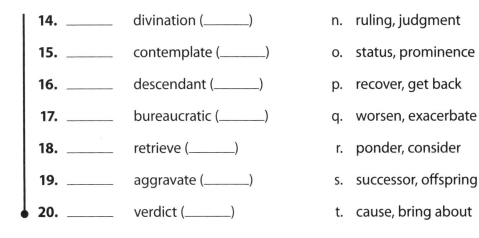

14. _____ divination (_____)   n. ruling, judgment

15. _____ contemplate (_____)   o. status, prominence

16. _____ descendant (_____)   p. recover, get back

17. _____ bureaucratic (_____)   q. worsen, exacerbate

18. _____ retrieve (_____)   r. ponder, consider

19. _____ aggravate (_____)   s. successor, offspring

20. _____ verdict (_____)   t. cause, bring about

EXERCISE 2-6

Identify the word that is *not* a synonym for the listed words. Then give the part of speech for each word. In the case of words that can function as two parts of speech, look at the synonyms for clues. Use a dictionary or thesaurus to check your answers.

1. _____ encounter (_____)

 - Ⓐ meet
 - Ⓑ run into
 - Ⓒ number

2. _____ random (_____)
 - Ⓐ unusual
 - Ⓑ unplanned
 - Ⓒ haphazard

3. _____ undergo (_____)
 - Ⓐ go below
 - Ⓑ endure
 - Ⓒ experience

4. _____ trigger (_____)

   Ⓐ set off

   Ⓑ activate

   Ⓒ damage

5. _____ emerge (_____)

   Ⓐ appear

   Ⓑ join

   Ⓒ surface

6. _____ draft (_____)

   Ⓐ plan

   Ⓑ sketch

   Ⓒ air

7. _____ access (_____)

   Ⓐ entrance

   Ⓑ code

   Ⓒ admission

8. _____ simulate (_____)

   Ⓐ arouse

   Ⓑ pretend

   Ⓒ replicate

9. _____ theory (_____)

   Ⓐ hypothesis

   Ⓑ proof

   Ⓒ premise

10. _____ voluntary (_____)

   Ⓐ optional

   Ⓑ unpaid

   Ⓒ unwanted

11. _____ adverse (_____)

   Ⓐ opposite

   Ⓑ unfavorable

   Ⓒ hostile

12. _____ fortify (_____)

   Ⓐ build

   Ⓑ strengthen

   Ⓒ invigorate

13. _____ dilemma (_____)

   Ⓐ problem

   Ⓑ disease

   Ⓒ predicament

14. _____ coerce (_____)

   Ⓐ pressure

   Ⓑ force

   Ⓒ persuade

15. _____ sacrifice (_____)

   Ⓐ sanctify

   Ⓑ relinquish

   Ⓒ surrender

EXERCISE 2-7

Read the following sentences and choose the word or phrase that is closest in meaning to the words in **bold type**.

1. _____ Tourism growth rates in increasingly popular developing countries are **projected** to surpass 6 percent through to 2020.

   (A) estimated

   (B) expected

   (C) planned

   (D) shown

2. _____ In the early 1900s, experiments with fruit flies **revealed** that chromosomes located in the cell's nucleus were made up of genes.

   (A) reviewed

   (B) proved

   (C) investigated

   (D) showed

3. _____ Religions have **evolved** to relieve people of their fear of death.

   (A) organized

   (B) emerged

   (C) developed

   (D) existed

4. _____ The early 1980s saw a proliferation of biotechnology companies in the fields of agriculture and pharmaceuticals where the potential successes of recombinant DNA promised to be as lucrative as they were **innovative**.

   (A) ingenious

   (B) practical

   (C) exciting

   (D) unusual

5. _____ More poems, stories, and songs have been written about the love between a man and woman than on any other **theme**.

   (A) issue

   (B) subject

   (C) pattern

   (D) argument

6. _____ Car manufacturing is responsible for one in ten manufacturing jobs, but along with car driving it is one of the biggest **contributors** to air pollution and global warming.

   (A) participants

   (B) supporters

   (C) causes of

   (D) answers to

7. _____ DNA evidence makes it difficult for lawyers to defend their clients and for the courts to guarantee a fair trial to anyone **implicated** in a crime on the basis of DNA fingerprinting.

   (A) accused of

   (B) involved

   (C) arrested for

   (D) judged

8. _____ After losing its bid for the Olympic Games, the city **administration** used its plans for the most sustainable games ever by initiating a pilot housing project on a former industrial site.

   (A) residents

   (B) office

   (C) police

   (D) management

9. _____ Sunlight is free, renewable, and available to everyone, **albeit** more plentiful in areas closest to the equator such as the Sahara Desert, which receives in excess of 4,000 hours of sunlight per year.

Ⓐ although

Ⓑ actually

Ⓒ except

Ⓓ occasionally

10. _____ Life is a process of continuous change, and with change comes **conflict**.

Ⓐ contraction

Ⓑ friction

Ⓒ difficulty

Ⓓ violence

11. _____ In large clinics and hospitals, where information is **accumulating** at a phenomenal rate, records are increasingly computerized for legal purposes and ease of access.

Ⓐ spreading

Ⓑ generating

Ⓒ gathering

Ⓓ appearing

12. _____ Even identical twins with the same genetic makeup are **distinct** in their thoughts, feelings, and behavior.

Ⓐ similar

Ⓑ different

Ⓒ special

Ⓓ unusual

13. _____ The invention of machines and their widespread adoption have **transformed** human society.

   Ⓐ changed

   Ⓑ influenced

   Ⓒ modernized

   Ⓓ moved

14. _____ Happiness **motivates** us; without it our lives would be empty and meaningless.

   Ⓐ entertains

   Ⓑ changes

   Ⓒ drives

   Ⓓ fascinates

15. _____ Overshoot is the result of rapid, uncontrolled growth, and when no one responds to the problem, the consequences of overshoot are **collapse**.

   Ⓐ breakdown

   Ⓑ reversal

   Ⓒ stagnation

   Ⓓ destruction

16. _____ The defense used DNA evidence to **ascertain** the defendant's innocence.

   Ⓐ question

   Ⓑ argue

   Ⓒ examine

   Ⓓ establish

17. _____ A group of **rebels** led a successful attack that overthrew the government.

 Ⓐ insurgents

 Ⓑ citizens

 Ⓒ youth

 Ⓓ soldiers

18. _____ In contact sports, a player can be injured **unintentionally**.

 Ⓐ seriously

 Ⓑ accidentally

 Ⓒ slightly

 Ⓓ consciously

19. _____ The report **unleashed** a controversy over the future of the planet.

 Ⓐ published

 Ⓑ opened

 Ⓒ questioned

 Ⓓ let loose

20. _____ You need to provide a **legitimate** excuse for handing in a late assignment.

 Ⓐ legal

 Ⓑ formal

 Ⓒ valid

 Ⓓ credible

EXERCISE 2-8

Substitute the most suitable word from the lists for the words in parentheses in the following two passages.

Passage 1

famous	profitable	attracted
voyages	approximately	prospective
embarked on	ran into	sign

Of the (1.) _____ (estimated) three million shipwrecks on the ocean floor, only the most (2.) _____ (commercially attractive) ones have (3.) _____ (captured) the attention of treasure hunters and salvagers. The most (4.) _____ (legendary) is the RMS *Titanic*. On April 14, 1915, the 882-foot, 46,392-ton luxury liner (5.) _____ (collided with) an iceberg and sank on its maiden voyage from Southampton to New York. Of the 2,223 people on board, 1,517 died in the tragedy. Lost but not forgotten, the *Titanic* and its treasures began to attract (6.) _____ (potential) salvagers in the 1960s, but it was not until the 1980s that Texas millionaire Jack Grimm (7.) _____ (undertook) three separate (8.) _____ (expeditions), only to find no (9.) _____ (trace) of the ship's remains.

Passage 2

came from   shipping   resistance
stimulates   adaptability   total
vital   set up   help
bought and sold   sustenance

An apple a day will keep the doctor away. In winter the antioxidant

vitamin C in oranges and citrus fruits (10.) _____ (boosts)

our (11.) _____ (immune system). Grapes are high in

(12.) _____ (nutrients), vitamins A, C, B6, foliate, flavonoids, and

(13.) _____ (essential) minerals. Pineapple is a natural healer

packed with vitamin C and bromelain, a natural anti-inflammatory. The

list of healthy, healing fruits goes on and on, but when it comes to health,

popularity, (14.) _____ (versatility), and (15.) _____

(overall) usefulness, none can beat the banana.

Bananas (16.) _____ (originated in) Malaysia as early as

2000 B.C., but the first banana plantations were (17.) _____

(established) in China around 200 A.D. In the early 1500s Portuguese and

Spanish explorers introduced bananas to the Caribbean and Americas.

The United Fruit Company, formed in 1899, was responsible for the

commercialization of Latin American bananas and controlled most of the trade

in tropical fruit into the mid-twentieth century. Nowadays bananas are

(18.) _____ (traded) as a commodity and, with the

(19.) _____ (aid) of refrigerated (20.) _____

(transport), bananas have conquered the world.

Antonyms

Antonyms are words with opposite meanings. It is sometimes easier to remember new words if we can associate them with their opposites, particularly if these words generate a strong visual image.

EXERCISE 2-9

Match the following words with their antonyms.

Set 1

1. _____ obvious	a. drawback
2. _____ purchase	b. limited
3. _____ uniform	c. confirm
4. _____ widespread	d. imperceptible
5. _____ acknowledge	e. general
6. _____ benefit	f. deny
7. _____ negate	g. superior
8. _____ specific	h. mild
9. _____ subordinate	i. sell
10. _____ intense	j. variable

Set 2

11. _____ cumbersome   a. latitude

12. _____ extinct   b. defend

13. _____ tangible   c. dignify

14. _____ longitude   d. abstract

15. _____ degrade   e. liberate

16. _____ evade   f. defeat

17. _____ accuse   g. confront

18. _____ conquest   h. existing

19. _____ merchant   i. purchaser

20. _____ oppress   j. manageable

EXERCISE 2-10

Indicate the synonyms (S) or antonyms (A) for the following words.

1. incorporate   _____ integrate   _____ separate

2. diminish   _____ increase   _____ decrease

3. diverse   _____ similar   _____ different

4. secure   _____ safe   _____ endangered

5. sufficient   _____ adequate   _____ meager

6. sole   _____ numerous   _____ single

7. visible   _____ hidden   _____ obvious

8. create   _____ destroy   _____ generate

9. eliminate   _____ include   _____ remove

10. dynamic   _____ energetic   _____ half-hearted

11. advocate _____ supporter _____ critic

12. coincide _____ differ _____ correspond

13. comprehensive _____ all-inclusive _____ limited

14. evident _____ imperceptible _____ obvious

15. implicit _____ inherent _____ explicit

16. integral _____ unified _____ peripheral

17. orient _____ direct _____ confuse

18. preliminary _____ final _____ initial

19. restore _____ bring back _____ abolish

20. unique _____ sole _____ common

21. impoverish _____ enrich _____ deplete

22. safeguard _____ threat _____ protection

23. incompetent _____ inept _____ adept

24. advent _____ arrival _____ disappearance

25. antipathy _____ affinity _____ animosity

26. perpetual _____ everlasting _____ temporary

27. insist _____ relent _____ demand

28. substantial _____ paltry _____ considerable

29. elaborate _____ ornate _____ simple

30. frustrate _____ facilitate _____ exasperate

3 How to understand the meaning of vocabulary from context

Objectives

To determine the meaning of new vocabulary from the context in which it is used

To identify context clues

What is context?

Using a dictionary is the most direct way to find the meaning of a word. However, you can't carry a dictionary around with you all the time, nor do you have time to stop and look up every unfamiliar word. You don't have time, either, to memorize long lists of words, some of which you may never use on a regular basis or come across again. Therefore, the best way to understand vocabulary is to become a "vocabulary Sherlock Holmes" and learn to figure out the word from the evidence at hand—that is, from context.

Context refers to the circumstances or setting in which the word is used. Returning to the Sherlock Holmes theme, context is the crime scene. To be a good vocabulary detective, you have to be able to pick up on all the clues. What are the advantages?

- It does not take a lot of skill to locate a word in a dictionary and copy down the definition. It certainly takes minimal skill to use a cell phone dictionary, but searching for clues and linking them require active thinking and inductive reasoning.
- Thinking reinforces memory: If you have to work for an answer, you are more likely to remember it.
- Understanding context develops global comprehension. Before you can comprehend the details, you need to see the "big picture."
- Stopping to look up every new word interrupts the flow of information. It is not only disrupting but also extremely frustrating, and you are more likely to give up in disgust than if you were to keep going until you reached a point where things start to make sense.

Developing a strategy

Before you start looking for clues, you need to know where to start and how to proceed.

1. Read the text or break it up into smaller, more manageable sections.
2. Determine the main idea from key words.
   - Who or what is the sentence or text about?
   - Which words are related to the main topic?
3. Determine the purpose of the passage:
   - To inform or instruct
   - To explain
   - To describe
   - To relate a series of events
   - To persuade
   - To compare and contrast
   - To stimulate thought or discussion
4. Determine the tone.
   - For the purpose of the TOEFL® test, tone is not an issue, whereas if you are reading fiction, tone is crucial to understanding.
5. Reread.
   - Remember that it is not necessary to understand or know every single word in a passage in order to understand its essential meaning. Rather, what you need to do is to make connections between key words and to use these connections to read between the lines.

TIP

When you travel somewhere for the first time, it's very useful to have a map, but maps, like dictionaries, have their limitations, and there are times when you have to look around you for information to help you find your way. When building vocabulary, you have to become intuitive and develop a "feeling" for English.

EXERCISE 3-1

Read the following texts in sections (separated by /). Identify the main idea and underline all related and important words. Then answer questions 1–3.

Text A

The responsibility for city management lies with municipal governments that derive revenue from service fees and property taxes. To build and maintain infrastructure, cities also depend on federal and state or provincial government payment transfers. / For several years now federal and state governments with high debt loads have offloaded more responsibilities onto already cash-strapped municipalities without providing the necessary financial support. / In addition to funding, city governments need a clear vision for the future and innovative public administrators who can see that vision through. Unfortunately elected public officials are more often bogged down in crisis management and Band-Aid solutions that they hope will get them reelected. / In the end, demands on failing services increase, an outdated infrastructure deteriorates, and poverty spirals downward into crime and despair.

1. What is the main idea?

_____

2. Which words are related to the main idea?

_____

3. What is the purpose of the text?

_____

Text B

From summer to fall, hurricanes—also called typhoons or tropical cyclones—form when hot air, often from the Sahara Desert, races over the Atlantic Ocean. As these columns of hot air spin, they pick up moisture and attract strong winds that bend as the storm travels. / At the center of the rotating storm is the eye, a deceptively calm area of low pressure that can stretch from 2 miles to 200 miles in diameter. Encircling the eye is the eye wall, the most intense part of the storm. Most hurricanes die at sea, but if they are sufficiently fueled with moisture and driven by tremendous winds, all hell breaks loose when they hit land. / In August 2005, Hurricane Katrina, the worst Atlantic hurricane on record, roared from the Bahamas toward Louisiana with winds up to 175 miles per hour and laid waste to the city of New Orleans. More than 1,800 people were killed, and property damage was estimated at more than $81 billion.

1. What is the main idea?

_____

2. Which words are related to the main idea?

_____

3. What is the purpose of the text?

_____

Context clues

When confronted with new vocabulary, you can use the following context clues to help you figure out the meaning:

- Your personal experience and general knowledge
- Definition, restatement, and synonyms
- Examples
- Comparison and contrast

In most cases you can use a combination of clues to understand vocabulary and the general meaning of a passage.

Clue 1: Your personal experience and general knowledge

Your basic tool as a vocabulary detective is what you already know. If, for example, you know nothing about geology or nuclear medicine, of course you will have difficulties understanding technical, scientific, or medical jargon that is specific to those topics. On the other hand, if you are already familiar with the subject matter, you can use your existing knowledge to help you figure out or, at least, to guess the meaning by associating something you don't know with something you do know.

Examine the following sentence:

In the story "The Reign of Superman," a homeless man, turned into a monster by a mad professor, uses his mental powers to **accumulate** great riches through dishonest means.

Most people have heard of Superman, and everyone is familiar with the classic plot in which the good superhero comes into conflict with an evil villain. So what do you know about villains? What do villains want? They want power or money. You know the word *rich*, so you can conclude that *riches* refers to money. When villains get money, what do they want? They want more and more money; in other words, their goal is to *accumulate* money until they become very, very rich. Can you picture a villain with a very huge pile of money?

The word *accumulate* in the preceding paragraph is closest in meaning to which of the following: spend, build up, invent, or save? Taking account of the context, you can predict that "build up" is the logical answer. If you check with a dictionary, you will see that *accumulate* means *to gather together a number or quantity of something*.

EXERCISE 3-2

Use your knowledge and experience of the world to figure out the meaning of the words in **bold type**. Try to formulate the meaning in your own words, without consulting a dictionary. Specify the clue that helped you come to your conclusion. Indicate how close your answer is to a dictionary definition by circling one of the following: Right on, Close, or A complete miss.

1. At the press conference the speaker nodded first to **acknowledge** questions from the reporters.

   Acknowledge probably means _____.

   Clue: _____

   How close is your definition?   Right on   Close   A complete miss

2. Please enclose a check with your application and **attach** it to the front page with a paper clip.

   Attach probably means _____.

   Clue: _____

   How close is your definition?   Right on   Close   A complete miss

3. Morning classes will **commence** at 9:00 and finish at 11:10.

   Commence probably means _____.

   Clue: _____

   How close is your definition?   Right on   Close   A complete miss

4. In the 2012 Summer Paralympic Games in London, 4,250 athletes from 164 countries **participated** in 20 sports and 503 medal events.

   Participated probably means _____.

   Clue: _____

   How close is your definition?   Right on   Close   A complete miss

5. The main **objective** of this book is to build vocabulary and to increase your chances of achieving a high score in the TOEFL® test.

   Objective probably means _____.

   Clue: _____

   How close is your definition?   Right on   Close   A complete miss

6. When the young man was arrested, it took three policemen to hold him down and **restrain** him while a fourth put him in handcuffs.

    Restrain probably means _____.

    Clue: _____

    How close is your definition?   Right on   Close   A complete miss

7. The theme of the Halloween party was the Monster Mash; everyone who came to the party wore **grotesque** masks and costumes.

    Grotesque probably means _____.

    Clue: _____

    How close is your answer?   Right on   Close   A complete miss

8. It isn't easy to get accepted into an **exclusive** golf and country club, unless you have a high income or belong to a prestigious profession.

    Exclusive probably means _____.

    Clue: _____

    How close is your definition?   Right on   Close   A complete miss

9. The police are offering a **reward** of $25,000 for information leading to the arrest and capture of the suspected bank robber.

    Reward probably means _____.

    Clue: _____

    How close is your definition?   Right on   Close   A complete miss

10. After the mother died during childbirth, the baby was cared for by her older **siblings**.

    Siblings probably means _____.

    Clue: _____

    How close is your definition?   Right on   Close   A complete miss

Clue 2: Definition, restatement, and synonyms

Sometimes texts, particularly those that introduce new subject matter in a textbook, include a definition of a specific word. This can take the form of:

- A direct definition: *which means* or *denotes; that is; i.e.; called, defined,* or *known as*
- A restatement: *or, in other words; that is to say*
- Verbs that link the subject with an equivalent: *be, appear, resemble, become, involve, signify, symbolize,* etc.

Look at the following example:

> **Amputees** are missing a **limb,** or part of an arm or leg, as a result of a congenital defect, an accident, or a medical condition such as cancer or diabetes.

In this example, you know that a limb is an arm or a leg. Assuming you don't understand the term *congenital defect,* you can figure out from your knowledge of the world that people can lose an arm or a leg when they've been in an accident or suffer a disease such as cancer or diabetes. If you check with a dictionary, you will find that *limb* means arm, leg, or wing, and an *amputee* is someone who has had a limb surgically amputated. You can probably guess from the context that *amputate* means to remove or cut off. You might be able to guess that *congenital defect* means a birth defect since some people are born with missing limbs.

TIP

Look for definitions set within commas, parentheses, or dashes:

> Every day 173,000 **megawatts** (a megawatt equals one billion watts) of energy strike the earth's surface in the form of sunlight.

EXERCISE 3-3

Use the definitions and restatements in the following sentences to work out the meaning of the word in **bold type** as you understand it. Do not copy the meaning from the sentence and do not consult a dictionary until you have completed the exercise. Give the clue that you used. Indicate how close your answer is to a dictionary definition by circling one of the following: Right on, Close, or A complete miss.

1. **Sustainable** tourism as identified in the Brundtland report to the 1987 World Commission on Environment and Development refers to development that "meets the needs of the present without compromising the ability of future generations to meet their needs."

   Sustainable means _____.

   Clue: _____

   How close is your definition?   Right on   Close   A complete miss

2. The healing circle is opened by a **facilitator**, or keeper, who ensures that participants show respect for each other and follow the guidelines.

   Facilitator means _____.

   Clue: _____

   How close is your definition?   Right on   Close   A complete miss

3. Simplicity refers to the lack of **clutter**—that is, all those nonessential things, patterns, habits, and ideas that take control of our lives and distract us from what is really important.

   Clutter means _____.

   Clue: _____

   How close is your definition?   Right on   Close   A complete miss

4. The government voted to **allocate** several million dollars for genetic research, which meant that significantly more money would go to developing cures for genetic diseases.

   Allocate means _____.

   Clue: _____

   How close is your definition?   Right on   Close   A complete miss

5. **Voluntary** denotes a free and conscious choice to make appropriate changes that will enrich life in a deeper, spiritual sense.

Voluntary means _____.

Clue: _____

How close is your definition?   Right on   Close   A complete miss

Although repetition should be avoided in academic writing, synonyms are sometimes used for emphasis. Common synonyms can also create a kind of bridge between the known and the unknown and reinforce meaning.

Examine the following sentence: Competitors in the Paralympics are **classified**, or organized, according to their level of disability.

Here it can be seen that another word for *classified* is *organized*. *According to their level of disability* is another clue that tells you that *classified* refers to a specific category. The root word, *class*, also tells you that the word has to do with a system of organization. If you check with a dictionary, you will see that the verb *classify* means:

- To arrange a group in classes according to shared characteristics
- To put in a particular class or category

EXERCISE 3-4

Use the synonyms in the following sentences to work out the meaning of the word in **bold type** as you understand it. Do not consult a dictionary until you have completed the exercise. Give the clue that you used. Indicate how close your answer is to a dictionary definition by circling one of the following: Right on, Close, or A complete miss.

1. Also known as "green" tourism, **ecotourism** promotes environmental protection, cultural sensitivity, and respect for the traditions and customs of the local population.

   Ecotourism means _____.

   Synonym: _____

   Clue: _____

   How close is your definition?   Right on   Close   A complete miss

2. In 2007, for the first time in history, the urban population **exceeded** 50 percent of the world's population. By 2050 it is estimated to go beyond 70 percent.

Exceed means _____.

Synonym: _____

Clue: _____

How close is your definition?   Right on   Close   A complete miss

3. Overnight the patient's condition worsened, and if it continues to **deteriorate** rapidly, he is not expected to survive another night.

Deteriorate means _____.

Synonym: _____

Clue: _____

How close is your definition?   Right on   Close   A complete miss

4. In the bomb attack, several bystanders were **injured** and two journalists were wounded.

Injure means _____.

Synonym: _____

Clue: _____

How close is your definition?   Right on   Close   A complete miss

5. Computer technology plays a **crucial** role in providing medical care, having become a key component of modern hospitals.

Crucial means _____.

Synonym: _____

Clue: _____

How close is your definition?   Right on   Close   A complete miss

Clue 3: Examples

Examples are the most graphic way to illustrate meaning, and they are often self-explanatory and more effective than complicated explanations. A good example will produce an "Aha, now I get it" reaction in the person to whom you're explaining something. Some lead-in words to examples are:

- Such as
- For example
- For instance
- Including
- As well as

Examples can also be separated by commas, parentheses, or dashes:

Eighty percent of the world's energy comes from fossil **fuels**, such as oil, coal, and natural gas.

These examples are self-explanatory; everybody knows that to get heat or energy we burn oil, coal, and natural gas, so *fuel* is a word for a material that people burn to produce energy, which is how it is defined in the dictionary.

In addition to a monthly salary, all employees receive standard **benefits**, including medical insurance, vacation pay, sick pay, and a Christmas bonus.

This example tells us that *benefits* are something extra that is good for us, and *standard* indicates that we are entitled to them—that is, everyone gets the same.

EXERCISE 3-5

Use the examples in the following sentences to work out the meaning of the word in **bold type** as you understand it. Do not consult a dictionary until you have completed the exercise. Give the clues that you used. Indicate how close your answer is to a dictionary definition by circling one of the following: Right on, Close, or A complete miss.

1. Superman's **exploits** focused on fighting crime syndicates, defeating evil megalomaniacs, and challenging alien forces with superpowers of their own.

   Exploits means _____.

   Examples: _____

   How close is your definition?　　Right on　　Close　　A complete miss

2. In a healing circle, a **symbol** of special meaning, such as an eagle's feather, a stone or crystal, or a figure, is used as a talking piece and passed from person to person.

   Symbol means _____.

   Examples: _____

   How close is your definition?　　Right on　　Close　　A complete miss

3. Getting a well-paid job is one of the main **incentives** to getting a college degree.

   Incentive means _____.

   Examples: _____

   How close is your definition?　　Right on　　Close　　A complete miss

4. Human rights legislation serves to protect people from various forms of **discrimination**—racial, sexual, religious, or economic, for instance.

   Discrimination means _____.

   Examples: _____

   How close is your definition?　　Right on　　Close　　A complete miss

5. College students have access to a wide range of research **resources**. In addition to its collection of books, the library has newspapers, magazines, journals, e-resources, and a staff of research librarians available to assist students.

   Resources means _____.

   Examples: _____

   How close is your definition?　　Right on　　Close　　A complete miss

Clue 4: Comparison and contrast

Another effective way to communicate meaning is to show how two concepts are either similar or different. If you are already familiar with one word, you should be able to understand its synonym or antonym from context.

SIGNAL WORDS FOR COMPARISON

- Similar(ly)
- Like, alike
- As well as, also
- The same, in the same way
- Likewise

Here is an example of comparison:

> The student's writing ability is **sufficient** to pass the test, and her reading comprehension is also **adequate**.

Sufficient and *adequate* are synonyms that mean *enough*.

SIGNAL WORDS FOR CONTRAST

- Different from
- Unlike
- Although
- However, but
- On the one hand, on the other hand
- While, whereas
- In contrast to, as opposed to

Here is an example of contrast:

> Whereas our supply of oil is **finite**, sunlight is a plentiful and **renewable** resource.

Your experience should tell you that oil is limited in supply, or *finite*. Sunlight, on the other hand, is unlimited, or *renewable*. The *renew* in *renewable* should also tell you that sunlight is something we can access again and again.

EXERCISE 3-6

Use the clues in the following sentences to work out the meaning of the word in **bold type** as you understand it. Indicate if there is a comparison or contrast clue in the sentence. Do not consult a dictionary until you have completed the exercise. Indicate how close your answer is to a dictionary definition by circling one of the following: Right on, Close, or A complete miss.

1. Our Literature teacher is very flexible about assignment deadlines if students have a valid excuse, whereas our history instructor insists **rigidly** that papers be handed in on time without exception.

   Rigid(ly) means _____.

   Clue: _____

   How close is your definition?　　Right on　　　Close　　　A complete miss

2. A suit and tie is considered suitable dress for a job interview. Likewise, for female applicants a pantsuit or dress with a jacket is **appropriate**.

   Appropriate means _____.

   Clue: _____

   How close is your definition?　　Right on　　　Close　　　A complete miss

3. Since the 1950s, tourism has experienced **enormous** growth rates, and huge increases are expected into the future, especially in Asian countries.

   Enormous means _____.

   Clue: _____

   How close is your definition?　　Right on　　　Close　　　A complete miss

4. Access to information on the Internet used to be limited, but thanks to wireless technology, Internet use has become **widespread**.

   Widespread means _____.

   Clue: _____

   How close is your definition?　　Right on　　　Close　　　A complete miss

5. Through genetic engineering, scientists can alter an organism's DNA at the cellular level and thereby **modify** plants so that they can withstand extreme climate conditions.

   Modify means _____.

   Clue: _____

   How close is your definition?　　Right on　　　Close　　　A complete miss

EXERCISE 3-7

Which of the context clues can you use to determine the meaning of the vocabulary in **bold type**? Do not use a dictionary to check your definition until you have completed the exercise. Indicate how close your answer is to a dictionary definition by circling one of the following: Right on, Close, or A complete miss.

1. The investigators began by collecting important **evidence**, such as fingerprints, hair, fibers, blood, and other DNA samples.

   Evidence means _____.

   Context clue: _____

   How close is your answer?   Right on   Close   A complete miss

2. Further research into restriction enzymes revealed that once an inserted gene was accepted by the host organism, it could be **replicated**, or copied, when the cells divided.

   Replicate means _____.

   Context clue: _____

   How close is your answer?   Right on   Close   A complete miss

3. Death is **irreversible**—that is, no one can come back to life to tell their tale.

   Irreversible means _____.

   Context clue: _____

   How close is your answer?   Right on   Close   A complete miss

4. In addition to being **toxic** to humans, herbicides and pesticides harm or kill birds, insects, butterflies, bees, and other animals, and threaten biodiversity.

   Toxic means _____.

   Context clue: _____

   How close is your answer?   Right on   Close   A complete miss

5. Men and women have been regarded throughout history as opposites. Women are emotional; men are **rational**.

   Rational means _____.

   Context clue: _____

   How close is your answer?   Right on   Close   A complete miss

6. Pilots flew in open cockpits exposed to all kinds of weather, with only maps and a compass to **navigate** by and find their destination.

Navigate means _____.

Context clue: _____

How close is your answer?　　　Right on　　　Close　　　A complete miss

7. *Toy Story* and its two **sequels,** *Toy Story 2* and *Toy Story 3*, recount the adventures and misadventures of a group of toys under the leadership of Woody and Buzz Lightyear.

Sequel means _____.

Context clue: _____

How close is your answer?　　　Right on　　　Close　　　A complete miss

8. The statue was built in honor of the young athlete's achievements in track and field sports and his humanitarian **accomplishments**.

Accomplishment means _____.

Context clue: _____

How close is your answer?　　　Right on　　　Close　　　A complete miss

9. On April 14, 1915, the *Titanic* **collided** with an iceberg and sank on its maiden voyage from Southampton, England, to New York City.

Collide means _____.

Context clue: _____

How close is your answer?　　　Right on　　　Close　　　A complete miss

10. The responsibility for city management lies with municipal governments that derive **revenue** from service fees and property taxes.

Revenue means _____.

Context clue: _____

How close is your answer?　　　Right on　　　Close　　　A complete miss

11. In 1990, the California Air Resources Board **stipulated** that 2 percent of all cars sold in California must be zero-emission in 1998, rising to 10 percent in 2003. Only electric cars would meet these requirements.

Stipulate means _____.

Context clue: _____

How close is your answer?　　　Right on　　　Close　　　A complete miss

12. Smoking is allowed outside the building, but it is strictly **prohibited** in any of the classrooms and common areas.

Prohibit means _____.

Context clue: _____

How close is your answer?   Right on   Close   A complete miss

13. If you do not include a transcript of your academic record, your application will be automatically **rejected**.

Reject means _____.

Context clue: _____

How close is your answer?   Right on   Close   A complete miss

14. Dietary **supplements**, such as vitamins and minerals, are recommended by most doctors.

Supplement means _____.

Context clue: _____

How close is your answer?   Right on   Close   A complete miss

15. Archeologists have discovered **traces**, or very small amounts, of gold dust in the gravesites.

Trace means _____.

Context clue: _____

How close is your answer?   Right on   Close   A complete miss

EXERCISE 3-8

Use context clues to determine the meaning of the academic word in **bold type**. Give the type of clue or clues that you used.

1. Fewer than 10 percent of urban dwellers are **residents** of megacities with populations exceeding ten million.

   The word *residents* is closest in meaning to _____:

   Ⓐ inhabitants

   Ⓑ supporters

   Ⓒ taxpayers

   Ⓓ visitors

   Clue: _____

2. Smaller and poorer countries depend on tourism as a major source of employment and as their only means of **diversifying** their limited economies.

   The word *diversifying* is closest in meaning to _____:

   Ⓐ supporting

   Ⓑ protecting

   Ⓒ varying

   Ⓓ containing

   Clue: _____

3. An effective public speaker makes use of various techniques, such as repetition, pauses, and increased volume, to **emphasize** significants points.

   The word *emphasize* is closest in meaning to _____:

   Ⓐ create

   Ⓑ stress

   Ⓒ like

   Ⓓ state

   Clue: _____

4. Near-death experiences follow a common pattern and contain any of ten to twelve elements that have been **compiled** from historical reports, experiments, and extensive interviews and surveys.

The word *compiled* is closest in meaning to _____:

Ⓐ collected

Ⓑ identified

Ⓒ recorded

Ⓓ produced

Clue: _____

5. Supporters of biotechnology argue that genetic engineering can **ensure** crops that will mature earlier, contain more nutrients, resist pesticides and herbicides used to control insects and weeds, and thus produce higher yields and prevent hunger in the future.

The word *ensure* is closest in meaning to _____:

Ⓐ prevent

Ⓑ produce

Ⓒ enable

Ⓓ guarantee

Clue: _____

6. In the meantime, the **controversy** over allowing DNA testing in court was still raging in the media, and lawyers Scheck and Neufeld were fighting for a moratorium on DNA evidence.

The word *controversy* is closest in meaning to _____:

Ⓐ question of

Ⓑ interest in

Ⓒ problem of

Ⓓ debate over

Clue: _____

7. More poems, stories, and songs have been written about the love between a man and a woman than about death, war, loss, or any other **theme**.

The word *theme* is closest in meaning to _____:

Ⓐ theory

Ⓑ problem

Ⓒ topic

Ⓓ idea

Clue: _____

8. Car sales **declined** between 2007 and 2009 due to a global financial crisis.

The word *declined* is closest in meaning to _____:

Ⓐ increased

Ⓑ stayed the same

Ⓒ decreased

Ⓓ rose

Clue: _____

9. Commitment to the development of solar energy has **fluctuated** in tandem with the volatility of oil prices.

The word *fluctuated* is closest in meaning to _____:

Ⓐ failed

Ⓑ varied

Ⓒ steadied

Ⓓ risen

Clue: _____

10. The incidence of accidents due to human error and negligence demonstrates that no human being is **infallible**.

The word *infallible* is closest in meaning to _____:

(A) unreliable

(B) permanent

(C) trustworthy

(D) perfect

Clue: _____

CHAPTER 4

How to overcome vocabulary challenges

Objectives

To identify different types of vocabulary according to their use

To identify essential academic and advanced words

To distinguish between easily confused words

To choose the correct meaning out of many possibilities

Different types of words

There is more to building vocabulary than simply sitting down with a dictionary or thesaurus and memorizing long lists of words. In the first three chapters, you learned to

- Identify and classify vocabulary according to parts of speech
- Recognize prefixes or suffixes that form nouns, adjectives, and verbs
- Understand words from their definitions and synonyms
- Understand vocabulary from context

TIP

To understand a text, you do not need to understand every single word. Nor is every word that you come across absolutely essential. Writing down all new words and looking each one up would be time-consuming and unproductive. Therefore, you need to be able to distinguish between different types of words and to focus on vocabulary that is most useful for your purposes.

Basic words

Basic words are high-frequency words that are used for everyday communication. These are the words that you learn first and use regularly.

In *Basic English: A General Introduction with Rules and Grammar* (1932), the English linguist, philosopher, and writer Charles K. Ogden identified 850 basic English words and classified them into three categories: operations, things, and qualities. (The list can be found at http://www2.educ.fukushima-u.ac.jp/~ryota/word-list.html. To get a good start, review that list and make a note of any basic words that are unfamiliar to you.)

A further resource for basic vocabulary is the General Service List (GSL), based on Michael West's 1953 text *A General Service List of English Words*. This list—updated in 1995 by John Bauman and Brent Culligan—consists of the 2,000 most frequently used words in English (see http://jbauman.com/gsl.html).

EXERCISE 4-1

In the following text identify the words that are already familiar to you. Underline the words you think belong in the list of basic words.

Bananas do not grow on a tree, as most people would imagine, but on a sturdy plant that can reach 6 to 7.6 meters in height with large leaves up to 0.6 meter wide and 2.75 meters long. In fact, the banana plant, *Musa acuminata*, is the world's largest perennial herb. Cultivation is best suited to tropical and subtropical areas with ample water, rich soil, and good drainage. Because bananas have been cultivated to become seedless, commercially grown bananas are propagated through division, a process of separating offshoots or "pups" from the mother plant.

EXERCISE 4-2

The following list identifies basic words that can be used in an academic context. Fill in the blanks with the part of speech and definition for each new word. Note that some words can be both nouns and verbs.

Part of speech   Definition

1. adjustment _____ _____

2. approval _____ _____

3. committee _____ _____

4. competition _____ _____

5. conscious _____ _____

6. damage _____ _____

7. development _____ _____

8. existence _____ _____

9. harmony _____ _____

10. impulse _____ _____

11. measure _____ _____

12. probable _____ _____

13. request _____ _____

14. responsible _____ _____

15. substance _____ _____

16. unit _____ _____

17. vessel _____ _____

EXERCISE 4-3

Complete each of the following sentences with the appropriate word from the list in Exercise 4-2. Be sure to use the correct form of the verb and to pluralize nouns, if necessary.

1. Before we order a new carpet, we have to _____ the floor and write down the dimensions.

2. Scientists dispute the _____ of life on other planets.

3. The social _____ will meet next Monday to discuss events for this year's Spring Festival Celebration.

4. Students wishing to discontinue their studies for personal reasons will need _____ from the dean's office before they can return and register for the following semester.

5. A higher education is an essential part of a student's personal and professional _____.

6. When the rescue crew pulled the driver out of the car, he was badly injured and barely _____.

7. What is the strange blue _____ in this bottle, and what is it used for?

8. Wouldn't it be wonderful if people could live with each other in perfect _____?

9. Many sunken _____ lying on the bottom of the ocean contain treasure that has been estimated to be worth millions of dollars.

10. If you can't find a book on the shelves in the library, you can _____ that it be put on hold for you as soon as it is returned.

11. It's possible, but not _____, that in our lifetime a large asteroid will hit and destroy the earth.

12. Human activity is largely _____ for global warming.

13. Hurricanes cause extensive _____ to the towns and surroundings in their path.

14. If you have made an overpayment to your account, we will make the necessary _____ to your next statement.

15. Are you going to enter your short story in this year's Creative Writing _____? It's so good that you should have a chance of winning.

16. The new apartment complex will contain eighty _____.

17. If you want to save money, you have to stop buying things on _____, and ask yourself first if you really need them.

Signal and transition words

Signal and **transition words** are particularly useful in writing, although of course they are also used in spoken English. Signal and transition words have distinct purposes:

- To link ideas
- To indicate a change in direction of thought
- To draw attention to an important point

These connectors make your thoughts flow. Without them, your thoughts would seem jumpy, disjointed, and difficult to follow.

Signal words can be compared to road signs, and they perform the following functions:

- Introduce examples: for example, such as, specifically
- Show agreement: of course, definitely
- Introduce additional information; and, in addition to, moreover
- Indicate order and sequence: first, then, after that
- Indicate time: before, after, finally
- Compare and contrast: like, similarly / although, however, on the one hand
- Demonstrate cause and effect: because, due to, on account of
- Demonstrate condition: if, unless, provided that
- Summarize and conclude: in conclusion, to summarize, in other words

EXERCISE 4-4

Underline the signal and transition words in the following texts.

Text A

Although Superman started out as an evil character, the second version was a savior in the tradition of Moses, Samson, or Hercules. This time he used his superpowers to fight for truth, justice, and the American way of life. In addition he wore his trademark bright blue costume with a red cape and a diamond-shaped **S** emblazoned on his chest. Because Superman's birth father, Jor-El, had sent his infant son, Kal-El, from the doomed planet of Krypton to the safety of Earth in a rocket, he was raised in an orphanage. Later the story changed, and Superman was raised by a kind elderly couple, Jonathan and Martha Kent, from Smallville, Kansas. Unaware of his powers until the age of eighteen, the boy grew up as Clark Kent and became a newspaper reporter for the *Daily Planet*. Unlike Superman, Clark Kent was myopic, socially awkward, and meek, but he was also intelligent, hard-working, and decent to the core— the kind of guy no one, including his pretty, feisty, and disdainful co-reporter, Lois Lane, would ever suspect of having superhuman powers.

Text B

First of all, a Pixar movie begins with an idea for a story. If the employee with the idea can sell it to the development team, different versions of the story, called treatments, are written in summary form. From there artists draw storyboards that resemble comic book sequences and develop the storyline and its characters. On condition that the story meets the director's approval, the script is written and then employees record the first voices. After that, the dialogue is perfected and professional actors are hired to read the parts. Next, the best versions are made into a videotape, or reel, which goes to editing for cleanup. Afterward the art department creates the visuals: characters, set, props, lighting—everything that appears on the movie screen.

International and foreign words

Language is a living organism that is continuously subject to change. English began as a Germanic language, and traces of its roots exist in many basic words, such as *water* and *door*. After the Normans under William the Conqueror invaded Britain in 1066, French became the language of the court, and as French became fashionable, it invaded the English language. With the Renaissance, English underwent a further transformation, incorporating scientific vocabulary borrowed from Greek and Latin. In the 1600s exploration took English sailors, and eventually settlers, to many parts of the world. When Britain established itself as a global empire, the English language assimilated words from other languages. The development of technology, beginning with the Industrial Revolution, created a need for more new words, and to this day English adds vocabulary on an ongoing basis.

As an international language, English has absorbed a considerable number of foreign words, and the list is growing. In addition to his Basic Word List, C. K. Ogden compiled a list of basic international words (http://ogden.basic-english.org/wordalpi.html). Of course this list is outdated. Unfortunately there is no definitive current list of international or foreign words in the English language. Because these words are generally recognized internationally, they are common to other languages with only small variations, mostly in pronunciation, from one language to another—for example, salad, salade, salata, insalata, салат.

Within the English language itself, there are regional differences, and we can think of English as American, British, Canadian, Australian, etc. There are also words and expressions that are used specifically in Ireland, Scotland, Wales, Newfoundland, the West Indies, New York, East London, or Johannesburg, for example.

EXERCISE 4-5

What is the origin of the following international words? The origins can be found in a dictionary.

1. chocolate _____

2. king _____

3. algebra _____

4. beer _____

5. automatic _____

6. economy _____

7. Gestalt _____

8. hygiene _____

9. influenza _____

10. camouflage _____

11. mammoth _____

12. kimono _____

13. sauna _____

14. propaganda _____

15. cafeteria _____

16. ombudsman _____

17. pariah _____

18. barbecue _____

19. assassin _____

20. juggernaut _____

Academic words

What is the difference between a basic word and an **academic word**? Basic words are used in informal everyday communication, whereas academic words are used in academic speech (at the university and college level). Sample words include *analyze, classify, discuss, compare*—words that can also be used across disciplines (whether it's an economics, literature, or biology class, a student must *analyze* a topic, for example). Frequently, academic vocabulary can be elevated or formal.

> **EXAMPLE**
>
> **Informal** Where did you **get** that information?
> **Formal**   Where did you **obtain** that information?

For your purposes, the **Academic Word List** (AWL) is your most useful resource. The AWL was developed in 1998 by Averil Coxhead as her M.A. thesis at Victoria University of Wellington, New Zealand. The AWL consists of 570 word families with a total of 3,000 words that do not necessarily belong to the 2,000 most frequently occurring words in English, but which appear with high frequency in the Arts, Commerce, Law, and Science faculty sections of the Academic Corpus (a collection of texts). These words were selected on the basis of their high frequency of use and are therefore considered critical if students are to understand and evaluate academic material (lectures, texts, papers, etc.) and to successfully carry out academic assignments (papers, discussions, presentations, examinations, etc.).

The AWL is divided into 10 sublists and can be found in its entirety on any of the following websites:

- https://www.vocabulary.com/lists/218701#view=notes
- http://www.victoria.ac.nz/lals/resources/academicwordlist/awl-headwords
- http://www.uefap.com/vocab/select/awl.htm

Appendix A has a list of the AWL words in this book. The AWL is addressed in more detail in Chapter 8.

Although the majority of vocabulary questions involve AWL words, a number of useful non-AWL words appear on the TOEFL® test as well. There is, however, no definitive list of these words, and as a result you need to be aware of words that you encounter repeatedly in your reading and listening.

EXERCISE 4-6

Underline the 17 academic words and circle the 11 useful words in the following text.

In 1990, the United States National Institutes of Health and the Department of Energy, in collaboration with partners from eighteen countries, embarked on the most ambitious venture to be undertaken since the Manhattan Project to develop the atom bomb or the Apollo project to put a man on the moon: the Human Genome Project. At an estimated cost of $3 billion to complete the task by 2005, leading scientists and researchers in the field of molecular biology set out to identify all 30,000 to 40,000 genes belonging to the human genome and to map the location of three billion bases of DNA; in other words, to write the Book of Life. This definitive resource was meant to lead to the understanding of genetic diseases, the creation of effective pharmaceuticals and medical treatments, and the alleviation and prevention of human suffering due to genetically transmitted diseases. In order to serve all mankind and to prevent control by any scientific, corporate, or national interests, all information was to be stored in public electronic databases and made freely and readily accessible to anyone who required it.

EXERCISE 4-7

Scan the following text. Identify the underlined words as basic, signal, international, academic, or useful.

As strange as the above elements may sound, near-death experiences (NDEs) can be scientifically verified. The cases of children, including very young children, who have had NDEs provide strong supporting evidence. Because children have neither preconceived notions nor previous knowledge of death or an afterlife, they cannot fake an experience that shares so many elements with adult NDEs. Furthermore, people who have been blind from birth have described visual experiences of color, shape, and form during NDEs that they could never have "seen" if their experience had not been real. Although they were under anesthesia, NDEers have accurately described objects unknown to them and located them in a place they could not have possibly observed in an unconscious, immobile state. While on the operating table, one woman described a pair of running shoes lying on the roof of the hospital building; this was later confirmed. The profound life-changing effect that NDEers carry with them also testifies to the validity of their experience. After having an NDE, individuals are said to be changed people. They tend to be more religious, more aware of how short life is, more determined to live their life fully, and less afraid of death. They become more caring, and show increased concern for others to the point of making personal sacrifices. Surely, no one can be so deeply affected by an event that has never happened to them.

BASIC	SIGNAL	INTERNATIONAL	ACADEMIC	USEFUL

BASIC	SIGNAL	INTERNATIONAL	ACADEMIC	USEFUL

Easily confused words

In the English language there are many words that can be easily confused.

- English not being a phonetic language, words are not consistently written the way they are spoken.
- Vowel sounds shift from region to region, so a word like *hot* can sound quite different depending on your location.

The most commonly confused words are **homonyms** (words that are spelled or pronounced the same but have completely different meanings), **homophones** (words that are pronounced the same but have different spellings and meanings), and **homographs** or **heteronyms** (words that are spelled that same but have different meanings and pronunciation).

The other category of easily confused words is words that are similar in spelling and pronunciation but very different in meaning or part of speech. Confusing these words can result in quite amusing, or ridiculous, statements.

- When words are intentionally confused, the result is a pun (a play on words) that can be clever and humorous, for example:

    Santa's helpers are subordinate clauses.

- When words are confused because the speaker doesn't know the difference, the result can be absurd, ridiculous, and even embarrassing. These linguistic *faux pas* are referred to as malapropisms, named after Mrs. Malaprop, a lower-class character in the seventeenth-century play, *The Rivals*, by Richard Sheridan. For example:

    No one knows exactly why dinosaurs became **distinct** (*distinct* is confused with the correct *extinct*).

Homonyms and homophones

For your purposes, homonyms and homophones will cause problems primarily in listening exercises, particularly if you are familiar with only one of the words. Most of these words are common one-syllable words.

EXAMPLES

In comparison to a day, a *minute* is *minute*.

Until it gets *light*, you have to have a *light* on in the room.

Well, he hasn't been feeling very *well* since he drank water from that *well*.

I can't *bear* it when people are cruel to *bears*.

In the event of a strong *wind*, it is necessary to *wind* up the flag and bring it indoors.

EXERCISE 4-8

Complete the sentences with the suitable homophone. Pluralize nouns and change the verb tense, if necessary. Record the definition of any words that you have trouble with.

1. affect, effect

Ⓐ Long periods of rain or sunshine

_____ our mood.

Ⓑ Weather has a significant

_____ on our mood.

2. air, err, heir

Ⓐ Prince William is _____ to the

throne of England.

Ⓑ Open the window and let in some fresh

_____.

Ⓒ To _____ is human; to forgive

is divine.

3. aloud, allowed

Ⓐ You can practice your pronunciation by

reading _____.

Ⓑ No one is _____ to smoke

inside the building.

4. aural, oral

Ⓐ The test consists of a written section and an

_____ interview.

Ⓑ When I had an ear infection, the doctor gave

me an _____ examination.

5. bases, basis

Ⓐ What is the _____ of your

assumption?

Ⓑ In the game of baseball, the runner must

touch all the _____ in order to

score a run.

6. brake, break

Ⓐ If you want to stop the car, you have to step

on the _____.

Ⓑ There is a 15-minute _____

between classes.

7. canvas, canvass

Ⓐ The tent is made of _____.

Ⓑ In North America it is a tradition for

political candidates to go door-to-door and

_____ before an election.

8. capital, capitol

Ⓐ What is the _____ of Venezuela?

Ⓑ The teams are debating the issue of

_____ punishment.

9. cede, seed

Ⓐ During the revolution, the president was

forced to _____ power to the

military.

Ⓑ Most plants grow from _____.

10. cent, scent, sent

Ⓐ We _____ an e-mail to all the

class members.

Ⓑ I love the _____ of lavender.

Ⓒ That poor man doesn't have a

_____ to his name.

11. censor, sensor

Ⓐ The robotic device contains a built-in

_____ that responds to light.

Ⓑ All films are reviewed by a

_____ before they are

catalogued and put on the library shelves.

12. cite, site, sight

(A) When you write an academic paper, you must _____ all of your sources according to APA style.

(B) There is no hope in _____ for lasting peace in the Middle East.

(C) The residential complex is an ongoing construction _____.

13. cereal, serial

(A) Most students eat _____ for breakfast.

(B) There is an interesting _____ on television about the American Civil War.

14. coarse, course

(A) This movie contains _____ language and graphic scenes of violence.

(B) I'm taking a _____ in nineteenth-century literature.

15. complacent, complaisant

(A) You shouldn't be so _____ about your grades if you want to graduate with honors.

(B) Sheri thinks that by being _____ to her instructors that she can get extra marks.

16. complement, compliment

(A) The bride received several _____ on her lovely wedding dress.

(B) Red and green _____ each other.

17. council, counsel

(A) Seth is running for student

_____.

(B) Student Services has a list of qualified

professionals who are available to

_____ students with personal

problems.

18. discreet, discrete

(A) When discussing personal problems, it is

necessary to be _____ and

keep all information confidential.

(B) The information is organized into

_____ categories.

19. discussed, disgust

(A) The movie was so violent that we walked

out in _____.

(B) In our last class we _____ the

negative effects of mass tourism on the

environment.

20. draft, draught

(A) You are required to hand in a first

_____ of your essay.

(B) Please close the window. There's a cold

_____ coming in.

21. earn, urn

(A) How much did you _____ in

your last job?

(B) After the cremation the ashes are put into

an _____.

22. elicit, illicit

(A) The gang was arrested for the trafficking of

_____ drugs.

(B) Instead of explaining new concepts at great

length, the professor asks leading questions

to _____ answers from the

class.

23. elude, allude

(A) No matter how hard he tries, success always

seems to _____ him.

(B) In his speech the president will only

_____ to a serious health

problem, rather than revealing any details.

24. incite, insight

(A) The discussion provided some interesting

_____ into the problem.

(B) A group of protesters threw stones and

various objects to _____ a full-

blown riot.

25. lessen, lesson

(A) The next _____ will cover

how to organize and remember vocabulary.

(B) In order to _____ anxiety, you

need to relax and focus on more positive

thoughts.

26. marshal, martial

(A) Mark has enrolled in a _____

arts course so that he can learn self-defence.

(B) To climb the mountain, the team had to

_____ all their strength and

inner resolve.

27. patience, patients

Ⓐ To master a foreign language, you need lots

of _____.

Ⓑ The doctor spent the morning visiting his

_____ in the hospital.

28. pedal, peddle

Ⓐ Nowadays there are not many salesmen

who _____ their products

from door to door.

Ⓑ To operate the machine, you have to step on

the foot _____.

29. precedence, precedents

Ⓐ The law has been changed by cases whose

decisions and outcomes have set historic

_____.

Ⓑ Sportsmanship should take

_____ over winning.

30. principal, principle

Ⓐ One of the _____ issues

in the solar energy debate is the cost to

consumers.

Ⓑ It is our _____ not to buy

products made in sweat shops.

Homonyms/ heteronyms

When confronted with a homograph that can have two meanings, you need to pay attention to the context. If you are familiar with only one meaning, you should be able to establish from context that there is a second meaning.

Let's assume that you know the word *desert*, as in Mojave Desert. If you come across the sentence "She was afraid that he was going to *desert* her and their children," then you can figure out that he was probably going to leave her, not bury her in the sand.

The following exercise contains some of the more useful homographs.

EXERCISE 4-9

Match the following sentences with the correct definition.

1. coordinates

_____ We need someone in the group who coordinates all activities.

_____ To solve the problem, you have to enter all the data under the right coordinates.

Ⓐ organize and bring together

Ⓑ a group of numbers

2. contract

_____ It is easy to contract an illness in crowded places, such as subways and airplanes.

_____ A lease is a rental contract between the tenant and the landlord.

Ⓐ a written legal agreement

Ⓑ catch or develop

3. converse

_____ It's difficult to converse in a noisy bar or disco.

_____ The converse of subjective is objective.

Ⓐ the opposite

Ⓑ hold a conversation

4. defect

_____ This product was recalled because of a manufacturing defect.

_____ During the Cold War, many Soviet artists and intellectuals tried to defect to the West.

Ⓐ flaw or imperfection

Ⓑ leave a country for political reasons

5. deliberate

_____ The jury must first deliberate before they can arrive at a verdict.

_____ The accident was caused by one driver's deliberate negligence.

Ⓐ consider carefully

Ⓑ intentional

6. entrance

_____ The ticket office is located at the gallery entrance.

_____ The magician proceeded to entrance the audience with his tricks.

Ⓐ cast a spell or fill with wonder

Ⓑ opening through which one can enter a building

7. incense

_____ We were incensed by his rudeness and lack of common consideration.

_____ When we entered the temple, we noticed the strong scent of burning incense.

Ⓐ make someone very angry

Ⓑ a substance burned for its sweet smell

8. invalid

_____ This permit is invalid and must be renewed as soon as possible.

_____ After he contracted polio as a child, Mark O'Brian remained an invalid and was confined to an iron lung for the rest of his life.

Ⓐ not officially recognized

Ⓑ a person made weak or disabled by illness

9. intimate

_____ The author's diaries contain intimate details of her love affairs.

_____ The young man intimated that he intended to marry his cousin.

Ⓐ private and personal

Ⓑ state in an indirect way

10. minute

_____ The man described his ordeal of his kidnapping to the police in minute detail.

_____ You have fifteen minutes to finish the examination.

Ⓐ a period equal to sixty seconds

Ⓑ very small

11. produce

_____ The farmer's market sells fresh produce from local farms and gardens.

_____ The team is going to produce a video as part of their communications assignment.

Ⓐ fruit and vegetables

Ⓑ create or make

12. project

_____ Biologists agreed that the Human Genome Project could be accomplished.

_____ Car sales are projected to reach 100 million by 2015.

Ⓐ estimate or forecast

Ⓑ an enterprise organized to achieve a particular aim

13. recreation

_____ Recreation facilities are located on campus next to the library.

_____ The model is an accurate re-creation of the Pyramids at Giza.

Ⓐ enjoyable leisure activity

Ⓑ a copy of something

14. refuse

_____ The instructor refused to extend the assignment deadline by another day.

_____ There are containers in all the classrooms for students to deposit their refuse.

Ⓐ say no

Ⓑ garbage

15. sewer

_____ The factory employs female sewers to make sports garments.

_____ Some people believe that there are alligators living in the New York sewers.

Ⓐ an underground pipe system for carrying waste water

Ⓑ someone who sews

Similar spelling

Words that have a slightly different spelling but a different meaning pose a major problem for English learners. Consider *compose* and *comprise*, *infect* and *infest*, or *persecute* and *prosecute*. In fact, these words cause problems for native English speakers.

The following exercise contains some of the most troublesome words that you should familiarize yourself with.

EXERCISE 4-10

Complete the sentences with the appropriate choice of word. Pluralize nouns and change the verb form or tense, if necessary. Record the definition of any words that you have trouble with.

1. action, activity

Ⓐ The class is involved in a writing

_____.

Ⓑ To solve the problem we need to take

immediate _____.

2. adverse, averse

Ⓐ Some drugs can create an

_____ reaction in the patient,

such as a skin rash or internal bleeding.

Ⓑ The filthy young boy appears to be

_____ to soap and water.

3. advise, advice

Ⓐ I have to make a decision and I need your

_____.

Ⓑ I strongly _____ you to be

organized and systematic if you want to

build your vocabulary.

4. alternately, alternatively

Ⓐ The recipe asks you to stir in the liquid and

flour _____.

Ⓑ If the Psychology 101 class is full, you can

sign up _____ for Sociology

101 or Anthropology 101.

5. amoral, immoral

Ⓐ Psychopaths and sociopaths are

_____ and show no

compassion for their victims.

Ⓑ The senator lost the election because

the press revealed a past incident of

_____ sexual behavior.

6. appraise, apprise

Ⓐ The president's advisor should

_____ him of the details of

the conflict.

Ⓑ Before we can act, we have to

_____ the situation.

7. assent, ascend

Ⓐ Early this morning the team of mountain

climbers began to _____

Mount Everest.

Ⓑ The committee is expected to give its

_____ to the proposal.

8. assume, presume

Ⓐ In a court of law the defendant is

_____ innocent until proven

guilty.

Ⓑ Let us _____ that everyone

will be coming to the meeting.

9. avoid, prevent

Ⓐ You should _____ eating too

much animal fat, salt, and sugar.

Ⓑ Cutting down on the intake of animal fat

will _____ heart disease.

10. climactic, climatic

(A) In the future we will experience significant _____ changes.

(B) Action movies have very _____ endings.

11. conscientious, conscious

(A) A young man does not have to serve in the military if he is a _____ objector.

(B) When I awoke, I was _____ of a strange presence in the room.

12. considerate, considerable

(A) When working in a group, it is important for everyone to be _____ of each other.

(B) There is a _____ amount of material to cover in our International Relations class.

13. continual, continuous

(A) The _____ rain led to severe flooding in low-lying areas.

(B) After years of negotiation, the _____ talks between the two countries have finally resulted in a peace treaty.

14. damage, injury, harm

(A) The severe head _____ resulted in permanent brain _____.

(B) No _____ will come to you if you are careful and do not tease the dog.

15. deduct, deduce

(A) The payroll clerk will automatically

_____ income tax from the

employees' wages.

(B) It is difficult to _____ what

happened at the crime scene without the

presence of sufficient evidence.

16. defuse, diffuse

(A) Before negotiations can proceed, it is

necessary to _____ any

tensions among the participants.

(B) Thanks to the Internet, music trends are

_____ across international

borders.

17. disinterested, uninterested

(A) _____ parties make good

negotiators in personal disputes.

(B) The class was totally _____ in

this morning's lecture, and half of them fell

asleep.

18. distinct, extinct

(A) Will human beings eventually become

_____ like dinosaurs did?

(B) This substance has a very _____

odor and taste.

19. economic, economical

(A) Many countries are experiencing a period of

slow or minimal _____ growth.

(B) In order to survive on a small pension,

seniors must be very _____.

20. emigration, immigration

Ⓐ Canada's population has increased due to _____—mostly from Asian countries.

Ⓑ Former communist countries have experienced a decline in population due to _____.

21. emit, omit

Ⓐ Do not _____ any information indicated by a red * on the application.

Ⓑ Factories and vehicles _____ greenhouse gases.

22. ensure, insure

Ⓐ Every vehicle owner is required by law to _____ his car in the case of an accident, theft, or damage.

Ⓑ Supporters of biotechnology argue that genetically engineered crops will _____ an adequate food supply for the future.

23. evoke, invoke

Ⓐ In October 1970 Prime Minister Pierre Trudeau believed it necessary to _____ the War Measures Act.

Ⓑ Holst's *Jupiter* _____ images of a joyous homecoming.

24. fictional, fictitious

Ⓐ Several great authors have written under _____ names.

Ⓑ The new novel is a _____ account of a historical event.

25. illusion, allusion

Ⓐ The poor boy's dream of becoming rich and famous is just an _____.

Ⓑ In his speech, the politician made an _____ to his opponent's involvement in a financial scandal.

26. immanent, imminent, eminent

Ⓐ If you look around you, you can see that in nature change is _____.

Ⓑ From the airplane's direction of flight, a disastrous collision with the tower was _____.

Ⓒ Professor Reid, an _____ criminologist, will be giving a lecture on serial killers this evening.

27. imply, infer

Ⓐ Are you _____ that I cheated on the exam?

Ⓑ We all could _____ from the teacher's offhand comment that he thought we were guilty of cheating on the exam.

28. permission, permit

Ⓐ In order to be excused from class, you need to get _____ from the Dean's office.

Ⓑ All students and faculty require a parking _____.

29. precede, proceed

Ⓐ When you have received your student I.D., you can _____ to the computer lab where you will take a placement test.

Ⓑ A _____ B.

30. prescribe, proscribe

Ⓐ The doctor _____ ibuprofen for the patient's inflammation.

Ⓑ Labor strikes are _____ in essential medical and emergency services.

31. priceless, worthless

A Vincent van Gogh painting is _____, whereas my amateur artwork is _____.

32. respectable, respectful, respective

Ⓐ Young people should be _____ of their elders.

Ⓑ Kevin's first effort at giving a presentation was _____ and worthy of a C+.

Ⓒ The graded papers will be returned to their _____ owners.

33. succeed, secede

Ⓐ In 1861 the southern slave states _____ and formed the Confederate States of America, resulting in the American Civil War which lasted until 1865.

Ⓑ If at first you don't _____, keep on trying.

34. subjective, objective

Ⓐ Grading essays can be a very _____ process unless the teacher has a rubric.

Ⓑ Journalists should be _____ when they report news events and not show any political or personal bias.

35. treat, cure

A medical doctor _____ an illness with the intention of _____ it.

Multiple meanings

Unfortunately there are very few words in English that have only one meaning.

A very simple example is the word, *bank,* which has three meanings in its noun form and also three as a verb. In addition there are several related words: *banker, bank card, bank holiday, banking, bank note, bank rate, bank roll*, and *bankrupt.* Also one word can also be used in different contexts.

So, what do you do? Dictionary definitions are given according to frequency of use, which may help you out in most cases. Otherwise you have to look at the context and use clues to help you determine which definition fits.

The following exercise deals with AWL words that have more than one meaning.

EXERCISE 4-11

Choose the definition that best fits the sentence. (Three definitions are given, but some words have as many as six or seven.)

1. abandon

   _____ As the storm closed in, the team was forced to abandon their climb.

   _____ The young dancers abandoned themselves to the music's rhythm.

   _____ The baby was abandoned by its mother and left on the church steps.

   Ⓐ desert or leave permanently

   Ⓑ give up a course of action

   Ⓒ make no attempt to resist

2. adjust

   _____ Someone from the insurance company is coming to adjust the damages to the car.

   _____ You should adjust your seatbelt so that it sits snugly.

   _____ After our flight, it took us a week to adjust to the time change.

   Ⓐ alter something slightly

   Ⓑ become used to a new situation

   Ⓒ assess loss or damages when assessing an insurance claim

3. appreciate

_____ This painting has appreciated considerably since I bought it.

_____ I really appreciate all your help.

_____ Unless you have lost a family member, you cannot really appreciate another person's grief.

Ⓐ be grateful for something

Ⓑ understand a situation fully

Ⓒ rise in value

4. approach

_____ If you want her to go out with you, you have to try a different approach.

_____ The yard was so overgrown that the driver couldn't find the approach to the house.

_____ We could hear the man's approach as he climbed the creaky stairs.

Ⓐ a way of dealing with something

Ⓑ the action of coming closer

Ⓒ a way leading to a place

5. commit

_____ The psychopath was committed to an institution for the criminally insane.

_____ The candidate is committed to reducing the deficit and balancing the budget.

_____ DNA evidence was used in a court of law to prove that the defendant did not commit the crime.

Ⓐ do something wrong or illegal

Ⓑ promise to do something

Ⓒ send someone to jail, a hospital, or court

6. conduct

_____ Students are required to conduct themselves in an orderly manner.

_____ The class is conducting a survey about time management.

_____ Daniel Barenboim will be conducting the symphony's performance of Beethoven's Fifth Symphony.

Ⓐ to organize and carry out

Ⓑ direct the performance of a piece of music

Ⓒ behave in a particular way

7. contract

_____ When we are cold, our veins contract.

_____ The city has contracted a company to build a new bridge.

_____ During the influenza outbreak, mostly old people and very young children contracted the disease.

Ⓐ decrease in size, number, or range

Ⓑ catch or develop a disease

Ⓒ enter into a legally binding agreement

8. credit

_____ Daisuke Inoue is given credit for inventing karaoke.

_____ You need between 108 and 120 credit hours to qualify for an Honors Bachelor's Degree.

_____ Years ago people could purchase food and clothing on credit.

Ⓐ an arrangement in which a store enables a customer to pay at a later date

Ⓑ public acknowledgement or praise

Ⓒ a unit of study counting toward a degree or diploma

9. depress

_____ Gray, rainy days depress me.

_____ To open the machine, you have to depress the lever.

_____ Contrary to what most people believe, alcohol actually depresses your body.

Ⓐ make someone feel very unhappy

Ⓑ reduce the level of activity in the system

Ⓒ push or pull something down

10. draft

_____ The holder of a bank draft can present it to any bank for cash.

_____ During the Vietnam war, many young Americans went to Canada to escape the draft.

_____ In the academic writing class all students are required to submit a first draft of their essay.

Ⓐ preliminary version of a piece of writing

Ⓑ a written order requesting a bank to pay a certain amount

Ⓒ compulsory recruitment for military service

11. element

_____ There is an element of danger in most sports activities.

_____ A near-death experience contains ten to twelve elements.

_____ There are distinct elements of dissension among the group.

Ⓐ an essential or typical part

Ⓑ a small amount

Ⓒ a distinct group within a larger one

12. expose

_____ When the doctor removed the man's hood, he exposed his extreme deformities to the audience.

_____ The journalist's reportage exposed widespread corruption in the government.

_____ Children who watch television without supervision can be exposed to excessive violence.

Ⓐ make visible by uncovering

Ⓑ reveal the true nature of

Ⓒ make someone vulnerable to possible harm or risk

13. file

_____ When the ceremony began, all participants filed into the auditorium.

_____ All examinations are filed in the office.

_____ A young woman filed a complaint of sexual harassment against her superior.

Ⓐ place a document in a file

Ⓑ officially place a legal document, application, or charge on record

Ⓒ walk one behind the other

14. fund

_____ The government funds sports and cultural events.

_____ Is there adequate money in the state pension fund?

_____ The project has run out of funds and will have to borrow money.

Ⓐ amount of money saved for a particular purpose

Ⓑ money that is available to be spent

Ⓒ provide money for something official

15. grant

_____ The refugees were granted political asylum.

_____ The student was granted a year's leave of absence.

_____ The instructor granted that the students presented a valid argument in favor of an extension on the assignment.

Ⓐ allow someone to do something

Ⓑ give something formally or legally

Ⓒ admit to someone that something is true

16. image

_____ Harvard has a prestigious image.

_____ This web page is full of interesting images.

_____ This poem contains a lot of powerful images.

Ⓐ a likeness of a person or thing in the form of a picture

Ⓑ the impression a person or company presents to the public

Ⓒ a picture in the mind

17. invest

_____ Prior to the dot.com crash, people invested a lot of money in Internet companies.

_____ King Arthur's sword, Excalibur, was invested with mythical powers.

_____ The students invested a lot of time and energy in their project.

Ⓐ put money into something with the intention of making a profit

Ⓑ devote time or energy to an undertaking with the expectation of a positive result

Ⓒ provide someone or something with a quality

18. issue

_____ The head of the department resigned due to issues of substance abuse.

_____ An interesting article on the global financial crisis appeared in the latest issue of *Business Week*.

_____ In this class we will be discussing current social and political issues.

Ⓐ an important topic or problem

Ⓑ personal problems or difficulties

Ⓒ each of a regular series of publications

19. margin

_____ Typewritten essays must have a 1-inch margin on all sides.

_____ The Huskies defeated the Lion Kings by a narrow margin.

_____ A safety margin has been built into the calculation.

Ⓐ the blank border on each side of a printed page

Ⓑ an amount by which something is won

Ⓒ an amount included so as to ensure success

20. period

_____ The Triassic Period was a time of major change in which 90 percent of the earth's species died out.

_____ An exam is scheduled for third period.

_____ Due to the fire, the cafeteria will be closed for an indefinite period.

Ⓐ a length or portion of time

Ⓑ a lesson in a school

Ⓒ a portion of time with particular characteristics

21. promote

_____ Companies promote their products through advertising.

_____ Ms. Campbell was promoted to Department Head.

_____ Greenpeace promotes the protection of the environment.

Ⓐ support or actively encourage a cause, venture, or aim

Ⓑ publicize a product or celebrity

Ⓒ appoint someone to a higher position

22. range

_____ There aren't many houses in our price range on the market.

_____ This store has a wide range of household appliances.

_____ The main issue with electric cars is their driving range.

Ⓐ a variety of things of a particular type

Ⓑ the limits between which something varies

Ⓒ the distance that a vehicle can travel before it needs fuel

23. register

_____ The earthquake registered 6.5 on the Richter scale.

_____ All students are required to register for classes this week.

_____ Tom showed such self-control that he didn't register so much as a smile.

Ⓐ detect and show a reading

Ⓑ express an emotion or opinion

Ⓒ put one's name on an official list

24. resource

_____ The library contains a wide variety of research resources.

_____ Canada has a lot of natural resources.

_____ After the tsunami people had to rely on their own resources to survive.

Ⓐ a country's means of supporting itself

Ⓑ a source of help or information

Ⓒ personal qualities that help one cope in difficult situations

25. shift

_____ You have to press _Shift_ to perform various functions.

_____ An earthquake results when two tectonic plates shift or rub against each other.

_____ The late shift begins at 8:00 p.m.

Ⓐ a slight change in position or direction

Ⓑ a period of time worked by a group of workers

Ⓒ a key used to switch between two characters or functions on a keyboard

26. suspend

_____ The light is suspended from the ceiling.

_____ Students who are caught smoking on the premises will be suspended.

_____ Due to construction work, bus service will be suspended until further notice.

Ⓐ stop something temporarily

Ⓑ temporarily bar someone from a job or attending school

Ⓒ hang from somewhere

27. trace

_____ The child disappeared without a trace.

_____ The lead investigator put a trace on all calls that were made to the victim's house in the last 24 hours.

_____ Investigators found traces of blood in the trunk of the suspect's vehicle.

Ⓐ a mark or other indication of the existence of something

Ⓑ a very small quantity

Ⓒ a procedure to follow or locate something

28. transfer

_____ You can transfer to Line 5 at the next subway station.

_____ When we were growing up, our father often got transferred to another city.

_____ The file will be transferred electronically.

Ⓐ move from one place to another

Ⓑ change to a different vehicle during a journey

Ⓒ copy information from one place to another

29. volume

_____ What is the volume of this barrel?

_____ So as not to disturb others you should turn down the volume.

_____ His silence speaks volumes.

Ⓐ the amount of space occupied by something within a container

Ⓑ degree of loudness

Ⓒ a book forming part of a multivolume work

30. welfare

_____ Homeless people are eligible to collect welfare.

_____ Parents are responsible for their children's welfare.

_____ The government has a social welfare program.

Ⓐ general health, happiness, and safety

Ⓑ practical or financial help provided by the government

Ⓒ money paid by the government to poor and needy people

PART 2

Building and recording vocabulary

How to record vocabulary

Objectives

To develop a systematic method of recording new vocabulary for study purposes

To create a personalized vocabulary journal

In order to remember vocabulary, you are well advised to keep a systematic record. There are of course various methods, and the one you use will depend on how much detail you need to include and whether the word is completely new to you or only somewhat familiar.

A vocabulary record should consist of the following:

1. **The word and its part of speech.** You should also make a note of prepositions that are used with the word (e.g., be in charge *of*) and if the verb is followed by a gerund or infinitive (e.g., consider *doing something*).
2. **Derivatives**, or related words in the word family.
3. **A definition that fits the context.** As you encounter the word again, you can add secondary definitions to your notes. (It is common for words to have more than one definition.)
4. **Useful synonyms and helpful antonyms.** *Note*: Not all words will have synonyms or antonyms.

5. **Examples.** Examples are different from sample sentences in that they tell you what the particular word refers to—in other words, what you can use the word to describe.

    Examples of the word *beverage* are beer, wine, juice, tea, coffee, etc.

    Examples of the word *humorous* are jokes, scenes from a movie, comedians, situations, etc.

    Examples are like collocations in that they remind you how to use a word. Learning to use words correctly is just as important as knowing what they mean. Although *humorous* is associated with funny and *beverage* with drink, you cannot say that a clown wears a humorous nose, or the horse took a beverage.

6. **Collocations** are companion words that typically occur together.

    Examples of collocations for *impression* are *positive, favorable, bad, first, lasting, positive, make.*

    Collocations can also include prepositions (e.g., be in charge *of,* look forward *to,* derive *from,* etc.).

    Collocations can be found in some dictionaries, including online collocation dictionaries (see the bibliography).

7. **Sample sentences containing the word.** Write down the sentence in which you originally found the word so that you have a reference, then look for more in textbooks, newspapers, magazines, etc. Try to make sentences of your own.

8. **A picture, drawing, or clue** that creates a clear graphic reminder or bridge. These visual associations can be particularly powerful and stay in your memory longer than sentences to which you have no personal association.

Note: For every vocabulary item that you want to record, there may be fewer than the preceding eight points.

A vocabulary record can, but does not necessarily have to, include the following:

*   The pronunciation, but only if phonetic symbols are meaningful to you
*   The register (formal vs. informal)
*   The type of language (e.g., medical, commercial, scientific)
*   A translation, if it helps you (Remember that translating only reinforces your dependence on your native language and prevents you from learning to think and express yourself in English.)

You can organize your vocabulary using any of the following methods:

- Alphabetically
- By subject
- Chronologically—that is, in the order in which you learn and record a new word

Keeping a vocabulary journal is like building your own personal dictionary. Depending on how imaginative you are, putting a vocabulary journal together can be a very creative exercise, and if you can make it fun, you will do it with more enthusiasm. Templates for vocabulary journals are given in Appendix B.

Vocabulary journal entry #1: A full-page entry

This type of vocabulary journal can be kept in a notebook or Word document. Because it contains more detail, a full-page entry is useful for recording words that are

- Completely new to you
- Very difficult to understand
- Hard to remember
- Used frequently

Journal entry

1. Word: **challenge** (n.)

2. Word family:

Noun	Adjective/adverb	Verb
challenger	challenging	challenge someone to something or to do something; challenged

3. Definition: a new or difficult task that tests someone's ability or skill

4. Synonyms: test, make demands on, stimulate

   Antonyms: effortless, easy

5. Examples of challenges: taking a TOEFL® test, climbing a mountain, learning a new language, running a race, participating in the Olympic Games

6. Collocations:

   adjectives: difficult, real, exciting, major, big, daunting, serious

   verbs: face, meet, welcome, accept, mount, look for, seek, look forward to

   nouns: an opponent

7. Sentences:

   The winning team accepted the loser's challenge to a rematch.

   The questions on the TOEFL® test are a real challenge.

8. Picture, clue, or personal association:

   Running my first marathon was a big challenge.

   If I don't have a challenge, I get bored easily.

EXERCISE 5-1

Using the earlier sample journal entry for **challenge** as a model, complete the templates for the following academic words.

Full-page entry #1

1. Word: **acquire** (_____)

2. Word family:

Noun	Adjective/adverb	Verb
_____	_____	_____
_____	_____	_____

3. Definition: _____

_____

4. Synonyms: _____

Antonyms: _____

5. Examples: _____

_____

6. Collocations: _____

_____

_____

7. Sentences: _____

_____

_____

8. Picture, clue, or personal association:

Full-page entry #2

1. Word: **context** (_____)

2. Word family:

Noun	Adjective/adverb	Verb
_____	_____	_____
_____	_____	_____

3. Definition: _____

_____

4. Synonyms: _____

Antonyms: _____

5. Examples: _____

_____

6. Collocations: _____

_____

_____

7. Sentences:

_____

_____

_____

8. Picture, clue, or personal association:

Full-page entry #3

---

1. Word: **domestic** (_____)

2. Word family:

Noun	Adjective/adverb	Verb
_____	_____	_____
_____	_____	_____

3. Definition: _____

_____

4. Synonyms: _____

Antonyms: _____

5. Examples: _____

_____

6. Collocations: _____

_____

_____

7. Sentences:

_____

_____

_____

8. Picture, clue, or personal association:

Full-page entry #4

1. Word: **inhibit** (_____)

2. Word family:

Noun	Adjective/adverb	Verb
_____	_____	_____
_____	_____	_____

3. Definition: _____

_____

4. Synonyms: _____

Antonyms: _____

5. Examples: _____

_____

6. Collocations: _____

_____

_____

7. Sentences: _____

_____

_____

8. Picture, clue, or personal association:

Vocabulary journal entry #2: Short-form entry

The short-form journal entry is useful for vocabulary items that require fewer details and for review or self-testing purposes.

TIP

If you record your vocabulary on paper, you can fold it lengthwise so that one half of the entry is hidden. Test yourself to see if you know the definition of the following word or can guess the word from the definition and synonyms.

Healing circles can be **adapted** to family situations, schools, the workplace, government agencies, churches, clubs, organizations, and prisons, and they embrace all ages, races, and walks of life.

Word: **adapt** to (v.)
Noun: adaptation, adaptor, adaptability
Adjective/adverb: adaptable, adaptive
Verb: adapted, adapting

1. Definition: change something in order to make it suitable for a new use or situation
2. Synonyms/antonymns: modify, change, adjust
3. Sentences:
   When we flew from Minnesota to Hawaii at Christmas, it took us a few days to adapt to the change in the climate.
   Animals adapt to their environment in order to survive.
4. Collocations:
   verbs: can, have to, must, need to
   adverbs: quickly, easily, readily, successfully

EXERCISE 5-2

Use the short-form template below to record the **AWL** (in bold type) and
<u>non-AWL</u> words (underlined) in the following text. See if you can figure out
the meaning of the word from the context.

The most practical form of solar energy is **passive** solar energy, which
occurs when natural light floods in through windows and is <u>absorbed</u> by
stone or concrete walls. In 1956 the world's first commercial solar building
was built in Albuquerque, New Mexico, by engineers Frank Bridgers and
Don Paxton. <u>Considered</u> ahead of its time, the design by architect Francis
Stanley provided for large, <u>sloping,</u> south-facing windows to capture infrared
radiation, following the same **principles** used by the ancient Romans to
heat their bathhouses. Passive solar energy is now being **incorporated**
into environmentally friendly building designs, which add double-glazed
windows and insulated walls and ceilings to trap heat, Trombe walls painted
black to **maximize** the absorption of infrared radiation, and mirrors or fiber
optics to **enhance** natural lighting.

1. Word: **passive** (_____)

    Noun: _____

    Adjective/adverb: _____

    Verb: _____

1. Definition: _____

_____

2. Synonyms/antonyms: _____

_____

3. Sentences: _____

_____

_____

_____

4. Collocations: _____

_____

_____

2. Word: **principle** (_____)

Noun: _____

Adjective/adverb: _____

Verb: _____

1. Definition: _____

_____

2. Synonyms/antonyms: _____

_____

3. Sentences: _____

_____

_____

_____

4. Collocations: _____

_____

_____

3. Word: **incorporate** (_____)

Noun: _____

Adjective/adverb: _____

Verb: _____

1. Definition: _____

_____

2. Synonyms/antonyms: _____

_____

3. Sentences: _____

_____

_____

_____

4. Collocations: _____

_____

_____

4. Word: **maximize** (_____)

Noun: _____

Adjective/adverb: _____

Verb: _____

1. Definition: _____

_____

2. Synonyms/antonyms: _____

_____

3. Sentences: _____

_____

_____

_____

4. Collocations: _____

_____

_____

5. Word: **enhance** (_____)

Noun: _____

Adjective/adverb: _____

Verb: _____

1. Definition: _____

_____

2. Synonyms/antonyms: _____

_____

3. Sentences: _____

_____

_____

_____

4. Collocations: _____

_____

_____

6. Word: **absorb** (_____)

Noun: _____

Adjective/adverb: _____

Verb: _____

1. Definition: _____

_____

2. Synonyms/antonyms: _____

_____

3. Sentences: _____

_____

_____

_____

4. Collocations: _____

_____

_____

7. Word: **consider** (_____)

Noun: _____

Adjective/adverb: _____

Verb: _____

1. Definition: _____

_____

2. Synonyms/antonyms: _____

_____

3. Sentences: _____

_____

_____

_____

4. Collocations: _____

_____

_____

8. Word: **sloping** (_____)

Noun: _____

Adjective/adverb: _____

Verbs: _____

1. Definition: _____

_____

2. Synonyms/antonyms: _____

3. Sentences: _____

_____

_____

_____

4. Collocations: _____

_____

_____

_____

Vocabulary journal entry #3: Flashcards

The handiest, most traditional way to record and review vocabulary is to use 3 × 5-inch flashcards, or index cards. While you can download the Language Lab app for this book with digital flashcards, it can be helpful to make your own, customized cards that reflect your personal learning needs.

Lined or unlined cards are available in different sizes and colors at any stationery or office supply store, or you can be creative and make your own. You can keep them like recipe cards in a small box, or use a small ring or ring binder that you can carry with you and flip through while you're sitting on the bus, waiting at the dentist's office, or taking a lunch break.

Flashcards are ideal for keeping a record of vocabulary as well as for reviewing and self-testing, and they lend themselves well to group and team work. To make learning more fun, they can be used in games and competitions.

Flashcards can be very simple. Depending on the size, they can contain only the most important information about a word for quick review. For your reference, the template in Appendix B includes as much detail as a full-page journal entry, but you can omit anything that you do not feel is necessary or helpful.

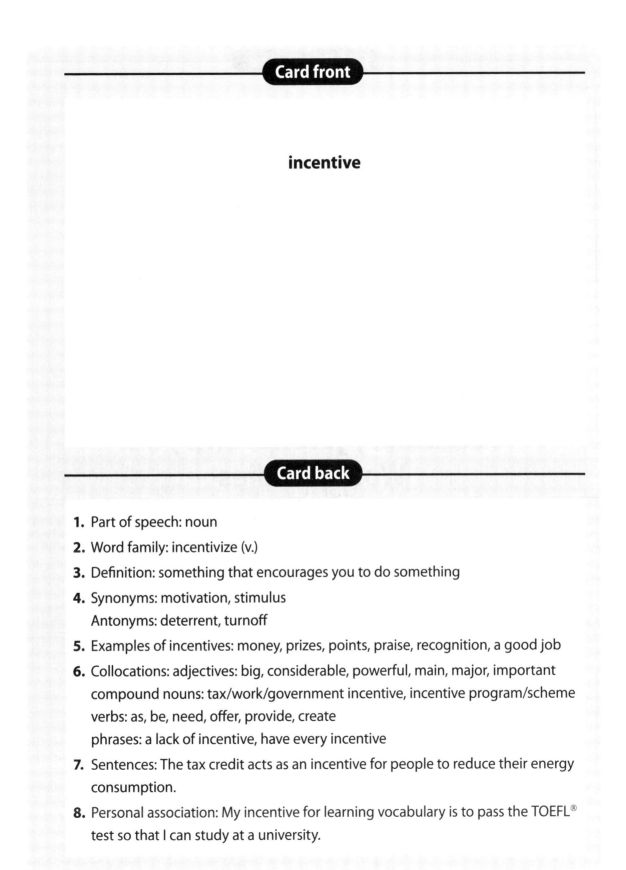

Card front

incentive

Card back

1. Part of speech: noun
2. Word family: incentivize (v.)
3. Definition: something that encourages you to do something
4. Synonyms: motivation, stimulus
   Antonyms: deterrent, turnoff
5. Examples of incentives: money, prizes, points, praise, recognition, a good job
6. Collocations: adjectives: big, considerable, powerful, main, major, important
   compound nouns: tax/work/government incentive, incentive program/scheme
   verbs: as, be, need, offer, provide, create
   phrases: a lack of incentive, have every incentive
7. Sentences: The tax credit acts as an incentive for people to reduce their energy consumption.
8. Personal association: My incentive for learning vocabulary is to pass the TOEFL® test so that I can study at a university.

EXERCISE 5-3

Make flashcards for the following words:

1. apparent
2. compromise
3. constitute
4. deviate
5. hierarchy
6. inherent
7. omnipotent
8. paradigm
9. reciprocal
10. scrutinize

Vocabulary journal entry #4: Word families

For words that you understand and can already use, you can record only the derivatives on a study sheet. This may seem like a lot of extra work, but writing down the various forms of a word reinforces learning and provides a quick overview.

EXAMPLE

Noun	Adjective/adverb	Verb
theory, theorist	theoretical	theorize
participation, participant	participatory, participative	participate
inflation	inflationary	inflate
stigma, stigmatization	—	stigmatize
loyalty, loyalist	loyal	—

EXERCISE 5-4

Complete the vocabulary chart with the derivatives of the given AWL and non-AWL words.

Noun	Adjective/adverb	Verb
1. objective	_____	_____
2. _____	radical	_____
3. _____	_____	violate
4. margin	_____	_____
5. _____	external	_____
6. _____	_____	exploit
7. insight	_____	_____
8. _____	approximate	_____
9. _____	_____	conceive
10. contamination	_____	_____
11. _____	spontaneous	_____
12. _____	_____	dispute
13. explosion	_____	_____
14. _____	relative	_____
15. _____	_____	endure

Vocabulary entry #5: Concordances

The *Oxford Advanced Learner's Dictionary* defines a concordance as "an alphabetical list of the principal words used in a book or body of work, showing where and how often these are used." These lists, which appear in language corpora, are produced using special computer software and are very useful for showing how a word is used and in which context it appears. A concordance appears in a grid with the word embedded in a sentence.

surrounding text	word	surrounding text
surrounding text	word	surrounding text
surrounding text	word	surrounding text

Compiling lists can be a very time-consuming process, but you can use the organizational principle of concordances to record vocabulary that you may find difficult to use.

EXAMPLES

Example 1: revenue

Countries depend on tourism for	**revenue**	and foreign investment.
Madagascar invests its tourist	**revenue**	in safeguarding its world-famous biodiversity.
Municipal governments derive	**revenue**	from service fees and property taxes.

Example 2: inevitable

The expansion of computer networks is made	**inevitable**	by their convenience to patients.
The only way humanity can avoid	**inevitable**	collapse is to reduce its ecological footprint.
Taxes and death are	**inevitable**.	

EXERCISE 5-5

Find or make three sentences using the following AWL and non-AWL words. The first sentence for each word is given as an example. Try to create your sentences so that the word lines up in each sentence.

1. elite

The Swiss Guard has served as an **elite** group of bodyguards since the late fifteenth century.

_____

_____

_____

2. occupy

The English Department **occupies** the fourth floor.

_____

_____

_____

3. parallel

College Drive runs **parallel** to Library Road.

_____

_____

_____

4. predicament

The hikers found themselves in a serious **predicament** after they ran out of drinking water.

_____

_____

_____

5. priority

Passing your exams should be your first **priority** if you want to graduate.

_____

_____

_____

Final word about vocabulary journals

No single method of keeping a vocabulary journal is necessarily the best. However, you should choose a method that allows you to find words quickly and to review and test yourself easily.

> **TIP**
>
> Using a ring binder lets you remove your recorded vocabulary and keep it up-to-date. Of course, you can keep your vocabulary on your computer, laptop, tablet or iPad, or smartphone if you prefer digital to paper.

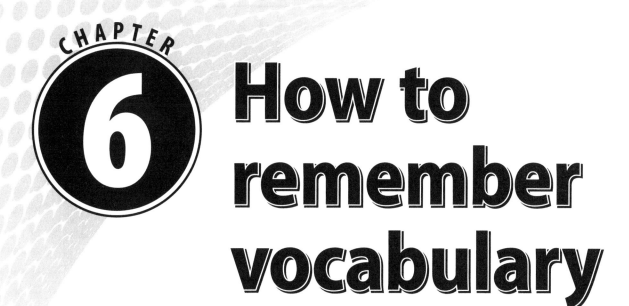

CHAPTER 6
How to remember vocabulary

Objectives

To improve your ability to retain and recall new vocabulary using strategies such as repetition, mnemonic devices, semantic connections, and practice

To remember collocations

Identifying academic words, understanding their meaning in a dictionary or a text, and recording them in a journal or list are fairly straightforward ways to learn new vocabulary. The more daunting task, however, is recalling the right words when you need them. You can memorize lists of words, but that's about as effective as memorizing dates for a history test. Once you've written the test, the dates vanish from your memory without a trace.

When you consider how many words you need to learn in order to answer a few questions on a test, coming up with the right word on the spot can be like searching for a needle in a haystack. Therefore, you need to start out with the attitude of learning words for life, not just for a test, and concentrate on words that you think will be of use to you in the future.

Techniques for remembering vocabulary

Repetition

The more often you see, hear, and say a word, the more likely you are to retain it. There are several strategies you can use.

- Choose a "word of the day" and repeat it to yourself as often as you can, like a song that gets stuck in your head.
- Repeat it to yourself silently if you feel uncomfortable about saying the word out loud. Try putting a face to it—the face of your favorite friend, teacher, singer, or movie star so that you will want to think of it more often.
- Post sticky notes on the bathroom mirror or your bedroom wall, your school locker, the dashboard of your car, your computer screen—anyplace where you will be sure to see them several times a day.
- Set a goal of using the word in a conversation between five and ten times a day, even if you're repeating the same sentence or question.
- Change the password for your laptop, cell phone, or e-mail account to the word you are learning so that you will have to use it frequently,
- Send the word you are learning several times as a text message to a friend who's also learning vocabulary, and have him or her do the same.
- Look purposefully for the word in anything you read or hear, and keep track of how many times you encounter it in one day.

All this may sound a little crazy, but if you have ever been obsessed with something or someone, you will know how difficult it was to banish the thought from your mind.

Mnemonics

Invented by the Greeks 2,500 years ago, **mnemonics** (the first "m" is silent) is a memory-improvement technique that makes use of rhymes, rules, phrases, diagrams, acronyms, and other associations to aid memory. Mnemonics connects powerful images to what you want to remember so that you can access information more quickly and permanently. The most effective associations are:

- Positive
- Vivid
- Pleasant
- Funny
- Even wacky and exaggerated

Associations also can involve the senses, enabling you to see, hear, taste, smell, and feel. Your most useful tool in creating effective images and strong connections is your imagination, and the more creative and crazy your connections are, the more likely you are to remember words.

Types of mnemonic methods are peg method, key word association, and visualization and association.

Peg method

The **peg method** works by relating two concepts that are basically unrelated. Since this method usually involves rhymes, it is more suitable for learning simple concepts such as numbers and one-syllable words. However, a vivid visual component with a humorous, even nonsensical, sentence will reinforce less complicated academic vocabulary.

EXAMPLES

Never *approach* a giant cockroach.

My little sister always needs a lot of *assistance*.

While walking through the forest, I became *aware* of a very angry grizzly bear.

There is a huge pile of *files* on my desk.

The neighbor's cows kept getting into our garden; *hence*, we built a fence.

EXERCISE 6-1

Match the rhyming words and create a nonsensical sentence for each.

1. _____ goal   **a.** towel

2. _____ pose   **b.** heavy

3. _____ brief   **c.** toad

4. _____ code   **d.** rose

5. _____ core   **e.** teacher

6. _____ grant   **f.** chief

7. _____ foul   **g.** goat

8. _____ quote   **h.** hole

9. _____ levy   **i.** ant

10. _____ feature   **j.** bore

1. _____

2. _____

3. _____

4. _____

5. _____

6. _____

7. _____

8. _____

9. _____

10. _____

Key word association

You can build vocabulary through word associations in which a known key word will evoke an unknown target word. This is, of course, a very personal process so what works for someone else may not necessarily be meaningful to you, and vice versa.

Take the following steps to form a key word mnemonic:

- Choose a word in your own language, or preferably in English if you can think of one, that contains a similar sound or spelling to the target word.
- Create a strong association that will readily remind you of the target word.
- Create a vivid visual image to reinforce the connection. Again, the funnier or crazier the image, the more likely you are to remember it.

EXAMPLES

Example 1: ambiguous

1. *Ambiguous* contains two words: *am* and *big*.

   In reality I am small, so to I say that I *am big*, *big* must have different meanings: powerful, popular, well-known, conceited.

2. A visual image could be myself as a miniature Statue of Liberty or Superman.

   Sentence: In this poem the poet uses *ambiguous* imagery, which makes it difficult to interpret.

Example 2: inclined

1. *Cline* sounds like *klein* in German.

2. The noun, *incline*, means a slope, so you can imagine a very small person standing helplessly on a steep slope or slide.

   Sentence: Most of the students are not *inclined* to do their homework on weekends after they've been out all night at a party.

EXERCISE 6-2

Give the definition for the following AWL and non-AWL words and create key word associations.

Word	Definition	Key word
1. terminate		
2. category		
3. rigid		
4. investigate		
5. migrate		
6. virtual		
7. malicious		
8. speculate		
9. responsible		
10. pattern		

Visualization and association

As can be seen from key word association, visual images are very effective mnemonic devices. If you have ever taken part in a play or a concert, you know how challenging it is to memorize your lines or lyrics, let alone recall them at the right moment on stage in front of an audience. We all wonder how actors and singers do it.

People with super memories are successful at remembering large amounts of information because they have trained their brains to create and store visual images. According to Tony Buzan, an expert on brain training and the inventor of mind mapping, "If the brain doesn't have an image, it can't remember. You've got to image, you've got to image." This accounts for the fact that most people can remember faces better than names, or a building and its surroundings rather than the street address or house number. It's just how the brain works!

Embellishing your images with all kinds of gory, absurd, naughty, hilarious, or outrageous details can make them more memorable.

EXAMPLES

Example 1: emerge

Emerge means *to come out of a dark, hidden, or confined space* and *to become known*. An image that everyone can relate to is a scene from a horror movie in which a creepy creature breaks the surface of a lake or swamp and rises up out of the water, dripping slime. Maybe it says, "Hi! My name's Bob!"

Sentence: During the journalist's investigation, it *emerged* that the prime minister was having an affair with a dancer from a striptease club.

Example 2: vicarious

Vicarious means a way in which *to feel or experience by watching or reading about someone else doing something*. A suitable image would be a fat, lazy couch potato lying on his back and stuffing his face from a huge bag of potato chips while watching a football or hockey game on television. You can even add a cartoon caption, in which the person tosses the empty bag onto the carpet and sighs, "That was the hardest I've ever played!"

Sentence: Parents derive a *vicarious* sense of achievement from their children's athletic and academic successes.

EXERCISE 6-3

Visualize the following AWL and non-AWL words and create a sentence to go with them.

Word	Visual image	Sentence
1. compatible		
2. reluctance		
3. voluntary		
4. precise		
5. comprise		
6. prohibit		
7. deny		
8. lethal		
9. immaculate		
10. explore		
11. surveillance		
12. assimilate		
13. catastrophic		
14. despise		
15. potent		

Making connections

In addition to associating words with powerful images, you can connect them to a group of words or concepts. It is much easier to remember things when they are related to other things than when they are isolated details.

List–group–label

This is a method for learning words in groups, and it helps to build background knowledge, expand vocabulary, and develop critical thinking. List–group–label works best in a group where everyone can combine their knowledge.

- Choose a subject and brainstorm as many related words as you can think of.
- Look at your words and group them into three categories. You will probably think of nouns first, but try to come up with verbs and adjectives as well to broaden your vocabulary.
- Give each category a descriptive label.

EXAMPLE

Example: environment

nature	atmosphere	pollution
ecology	animals	water
global warming	natural disasters	carbon dioxide
laws	conservation	trees
oil spills	rain	mountains

Categories

Problems	**Components**	**Protection**
pollution	nature	ecology
global warming	animals	laws
oil spills	trees	conservation
carbon dioxide	mountains	
natural disasters	rain	
	water	
	atmosphere	

EXERCISE 6-4

Make a list of words that relate to the following subjects.

1. crime _____

2. genetics _____

3. advertising _____

4. jobs _____

5. money _____

Grouping or semantic mapping

It is much easier to remember new information when it is related to something you already know than when it occurs in isolation. One technique that visually links words and establishes relationships is called **semantic mapping**. You may have used this technique, also called **mind mapping**, to brainstorm ideas for writing assignments. The organizing principle behind semantic mapping is not really all that different from list–group–label; the only feature that distinguishes semantic mapping is the graphic layout. A semantic map looks something like the solar system with the sun in the middle, the planets orbiting around the sun, and the moons revolving around the planets.

Semantic mapping uses three elements to categorize vocabulary:

1. A target phrase or word that is the central focus (like the sun).
2. Strands that provide additional information about the central concept, such as a definition or characteristic (like the planets)
3. Supporting details or examples for each strand (like the moons)

How to create a semantic map

1. Draw a circle in the middle of a piece of paper and write the key concept inside the circle.
2. Draw lines like spokes in a wheel from the central circle, and at the end of each line draw another circle for the related words.
3. Draw radiating lines from the smaller circles, and at the end draw more circles to contain details and examples.

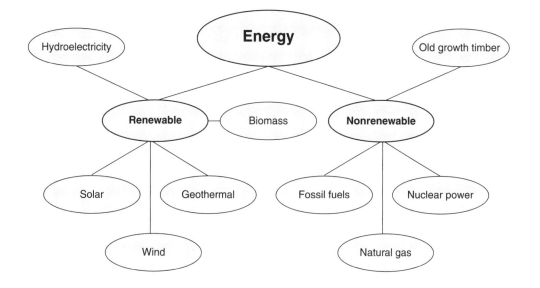

Depending on the subject matter, semantic maps can range from basic and simple to complicated, and they can consist of more than three levels. For example, the preceding map could include examples of fossil fuels and biomass fuels.

EXERCISE 6-5

Create a semantic map for the following topics using the clues to subcategories provided for you. You just need to fill in the specifics and examples.

1. Government: levels of government, responsibilities
2. Personality: types of personality, personality traits
3. Human rights: types of rights (political), examples
4. Communications: sources of communication, characteristics

Chunking (clustering)

Chunking, also known as **clustering**, involves learning concepts in units. Research shows that we learn best in chunks and that we are able to process seven to nine unrelated units at a time, depending upon their complexity. This principle is something you can keep in mind when studying; in other words, don't overload yourself with information.

Language is learned in chunks. An example would be: *How are you today?* which probably sounds more like: *how'r'u t'day?* Together these words convey a specific meaning, and therefore they are more meaningful than if you were to learn each word individually. Frequently used for remembering numbers, chunking is an attempt to find meaning or patterns in pieces. Neuroscientist Daniel Bor, author of *The Ravenous Brain: How the New Science of Consciousness Explains Our Insatiable Search for Meaning*, argues that humans look for patterns and that finding patterns is the basis of creativity.

Vocabulary can be learned in chunks based on what the units have in common.

1. Prefixes

    Overall, overlap, overseas, overload, overwhelm

    Expand, expire, exploit, export, expose

2. A common subject

    Sources of energy: oil, coal, gas, nuclear power, old growth timber

    Seven deadly sins: envy, avarice, lust, anger, gluttony, sloth, pride

3. Meaning

    Notion, idea, concept, thought

    Confine, limit, contain, enclose, restrict

A challenging, but creative, way to use chunking to learn vocabulary is to make a sentence using a specific group of words. The sentence doesn't have to make complete sense, but the words have to be used correctly. In fact, you are more likely to remember sentences that are a little crazy or that evoke an unusual image.

EXAMPLES

I gave my **consent** to **conduct** a **survey** with a **team** of **temporary psychology** professors.
The **lecture** had a **positive impact** on the younger **generation** of **ethnic colleagues**.
The **adjacent academy** was **abandoned** after an incident with a **chemical** substance that had **widespread medical consequences**.

Another activity is to create news headlines with new vocabulary.

EXAMPLES

Citizens claim **federal subsidies** are **insufficient**.
Student **suspended** for **transmitting revolutionary research**.
Demonstrating protestors **occupy legislative assembly**.

EXERCISE 6-6

Create sentences or headlines using the following AWL words.

1. overseas, partner, participate, previous, scheme

   _____

   _____

2. vehicle, technical, transport, regulate, panel

   _____

   _____

3. investigate, injure, identity, evident, authority

   _____

   _____

4. benefit, aid, financial, majority, corporate

   _____

   _____

5. create, diverse, domestic, flexible, framework

   _____

   _____

Collocations

Collocations refer to groupings of words that typically occur together. For example, we *make a mistake* (not do a mistake); we *commit a crime* (not make a crime); we look *at* our watch (not on or to our watch); we can have a *strong* or *stiff* drink (not a heavy or powerful drink). Because you can't necessarily figure them out logically or explain why one word is used instead of another, collocations have to be learned as a unit. This is especially true of verbs, nouns, and adjectives that are accompanied by prepositions, which is why Chapter 5 suggested that you record prepositions in your vocabulary journal. Since collocations are so particular to one language, they are very difficult to translate, and you can run into some serious, and amusing, problems if you try to translate directly from your native language into English.

> **TIP**
>
> To master collocations you have to read extensively, watch television and movies, and develop a good feeling for the language. Also, you must pay careful attention to what native speakers say in conversation.

There are seven types of collocations.

1. Adverb and adjective
   - We weren't *fully aware* of the consequences.
   - I was *completely surprised* when I opened the door.
2. Adjective and noun
   - I need to get some *fresh air*.
   - Everyone should eat a *healthy diet*.
3. Noun and noun
   - We need a *bar of soap*, a *tube of toothpaste*, and a *bottle of aspirin*.
   - He lost his *cigarette lighter*, *car keys*, and *driver's licence*.
4. Noun and verb
   - Dogs *bark*, snow *falls*, and planes *take off*.
5. Verb and noun
   - We have *to do our homework* and *make our beds*.
6. Verb and preposition
   - Most people *believe in God*.
   - I'm *looking forward to* seeing you.

7. Verb and adverb
   • Listen *carefully*!

There are also fixed expressions that contain inseparable collocations.

EXAMPLES

I feel toward one of my students as if he were my own *flesh and blood.*
The team's determined to win come *hell or high water.*
The hostages came out of the ordeal *alive and kicking.*
The *high and mighty* live in this upscale neighborhood.
Janice *has her feet on the ground*, whereas James usually *has his head in the clouds.*

As you learned in Chapter 5, collocations can be found in learner's dictionaries and specific online collocation dictionaries.

EXERCISE 6-7

Make a note of the parts of speech and find collocations for the following AWL words.

1. attitude (_____) _____

_____

2. civil (_____) _____

_____

3. confirm (_____) _____

_____

4. define (_____) _____

_____

5. erode (_____) _____

_____

6. fee (_____) _____

_____

7. implement (_____) _____

_____

8. index (_____) _____

_____

9. mechanism (_____) _____

_____

10. network (_____) _____

_____

11. option (_____) _____

_____

12. phenomenon (_____) _____

_____

13. range (_____) _____

_____

14. schedule (_____) _____

_____

15. target (_____) _____

_____

EXERCISE 6-8

Fill in the blanks with the AWL and non-AWL words from the following list for their collocations.

deteriorate (v.)   compromise (n.)   pursue (v.)
nutrition (n.)   annual (adj.)   sacrifice (n.)
portion (n.)   deny (v.)   challenge (n.)
conclusion (n.)   predict (v.)   evade (v.)
uniform (n.)   approval (n.)   bureaucratic (adj.)
release (n.)   essential (adj.)   rate (n.)
accomplishment (n)   pattern (n.)

1. income, precipitation, report, expenditures, budget _____

2. a goal, fugitive, hobby, interest, actively, vigorously _____

3. immediate, slow, welcome, emotional, a sense of _____

4. full, standard, traditional, military, in / out of _____

5. considerable, sizeable, generous, individual, of _____

6. with accuracy, fail to, difficult to, the weather, the future _____

7. firmly, emphatically, vehemently, publicly, explicitly _____

8. great, serious, major, pose, rise to the _____

9. acceptable, reasonable, agree on, reach, work out _____

10. reasonable, obvious, foregone, come to, jump to _____

11. interest, daily, exchange, birth, failure _____

12. seriously, dramatically, rapidly, continue to, be likely to _____

13. sufficient, adequate, proper, good, a source of _____

14. geometric, floral, basic, fall into, establish, emerge _____

15. total, overwhelming, full, seek, gain _____

16. extremely, highly, somewhat, necessarily, be/become _____

17. deem / regard something as, absolutely, for, to _____

18. narrowly, successfully, attempt to, try to, manage to _____

19. considerable, real, major, of, in _____

20. enormous, personal, ultimate, make, offer something as _____

Practice

Taking tests and doing exercises are not the most exciting ways to remember vocabulary. Since tests are associated with stress and hard work, they are not particularly enjoyable, nor would you want to spend your free time taking tests when there are several activities you would rather do. Tests, however, can help you practice answering questions within a given time limit and measure your progress, and should you do better than expected, they can give you a feeling of accomplishment. The same applies to vocabulary exercises, which remind one of the onerous task of doing homework.

TIP

To lessen the anxiety of tests and the drudgery of exercises, approach them in small doses—say, at the end of a unit of study or once a week.

- Set aside a specific time in your study schedule, and give yourself a reward or special treat, even if you don't do as well as you'd like to.
- Keep track of your progress on a graph.
- Do exercises and tests with a partner; combining your knowledge or competing for the best score can make studying more fun.

McGraw-Hill Education: TOEFL® iBT (2014) provides three practice TOEFL® tests as well as preparation on specific parts of the test. There are also many websites where you can find practice vocabulary tests and exercises for the TOEFL® test. See the bibliography and online resources at the end of the book for some suggested sites.

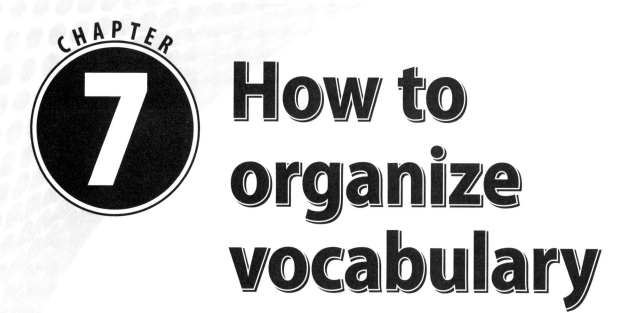

CHAPTER 7

How to organize vocabulary

Objective

To organize vocabulary according to academic subject

As you saw in Chapter 6, associating vocabulary with powerful images and connecting it with other words can help you remember more easily. It also helps if you learn words that are related to the same subject. In this chapter you will group words according to academic disciplines.

Agriculture

Art, Music, and Theater

Business and Economics

Communications

Computer Science and Technology

Education

Environmental Science

Engineering and Architecture

History, Government, and Politics

Law and Justice

Language and Literature

Mathematics

Medicine

Philosophy and Religion

Natural and Life Sciences (Biology, Chemistry, Geology, Geography, Physics)

Rhetoric

Social Sciences (Psychology, Sociology, Anthropology)

Of course, individual words can refer to more than one subject, and you will not be able to list *all* the words that fall under one subject heading, nor will they all fit on one page. The exercise in this chapter is meant to get you going. Start with the words that you have learned so far in this book and that are contained in Appendix A. As you come across new words in your studies, add them to your lists. You can also make new categories if you find them useful. Be sure to record a sample sentence or some examples of how the word is used, rather than only a definition. Try to make your sentence as graphic and personal as you can.

For each subject five words are given as an example. These words have been taken from the AWL and from the vocabulary.com Top 1000, which appear most frequently on SAT, ACT, GRE, and TOEFL® tests (https://www.vocabulary.com/lists/52473#view=notes).

Agriculture

Word	Example
fertilize (v.)	If the soil lacks organic matter, you will need to **fertilize** it.
flourish (v./n.)	Plants cannot **flourish** without sunlight, water, and nutrients.
horticulture (n.)	Sarah is studying **horticulture** so that she can become a gardener.
modify (v.)	Biotech companies genetically **modify** their seeds to resist pests and chemicals.
yield (v./n.)	Hybrid varieties were developed to increase **yield** and resistance to harsh weather conditions.

Art, Music, and Theater

Word	Example
contemporary (adj.)	I prefer **contemporary** art to the works of classical artists.
exhibit (n./v.)	The museum is holding an interesting **exhibit** of Emily Carr's early paintings.
graphic (adj.)	Quentin Tarantino's movies contain scenes of **graphic** violence.
pastoral (adj.)	Many of Monet's paintings depict **pastoral** scenes.
perform (v.)	The orchestra will **perform** works by Beethoven, Bach, and Mozart.

Business and Economics

Word	Example
expand (v.)	The Asian market is **expanding**.
income (n.)	The company relies on its sales **income**.
incorporate (v.)	We are going to **incorporate** your suggestions into our plans.
invest (v.)	The company has **invested** heavily in new technology.
revenue (n.)	Our **revenues** are expected to grow over the next ten years.

Communications

Word	Example
comment (n./v.)	Do you have any further **comments**?
correspond (v.)	We can **correspond** regularly by e-mail.
edit (v./n.)	You need to **edit** your essay before you prepare a final draft.
media (n.)	We rely on electronic **media** for news.
transmit (v.)	We cannot **transmit** your message due to a technical problem.

Computer Science and Technology

Word	Example
automate (v.)	Nowadays most factories are **automated.**
capacity (n.)	This laptop has a storage **capacity** of 640 GB.
device (n.)	A cell phone is a very versatile and handy **device**.
input (n./v.)	Before you can do the calculation, you have to **input** all the data.
operate (v.)	A laptop is easy to **operate**.

Education

Word	Example
discipline (n./v.)	The vocabulary in this exercise is organized according to academic **discipline**.
evaluate (v.)	The teacher will **evaluate** the class's progress at the end of each month.
instruct (v.)	Who's going to **instruct** the Academic Writing class?
institute (n.)	Joseph is a researcher at the **Institute** for Regenerative Medicine.
objective (n.)	The **objectives** are listed on the first page of the course outline.

_____   _____

_____   _____

_____   _____

_____   _____

_____   _____

_____   _____

_____   _____

_____   _____

_____   _____

_____   _____

_____   _____

_____   _____

_____   _____

_____   _____

Environmental Science

Word	Example
adapt (v.)	Animals survive by **adapting** to their environment.
contaminate (v.)	Pesticides and herbicides **contaminate** the soil and groundwater.
evolve (v.)	Do you think that man **evolved** from the ape?
migrate (v.)	Swallows **migrate** southward at the end of the summer.
monitor (v./n.)	To understand what is happening in the environment, it is necessary to **monitor** changes on a continual basis.

Engineering and Architecture

Word	Example
artificial (adj.)	The new park will include an **artificial** lake for recreational water sports.
construct (v.)	The Eiffel Tower was **constructed** between 1887 and 1889.
infrastructure (n.)	The city government will have to invest heavily in upgrading the aging **infrastructure.**
mechanical (adj.)	My brother has always been interested in **mechanical** equipment.
scale (n.)	The model of the new library was built exactly to **scale**.

History, Government, and Politics

Word	Example
conflict (n./v.)	The course of human history is characterized by a series of **conflicts**.
legislate (v.)	The government has the power to **legislate** striking civil servants back to work.
regulate (v.)	GE foods are not as strictly **regulated** as additives and preservatives.
revolution (n.)	History has witnessed major **revolutions** in America, France, and Russia, among others.
successor (n.)	Will Prince Charles or Prince William be the **successor** to the throne of England when Elizabeth II dies?

Law and Justice

Word	Example
discriminate (v.)	It is illegal to **discriminate** against people on the basis of race, color, religion, gender, and sexual orientation.
equality (n.)	The Constitution guarantees **equality** for all people before the law.
implicate (v.)	Three foreigners were **implicated** in the terrorist attack.
motive (n.)	To get a conviction, the prosecution has to prove that the defendant had a **motive** for committing the crime.
violate (v.)	Repressive regimes have a record of **violating** human rights.

Language and Literature

Word	Example
drama (n.)	Ancient Greek **drama** had a strong influence on modern theater.
interpret (v.)	On the exam you will be required to **interpret** several passages from *Macbeth*.
metaphor (n.)	A long, hard journey is a common **metaphor** for the challenges of life.
publish (v.)	The first edition of Walt Whitman's *Leaves of Grass* was **published** in 1855.
satire (n.)	Jonathan Swift was a master of social **satire**.

Mathematics

Word	Example
dimension (n.)	We have to measure the **dimensions** of this container to calculate the volume it can hold.
exceed (v.)	This year's enrollment **exceeds** that of last year.
random (adj.)	Gambling games deal with **random** numbers.
ratio (n.)	The student:teacher **ratio** in this class is 32:1.
sequence (n.)	1, 2, 4, 8, 16 begins an infinite **sequence**.

Medicine

Word	Example
detect (v.)	CT scans can **detect** tumors of a certain size.
malignant (adj.)	The patient's results came back showing that her tumor was **malignant**.
practitioner (n.)	Tony wants to become a general **practitioner** and go into family medicine.
recover (v.)	It took me two weeks to **recover** from the flu.
therapeutic (adj.)	When I'm under a lot of stress, I find doing yoga very **therapeutic.**

Philosophy and Religion

Word	Example
contemplate (v.)	Throughout human history people have **contemplated** the meaning of death.
ethical (adj.)	Many people disagree about the **ethical** implications of applying genetic research.
logic (n.)	I don't understand the **logic** behind your reasoning.
perceive (v.)	Everyone has a different way of **perceiving** reality.
valid (adj.)	In order to be **valid**, an argument must be based on factual evidence.

Natural and Life Sciences (Biology, Chemistry, Geology, Geography, Physics)

Word	Example
diverse (adj.)	Nature is **diverse**, and this diversity allows life to continue.
empirical (adj.)	Good science requires **empirical** evidence and sound conclusions.
extract (v./n.)	Embryonic stem cells can only be **extracted** from the umbilical cord of aborted fetuses.
nuclear (adj.)	Many people are opposed to **nuclear** power out of safety concerns.
trigger (v.)	Subterranean atomic tests are suspected of **triggering** earthquakes.

Rhetoric

Word	Example
coherent (adj.)	The opposing side's argument was **coherent** and well substantiated.
convince (v.)	You cannot **convince** me of your opinion without facts to back it up.
debate (n./v.)	The government's support of stem cell research has unleashed a **debate** in the media.
justify (v.)	He **justified** his decision to take a temporary leave from his studies by claiming that he had personal issues to deal with.
presume (v.)	Unless there is strong evidence to the contrary, we have to **presume** that someone is innocent until proven guilty.

Social Sciences (Psychology, Sociology, Anthropology)

Word	Example
conform (v.)	In a group the members are under pressure to **conform**.
statistics (n.)	A report should include relevant facts and **statistics**.
tension (n.)	Mounting **tension** between the two groups led to outright conflict.
tradition (n.)	It's a **tradition** to initiate members into a group by having them undergo some kind of test or challenge.
trend (n./v.)	It's a **trend** for all students to carry a cell phone with them at all times.

PART 3

Using vocabulary

CHAPTER 8

How to use vocabulary from the Academic Word List

Objectives

To use AWL vocabulary correctly

To accustom yourself to academic-type readings and lectures in a short form

Regular reading and listening can increase your exposure to vocabulary, but the only way to retain new words is to use them repeatedly and regularly. Simply put, if you don't use it, you lose it.

Unfortunately, it takes a considerable amount of time before you can use new vocabulary correctly and spontaneously. Furthermore, when you are preparing for a test, unless you start very early, you have to cram a lot of words into a short period of time. So, you can only do the best you can.

The ten readings that follow range from 200 to 350 words and are meant to help provide vocabulary acquisition using AWL words. They feature the kinds of content to be found in the TOEFL® test reading and listening (lecture) sections. (The TOEFL® test reading section features three readings of about 700 words and the listening section features four academic lectures to listen to. The TOEFL® test writing section includes shorter 200- to 300-word texts and lectures to respond to.)

The AWL words in the following readings are indicated in **bold type.** Other useful words are <u>underlined</u>. Do not consult a dictionary as you do the exercises; rather, try to use the strategies in Chapter 3 to determine the meaning from context or eliminate words that you know are wrong.

The audio icon indicates that you can also listen to recordings of these readings.

Reading 1:
Albert Einstein's theory of relativity

In 1905, German-born physicist Albert Einstein published his "special theory of relativity," which forced scientists to **revise** long-held notions related to mass and energy, and gave the world its most <u>recognizable</u> equation.

For centuries, scientists **considered** mass and energy to be **distinct** and unrelated **concepts**. Einstein's theory, however, revealed that these building blocks of the physical world were actually the same thing, just in different forms. Einstein **demonstrated** that mass (m) and energy (E) are equal, as long as they are multiplied by the speed of light (c) times itself (^{2}). The mathematical result was the now famous equation $E = mc^2$.

The simplicity of Einstein's short equation would seem to **contradict** its **inherent** complexity and <u>far-reaching</u> implications into space, time, energy, and mass. Put simply, $E = mc^2$ means that if a tiny amount of mass is multiplied by the speed of light squared, it can be **converted** into huge amounts of energy—with dramatic results. The consequences of this "simple" conversion can be seen in an atomic bomb's massive power or in the Big Bang theory of the origins of the universe.

Einstein's theory of relativity has held up for a century. Numerous experiments have been **conducted** over the past hundred years to test Einstein's ideas, and all have **confirmed** that the speed of light is constant, regardless of the observer's motion.

EXERCISE 8-1

Choose the word that is closest in meaning to the word from Reading 1.

1. _____ **revise**   a. reread   b. rethink   c. reduce

2. _____ **consider**   a. regard   b. allow   c. measure

3. _____ **distinct**   a. separate   b. unusual   c. unpleasant

4. _____ **concept**   a. theory   b. plan   c. idea

5. _____ **demonstrate**   a. protest   b. show   c. question

6. _____ **contradict**   a. explain   b. confirm   c. refute

7. _____ **inherent**   a. apparent   b. intrinsic   c. obvious

8. _____ **convert**   a. transform   b. adapt   c. redeem

9. _____ **conduct**   a. initiate   b. carry out   c. transmit

10. _____ **confirm**   a. validate   b. approve   c. deny

EXERCISE 8-2

Complete each of the following sentences with the appropriate choice from the words listed in Exercise 8-1. Be sure to use the correct form of each verb and to pluralize nouns if necessary.

1. Every person has a/an _____ personality that makes him or her stand out from the rest.

2. After analyzing the data, the team had to _____ their original hypothesis.

3. His rude behavior only _____ our negative first impression of him.

4. Some people have no _____ of what it means to respect others' privacy.

5. Almost everyone has a/an _____ fear of death that is not so easy to overcome.

6. When people travel to foreign countries, it is natural for them to _____ the local currency into their own.

7. Part of our assignment in Study Skills is to _____ a survey about time management.

8. When you write a refutation, you are supposed to come up with arguments that _____ your thesis.

9. The experiment is designed to _____ how two chemical substances interact.

10. Before you make an important decision concerning your future, you need to _____ all your options.

EXERCISE 8-3

Choose the word that corresponds to the best answer.

1. The word *recognizable* in the passage is closest in meaning to _____.

    (A) popular

    (B) appreciated

    (C) distinct

    (D) understood

2. The word *far-reaching* in the passage is closest in meaning to _____.

    (A) extensive

    (B) novel

    (C) significant

    (D) devastating

Reading 2:
The effects of meteorite impacts on biological evolution

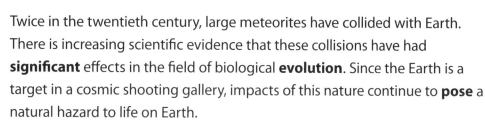

Twice in the twentieth century, large meteorites have collided with Earth. There is increasing scientific evidence that these collisions have had **significant** effects in the field of biological **evolution**. Since the Earth is a target in a cosmic shooting gallery, impacts of this nature continue to **pose** a natural hazard to life on Earth.

If a meteorite **impact** is sufficient in magnitude, it can cause an ecological catastrophe. The best-documented case occurred 65 million years ago at the end of the Cretaceous period of geological history when a meteorite in **excess** of a trillion tons and at least 10 kilometers in diameter crashed into the Earth. This break in geological history is marked by a mass <u>extinction</u>, when as many as half the species on the planet perished. While a dozen or more mass extinctions have since been recorded, the Cretaceous mass extinction has always <u>intrigued</u> paleontologists because it marks the end of the age of the dinosaurs. For tens of millions of years, those great creatures had <u>flourished</u>, only to disappear suddenly and mysteriously.

According to some **estimates**, the majority of all extinctions may be **attributed** to such impacts. Such a **perspective** fundamentally **alters** our view of biological evolution. The standard **criterion** for the survival of a species is its success in competing with other species and adapting to slowly changing environments. Yet an equally important criterion is the ability of a species to survive random global ecological catastrophes.

EXERCISE 8-4

Choose the word that is closest in meaning to the word from Reading 2.

1. _____ **significant**   a. important   b. sudden   c. symbolic

2. _____ **evolution**   a. history   b. revolution   c. development

3. _____ **pose**   a. raise   b. present   c. constitute

4. _____ **impact**   a. collision   b. effect   c. explosion

5. _____ **excess**   a. extravagance   b. surplus   c. remainder

6. _____ **estimate**   a. opinion   b. acclaim   c. approximation

7. _____ **attribute**   a. characterize   b. explain   c. ascribe to

8. _____ **perspective** a. outlook   b. understanding   c. image

9. _____ **alter**   a. change   b. evolve   c. refute

10. _____ **criterion**   a. condition   b. measure   c. censure

EXERCISE 8-5

Complete each of the following sentences with the appropriate choice from the words listed in Exercise 8-4. Be sure to use the correct form of each verb and to pluralize nouns if necessary.

1. The weather has a major _____ on people's health and

   well-being.

2. She _____ her successful career to the encouragement

   and support she received from her parents.

3. Scientists have recorded a/an _____ increase in the

   average global temperature.

4. By 2020 it is _____ that global tourist revenues will

   reach in _____ of $2 trillion.

5. Nuclear waste that is improperly disposed of _____ a

serious hazard to the environment and the health of human beings.

6. What _____ do the professors use to evaluate the

students' overall performance?

7. Everyone has a different _____ on life and its challenges.

8. The instructor is going to _____ the course content for

next semester to make it more relevant to contemporary issues.

9. Darwin's theory of _____ changed the way humans

regarded the creation of man.

EXERCISE 8-6

Choose the word that corresponds to the best answer.

1. The word *extinction* in the passage is closest in meaning to _____.

   Ⓐ movement

   Ⓑ distinction

   Ⓒ change

   Ⓓ disappearance

2. The word *flourish* in the passage is closest in meaning to _____.

   Ⓐ exist

   Ⓑ thrive

   Ⓒ wither

   Ⓓ wield

3. The word *intrigue* in the passage is closest in meaning to _____.

   Ⓐ fascinate

   Ⓑ challenge

   Ⓒ frustrate

   Ⓓ amuse

Reading 3:
The United States voting system

Critics say that current voting systems in the United States are inefficient and responsible for the inaccurate counting of votes. Miscounts can be especially damaging if an election is closely <u>contested</u>. Instead of **conventional** ballot systems, critics would like to see the widespread **implementation** of computerized voting systems.

In traditional voting, frequent errors can occur by sheer accident. Voters usually have to locate and **indicate** their choice of candidate by marking an X on a large sheet of paper, or ballot, containing a list of many names. People with poor eyesight can easily mark the wrong name. Conversely, computerized voting machines employ easy-to-use touch-screen technology. To cast a vote, a voter needs only to touch the candidate's name on the screen to record a vote. Voters can even have the computer <u>magnify</u> the name for easier viewing.

Another major problem with old voting systems is that they **rely** heavily on people to <u>tally</u> the votes. Officials must often count ballots and record votes individually. Since they have to deal with thousands of ballots, mistakes are **inevitable**. If an error is **detected**, a time-**consuming** and expensive recount has to take place. In **contrast**, computerized systems remove the **incidence** of human error, since all the vote counting is done quickly and automatically.

Finally some people **maintain** that installing voting technology nationwide is too risky. However, without giving it a thought, governments and individuals alike trust complex computer technology to be perfectly accurate in daily banking transactions as well as in the communication of highly sensitive information. So, why not entrust computers with our elections?

EXERCISE 8-7

Choose the word that is closest in meaning to the word from Reading 3.

1. _____ **conventional** a. convenient b. accepted c. traditional

2. _____ **implementation** a. application b. agreement c. consequence

3. _____ **indicate** a. express b. specify c. direct

4. _____ **rely** a. relieve b. depend c. expect

5. _____ **inevitable** a. uncertain b. possible c. unavoidable

6. _____ **detect** a. notice b. expose c. ignore

7. _____ **consume** a. waste b. expend c. devour

8. _____ **contrast** a. opposition b. similarity c. tandem

9. _____ **incidence** a. absence b. frequency c. experience

10. _____ **maintain** a. sustain b. service c. claim

EXERCISE 8-8

Complete each of the following sentences with the appropriate choice from the words listed in Exercise 8-7. Be sure to use the correct form of each verb and to pluralize nouns if necessary.

1. There are people who _____ that solar energy is neither economic nor feasible on a large scale.

2. Nowadays most people _____ on their cell phones for more than just making calls.

3. The red arrow _____ the direction in which you have to go.

4. E-mail has replaced _____ communication, such as letters and cards.

5. These exercises may _____ a lot of time, but doing them is worth the effort.

6. The _____ of cancer is higher among people living

    in heavily polluted environments than among those who are not exposed to

    chemicals on a daily basis.

7. A CT scan can _____ tumors in the body if they are of

    sufficient size.

8. The widespread _____ of computer technology in the

    medical field has made it easier to locate, copy, file, and archive patient records.

9. Although many people would like to live forever, death is

    _____.

10. In our Academic Writing class, our first assignment is to write a compare-and-

    _____ essay.

EXERCISE 8-9

Choose the word that corresponds to the best answer.

1. The word *contest* in the passage is closest in meaning to _____.

    (A) compete

    (B) match

    (C) challenge

    (D) supervise

2. The word *magnify* in the passage is closest in meaning to _____.

    (A) enlarge

    (B) duplicate

    (C) minimize

    (D) intensify

3. The word *tally* in the passage is closest in meaning to _____.

    (A) correspond

    (B) count

    (C) qualify

    (D) verify

Reading 4:
The legacy of the Chernobyl nuclear disaster

On April 26, 1986, the worst nuclear accident in history **occurred** at the Chernobyl nuclear power plant outside Pripyat, Ukraine, when a powerful explosion **released** four hundred times the amounts of radiation that fell in the atomic bomb attack on Hiroshima at the end of World War II. Although a relatively small number of people died in the blast, the long-term repercussions on humans and the environment will be felt for centuries.

Shortly after 1:00 a.m., a steam explosion during a routine test in the plant's No. 4 reactor **triggered** a second explosion and ignited a massive fire. Unaware of lethal radiation levels, firefighters, rescue workers, and cleanup crews arrived without protective clothing. As a result, 28 of the 31 reported deaths were a direct result of radiation exposure.

The Soviet government was slow to warn the public about hazardous radiation in the air. Thirty-six hours after the explosion, 45,000 residents (mostly from Pripyat) were evacuated from a 10-kilometer area around the plant. Two days later, more than 100,000 other citizens were evacuated from an **established** 30-kilometer "**exclusion** zone."

In the years following the disaster, the effects of radiation have been devastating. Many babies in Belarus were born with multiple holes in their hearts—a condition known as "Chernobyl heart." The number of thyroid cancer cases in victims younger than 14 at the time of the explosion **exceeds** the national average. Many of the 600,000 "liquidators" who helped clean up over the years have reported numerous health problems. Their children's health has been affected as well.

The accident contaminated farmlands and endangered water supplies in much of Belarus, Ukraine, and Russia. **Initially** animals were exposed to harmful radiation, but later, in the absence of humans in the 30-km exclusion zone, their populations recovered and flourished.

Today, reactor No. 4 is still encased in an aging concrete sarcophagus. **Despite** radiation warnings, some residents have returned to the 30-km zone. But no one is permitted to live in the more strictly **enforced** 10-km zone where radiation levels **prohibit** human habitation for the next 100 to 200 years.

EXERCISE 8-10

Choose the word that is closest in meaning to the word from Reading 4.

1. _____	**occur**	a. exist	b. happen	c. appear
2. _____	**release**	a. launch	b. provide	c. free
3. _____	**trigger**	a. provoke	b. avoid	c. set off
4. _____	**establish**	a. confirm	b. set up	c. recognize
5. _____	**exclusion**	a. prohibition	b. elite	c. omission
6. _____	**exceed**	a. surpass	b. accelerate	c. excel
7. _____	**initially**	a. primarily	b. at first	c. originally
8. _____	**despite**	a. because of	b. apart from	c. notwithstanding
9. _____	**enforce**	a. impose	b. require	c. organize
10. _____	**prohibit**	a. prevent	b. ban	c. inhibit

EXERCISE 8-11

Complete each of the following sentences with the appropriate choice from the words listed in Exercise 8-10. Be sure to use the correct form of each verb and to pluralize nouns if necessary.

1. During examinations, communicating with another student is strictly

   _____.

2. The drivers was stopped and fined by police for _____

   the speed limit.

3. Exam protocol requires that the _____ of digital

   devices during examinations be strictly _____.

4. Most car accidents _____ because drivers exceed the

   speed limit or do not pay attention to the road.

5. In what year was the United Nations _____?

6. Eating peanuts can _____ an extreme or fatal reaction

   in people who are allergic.

7. _____ we didn't like our instructor, but by the end of the term we changed our minds.

8. _____ the fact that I didn't really need one, I decided to buy a new cell phone.

9. Factories and power plants _____ carbon dioxide into the atmosphere.

EXERCISE 8-12

Choose the word that corresponds to the best answer.

1. The word _repercussions_ in the passage is closest in meaning to _____.

    Ⓐ rewards

    Ⓑ benefits

    Ⓒ possibilities

    Ⓓ consequences

2. The word _lethal_ in the passage is closest in meaning to _____.

    Ⓐ fatal

    Ⓑ safe

    Ⓒ legitimate

    Ⓓ excessive

3. The word _evacuate_ in the passage is closest in meaning to _____.

    Ⓐ clean

    Ⓑ abandon

    Ⓒ remove

    Ⓓ escape

4. The word _devastating_ in the passage is closest in meaning to _____.

    Ⓐ disastrous

    Ⓑ permanent

    Ⓒ unprecedented

    Ⓓ significant

Reading 5:
The stock market crash of 1929

The financial <u>exuberance</u> and prosperity of the late 1920s came to an abrupt halt on Thursday, October 24, 1929—dubbed "Black Thursday"—when the stock market lost 23 percent of its value. The crash devastated the global economy and sent much of the world spiraling into an economic **depression**.

Following World War I, increased industrial and agricultural production <u>propelled</u> **dramatic** economic growth in the United States. Wages increased and American **consumers purchased** homes, automobiles, household appliances, and stock on **credit**. Between 1920 and 1929, the stock market was considered a sure bet, and inexperienced working-class American investors staked their life savings or borrowed heavily from banks in hopes of making a killing on the booming market.

The combination of wild spending and easily **obtainable** credit was a recipe for disaster. Banks <u>obliged</u> eager investors who were caught up in the borrowing and buying frenzy but who failed to recognize—or even consider—that the bubble would ever burst. Stock values for some companies inflated by as much as 450 percent, but when **irrational** market values were realized, share prices <u>plummeted</u> as investors panicked and pulled out of the market. On October 24 the market buckled, and on October 29, 1929—known now as "Black Tuesday"—it **collapsed**.

By the end of 1929 investors had lost $100 billion in assets. The crash left many families in financial ruin, and Black Tuesday is generally considered the beginning of the Great Depression. Not only was investor confidence shaken, but consumer demand for goods also **declined**, production decreased, and unemployment in the United States jumped from just 3 percent in 1929 to 25 percent by 1933. It wasn't until after the United States entered World War II in late 1941 that the economy finally began to **stabilize.**

EXERCISE 8-13

Choose the word that is closest in meaning to the word from Reading 5.

1. _____ **depression**   a. recession   b. desolation   c. indentation

2. _____ **dramatic**   a. theatrical   b. exciting   c. significant

3. _____ **consumer**   a. end user   b. consultant   c. retailer

4. _____ **purchase**   a. acquire   b. buy   c. utilize

5. _____ **credit**   a. loan   b. recognition   c. recommendation

6. _____ **obtainable**   a. disposable   b. inevitable   c. available

7. _____ **irrational**   a. radical   b. illogical   c. incompatible

8. _____ **collapse**   a. break down   b. recover   c. hesitate

9. _____ **decline**   a. level out   b. refuse   c. lessen

10. _____ **stabilize**   a. change   b. regain balance   c. improve

EXERCISE 8-14

Complete each of the following sentences with the appropriate choice from the words listed in Exercise 8-13. Be sure to use the correct form of each verb and to pluralize nouns if necessary.

1. After receiving antibiotics, the patient's condition is beginning to

    _____ and his health should improve within a few

    days.

2. In his address the president attempted to reassure

    _____ and rebuild confidence in the economy.

3. The financial crisis is having a/an _____ effect on real

    estate prices.

4. I don't like to buy expensive things on _____ if I can't

    pay it off without having to pay interest.

5. Where did you _____ your new laptop?

6. The country is experiencing an economic _____ due

    to a prolonged financial crisis.

7. Inflated stock valuations eventually lead to a bubble after which the stock

    market _____.

8. The American manufacturing sector has been in _____

    ever since China entered the World Trade Organization.

9. Bus passes are _____ at the Student Union building.

10. What's wrong with Edward? Lately his behavior has been

    _____, and he's been doing things that are completely

    out of character.

EXERCISE 8-15

Choose the word that corresponds to the best answer.

1. The word *exuberance* in the passage is closest in meaning to _____.

Ⓐ affluence

Ⓑ stability

Ⓒ enthusiasm

Ⓓ health

2. The word *propel* in the passage is closest in meaning to _____.

Ⓐ project

Ⓑ drive

Ⓒ promote

Ⓓ guide

3. The word *oblige* in the passage is closest in meaning to _____.

Ⓐ accommodate

Ⓑ compel

Ⓒ observe

Ⓓ caution

4. The word *plummet* in the passage is closest in meaning to _____.

Ⓐ waver

Ⓑ plunge

Ⓒ decline

Ⓓ increase

Reading 6:
AIDS in America

AUDIO TRACK 6

On July 3, 1981, the *New York Times* reported that a rare form of skin cancer had mysteriously appeared in forty-one homosexual men in New York City and San Francisco. Although very little was known about the disease at the time, the article was one of the first to spotlight the now-global AIDS epidemic.

In the fall of 1981, the Centers for Disease Control (CDC) declared the unknown disease an epidemic. A year later, the CDC **linked** the disease to blood and gave it the name Acquired Immune Deficiency Syndrome (AIDS). Even though the CDC had **assumed** early on that AIDS was **transmitted** through sexual activity, the actual cause and transmission route remained undetermined until 1984, when Dr. Robert Gallo at the National Cancer Institute and Dr. Luc Montagnier at the Institut Pasteur in Paris, France, announced they had co-discovered the virus that caused AIDS. The following year, the name Human Immunodeficiency Virus (HIV) was coined.

By 1983, intravenous drug users, Haitians, hemophiliacs, and women who had AIDS-infected partners were considered at high risk of contracting the disease. Because gay men were the first to **exhibit** symptoms, media reports often referred to AIDS as "Gay Cancer" or Gay-Related Immunodeficiency Disease, and these **biased** reports precipitated a social backlash against homosexuals.

Despite national media attention, public concern, and thousands of deaths around the world, including that of popular actor Rock Hudson in 1985, the U.S. government did little to make HIV/AIDS a national and global health **priority**. President Ronald Reagan did not mention AIDS publicly until 1987, and Republican Senator Jesse Helms of North Carolina cut federal funding for

AIDS educational materials that "**promote** or encourage, directly or indirectly, homosexual activities." The so-called "no promo homo" **amendment required** materials to remove any mention of anal intercourse, which by that time was known to be a **primary** way in which HIV/AIDS was transmitted.

According to the AIDS.gov website, approximately 1.2 million adults and adolescents in the United States were living with HIV at the end of 2008. Thanks to improved funding for education, fewer Americans are dying of AIDS. In parts of the world, however, the epidemic is severe. More than 25 million of the estimated 39.4 million people in the world who have HIV live in sub-Saharan Africa.

EXERCISE 8-16

Choose the word that is closest in meaning to the word from Reading 6.

1. _____ **link**   a. transport   b. suggest   c. connect

2. _____ **assume**   a. accept   b. conclude   c. adopt

3. _____ **transmit**   a. send   b. transfer   c. carry

4. _____ **exhibit**   a. demonstrate   b. display   c. describe

5. _____ **biased**   a. false   b. ridiculous   c. prejudiced

6. _____ **priority**   a. preference   b. main concern   c. issue

7. _____ **promote**   a. further   b. upgrade   c. publicize

8. _____ **amendment**   a. adaptation   b. change   c. prohibition

9. _____ **require**   a. acquire   b. desire   c. need

10. _____ **primary**   a. predominant   b. first   c. elementary

EXERCISE 8-17

Complete each of the following sentences with the appropriate choice from the words listed in Exercise 8-16. Be sure to use the correct form of each verb and to pluralize nouns if necessary.

1. Attending classes instead of going to every social function around campus should be your first _____.

2. Students wishing to take a temporary leave of absence _____ approval from the dean's office.

3. At its meeting, the city council passed a/an _____ to the environmental waste and recycling bylaw.

4. From the survey results, we can safely _____ that students would frequent the cafeteria more regularly if it offered a more international menu.

5. The _____ causes of accidents are human error and failure to pay attention to traffic.

6. The articles in this newspaper are definitely _____ in favor of the business community.

7. The university's recreation program _____ physical fitness and good mental health.

8. Cigarette smoking is _____ to lung cancer and lung disease.

9. The participants in the psychological test _____ signs of distress and discomfort when they heard a scream in the next room.

10. Diseases can easily be _____ when people fail to wash their hands properly.

EXERCISE 8-18

Choose the word that corresponds to the best answer.

1. The word *deficiency* in the passage is closest in meaning to _____.

Ⓐ lack

Ⓑ limitation

Ⓒ surplus

Ⓓ resistance

2. The word *epidemic* in the passage is closest in meaning to _____.

Ⓐ rise

Ⓑ occurrence

Ⓒ problem

Ⓓ outbreak

3. The word *precipitate* in the passage is closest in meaning to _____.

Ⓐ cause

Ⓑ trigger

Ⓒ increase

Ⓓ follow

Reading 7: The Lewis and Clark expedition of 1803–1806

When Thomas Jefferson became president of the United States in 1801, about two thirds of the American population was **confined** to an area within 50 miles of the Atlantic Ocean. Two years into his presidency, and interested primarily in the port of New Orleans, Jefferson agreed to **acquire** the entire 820,000-square-mile Louisiana Territory from Napoleon Bonaparte. On April 30, 1803, the Louisiana Purchase was signed; at a cost of $15 million, Jefferson's deal doubled the size of the United States.

In a confidential letter to Congress, Jefferson requested **funds** for an exploratory expedition from the Mississippi River to the Pacific Ocean. With the approved $2,500 as financing, Jefferson chose his private secretary, Captain Meriwether Lewis, and Lewis's friend, Lieutenant William Clark, to head up what was called the Corps of Discovery.

With few reliable maps of the region in existence, the journey of the Corps of Discovery would prove to be an ambitious **undertaking** beset with hardship. On May 14, 1804, Lewis and Clark set out with a team of thirty-three members trained in botany, zoology, outdoor **survival**, and other scientific skills in search of a passage between the Mississippi and the Pacific.

Their mission included **instructions** to collect data on the Native American population, indigenous plant and animal life, minerals, rivers, lakes, and trade possibilities. By November 1805 their journey had taken them 8,000 miles up the Missouri River, over the Continental Divide, and along the Columbia River to the Pacific Ocean. Trapper and guide Toussaint Charbonneau assisted the expedition and his Shoshone wife, Sacagawea, **interpreted**, providing valuable advice on edible and medicinal native plants. Despite hunger, sickness, and the hardships of a difficult terrain, the expedition returned amid fanfare to St. Louis on September 23, 1806.

Not only did Clark's detailed maps lay the groundwork for future **migration** westward, but the expedition fulfilled Manifest Destiny, a popular **ideology** at the time that Anglo Americans would **expand** their civilization across the North American continent.

EXERCISE 8-19

Choose the word that is closest in meaning to the word from Reading 7.

1. _____ **confine**   a. incarcerate   b. enclose   c. limit

2. _____ **acquire**   a. purchase   b. request   c. forfeit

3. _____ **funds**   a. supply   b. financing   c. organization

4. _____ **undertaking**   a. prospect   b. venture   c. agreement

5. _____ **survival**   a. exercise   b. skill   c. endurance

6. _____ **instruction**   a. directions   b. lesson   c. guidance

7. _____ **interpret**   a. explain   b. understand   c. translate

8. _____ **migration**   a. navigation   b. relocation   c. exploration

9. _____ **ideology**   a. belief   b. idea   c. theory

10. _____ **expand**   a. spread out   b. elaborate   c. inflate

EXERCISE 8-20

Complete each of the following sentences with the appropriate choice from
the words listed in Exercise 8-19. Be sure to use the correct form of each verb
and to pluralize nouns if necessary.

1. You can _____ a broader vocabulary through extensive

   reading and daily exposure to the language.

2. Fortunately the outbreak has been _____ to a small area.

3. Abstract paintings are difficult to _____.

4. Every creature is concerned first and foremost with its own

   _____.

5. The government provides _____ to students who need

   financial assistance.

6. Heat causes materials to _____.

7. Every political party has its own distinct _____.

8. When you take an examination, it is very important to read and follow the

   _____ exactly.

9. At the end of summer a mass _____ of birds occurs from

   northern to southern climates.

10. When Europeans first came to North America, settling in a hostile environment

    was a risky and uncertain _____.

EXERCISE 8-21

Choose the word that corresponds to the best answer.

1. The word *confidential* in the passage is closest in meaning to _____.

   Ⓐ detailed

   Ⓑ private

   Ⓒ conventional

   Ⓓ public

2. The word *expedition* in the passage is closest in meaning to _____.

   Ⓐ journey

   Ⓑ mission

   Ⓒ group

   Ⓓ race

3. The word *indigenous* in the passage is closest in meaning to _____.

(A) threatened

(B) native

(C) rare

(D) useful

4. The word *manifest* in the passage is closest in meaning to _____.

(A) true

(B) secret

(C) predestined

(D) obvious

Reading 8:
Alan Turing and the test for artificial intelligence

AUDIO TRACK 8

Although the term was coined by American visionary and computer scientist John McCarthy, artificial intelligence was pioneered by British mathematician, logician, and cryptographer Alan Turing, a <u>preeminent</u> thinker who was well ahead of his time.

Turing earned degrees at Cambridge and Princeton in mathematics and mathematical **logic**, and in 1936 he **conceived** the "Turing Machine," an **abstract** information-processing mathematical model that foreshadowed digital computers. During World War II, Turing was a member of the top-secret code-breaking team at England's Bletchley Park, where he and his comrades were able to create a machine that could decode Germany's "Enigma" machine. In 1945, he **designed** the Automatic Computing Engine, which was too expensive to build at the time. In the 1950s, he turned his intellect to theories of artificial intelligence, and in order to provide **empirical evidence** to support his ideas, he devised the first test to determine if machines could think. The Turing Test was an **adaptation** of a Victorian game called the imitation game, in which an <u>interrogator</u> asks two secluded participants questions and guesses from their written answers which is the man and which the woman.

In the Turing Test, a computer takes the place of the male contestant. If the interrogator cannot **differentiate** between the human and the computer, it could be **concluded** that the computer was thinking. So far computers have performed badly in the Turing Test; however, their inability to fool people does not <u>preclude</u> the possibility that one day machines will be able to think independently and creatively.

In 1952, Turing, who was openly gay, was prevented from **pursuing** his progress in computers after he was <u>convicted</u> of "gross indecency" and stripped of his British government security clearance. On June 7, 1954, he committed suicide by eating an apple dipped in cyanide. Despite his untimely death, his far-reaching ideas continue to have an impact on the development of intelligent machines to this day.

EXERCISE 8-22

Choose the word that is closest in meaning to the word from Reading 8.

1. _____ **logic**   a. prediction   b. reason   c. sanity

2. _____ **conceive**   a. create   b. imagine   c. admit

3. _____ **abstract**   a. actual   b. obscure   c. intellectual

4. _____ **design**   a. plan   b. pattern   c. embellish

5. _____ **empirical**   a. essential   b. theoretical   c. experiential

6. _____ **evidence**   a. argument   b. proof   c. clue

7. _____ **adaptation**   a. modification b. utilization   c. copy

8. _____ **differentiate**   a. change   b. distinguish   c. confuse

9. _____ **conclude**   a. formulate   b. terminate   c. deduce

10. _____ **pursue**   a. research   b. follow   c. chase

EXERCISE 8-23

Complete each of the following sentences with the appropriate choice from the words listed in Exercise 8-22. Be sure to use the correct form of each verb and to pluralize nouns if necessary.

1. Gregor Mendel's experiments with garden peas provided _____ evidence that traits were passed from the parent plant to its offspring.

2. Pablo Picasso was a/an _____ painter.

3. The movie is a/an _____ of a famous novel by Thomas Hardy.

4. Nowadays computers are used to _____ machines and buildings.

5. After graduation, I intend to _____ a career in international development.

6. Good academic writers will provide _____ in the form of examples and citations to support their arguments.

7. An astounding number of babies are _____ during times of extreme hardship, such as war or disaster.

8. It is very difficult to _____ between two identical twins.

9. We can _____ from the improvement in the students' performance that they have started to take their studies seriously and have been working much harder.

10. In order to solve mathematical problems, you have to use straightforward

_____.

EXERCISE 8-24

Choose the word that corresponds to the best answer.

1. The word *preeminent* in the passage is closest in meaning to _____.

   (A) well-known

   (B) unusual

   (C) clear

   (D) outstanding

2. The word *interrogator* in the passage is closest in meaning to _____.

   (A) torturer

   (B) instructor

   (C) questioner

   (D) interlocutor

3. The word *preclude* in the passage is closest in meaning to _____.

   (A) prevent

   (B) signify

   (C) involve

   (D) conclude

4. The word *convicted* in the passage is closest in meaning to _____.

   (A) absolved

   (B) sentenced

   (C) confined

   (D) accused

Reading 9:
The legacy of William Shakespeare

Almost four hundred years after his death, William Shakespeare's dramas still draw crowds, and details about his life continue to **reinforce** the reputation of the world's most renowned playwright. Shakespeare's exact birth date is unknown, but it is believed to be April 23, 1564, as it is close to his baptismal date, April 26. His supposed birth date **coincides** with the date of his death, which is also April 23.

Few official documents apart from sundry property records, court documents, tax records, and a will exist to substantiate the details of Shakespeare's life. Born and raised at Stratford-upon-Avon, England, he **presumably** attended Stratford Grammar School. Church records show that in November 1582, at age 18, he married Anne Hathaway. By 1594, Shakespeare was an actor, **published** poet, and playwright, and beginning in 1599, he became part owner of the Globe Theatre. Because the few known facts about his life are so prosaic, speculation about "the real Shakespeare" abounds with an almost cultlike fervor.

While details of his life are sparse, the brilliance of Shakespeare's work goes unchallenged. Shakespeare's canon currently **comprises** thirty-eight plays written between 1590 and 1612 and **consists** of histories, comedies, tragedies, and romances. Shakespeare **contributed** thousands of words to the English language (*fanged, birthplace, arch-villain*) and expanded the dramatic possibilities of blank verse, making it mimic the rhythm of speech even as he elevated speech to poetry. He heightened the **psychological** realism of his characters, making their struggles endlessly adaptable to theater in different times and places.

Shakespeare discoveries, though rare, continue to make news. In June 2012, archaeologists finally located the **foundation** of the lost Curtain Theatre in London, where *Henry V* and *Romeo and Juliet* would have first been staged.

One wonders if Shakespeare foresaw his legacy when he composed these lines in *Julius Caesar*: "How many ages **hence**/Shall this our lofty scene be acted over/In states unborn and accents yet unknown!"?

EXERCISE 8-25

Choose the word that is closest in meaning to the word from Reading 9.

1. _____	**reinforce**	a. reiterate	b. confirm	c. strengthen
2. _____	**coincide**	a. collide	b. match up	c. conclude
3. _____	**presumably**	a. supposedly	b. possibly	c. boldly
4. _____	**publish**	a. disseminate	b. print	c. advertise
5. _____	**comprise**	a. encompass	b. include	c. be made up
6. _____	**consist**	a. be composed	b. conform	c. deliver
7. _____	**contribute**	a. cause	b. furnish	c. donate
8. _____	**psychological**	a. mental	b. imaginary	c. deviant
9. _____	**foundation**	a. justification	b. agency	c. base
10. _____	**hence**	a. presumably	b. therefore	c. from now on

EXERCISE 8-26

Complete each of the following sentences with the appropriate choice from the words listed in Exercise 8-25. Be sure to use the correct form of each verb and to pluralize nouns if necessary.

1. The Introduction to Academic Writing class is designed to give students a

   solid _____ on which they can build when doing

   research and writing academic papers.

2. Our Geography class _____ of nothing but dry, boring

   lectures.

3. _____ pain is often more difficult to bear than physical

   discomfort.

4. I'm very excited that the college newspaper is going to

_____ my article in the upcoming edition.

5. My brother's birthday _____ with Independence Day.

6. In this class everyone is expected to _____ actively to

the discussion rather than just sit there and stare into space.

7. A water molecule is _____ of one oxygen and

two hydrogen atoms.

8. These three papers contain exactly the same answers;

_____ my suspicion that the students were copying

from each other.

9. Mnemonic techniques such as pictures or key words can

_____ your memory and understanding of a new word.

10. _____ the instructor will tell us what sections of the

book we should study before we take the test.

EXERCISE 8-27

Choose the word that corresponds to the best answer.

1. The word *substantiate* in the passage is closest in meaning to _____.

   Ⓐ document

   Ⓑ verify

   Ⓒ disprove

   Ⓓ confirm

2. The word *sundry* in the passage is closest in meaning to _____.

   Ⓐ various

   Ⓑ dubious

   Ⓒ distinct

   Ⓓ specific

3. The word *prosaic* in the passage is closest in meaning to _____.

Ⓐ obvious

Ⓑ curious

Ⓒ unclear

Ⓓ mundane

4. The word *mimic* in the passage is closest in meaning to _____.

Ⓐ imitate

Ⓑ satirize

Ⓒ improvise

Ⓓ reproduce

Reading 10:
The Panama Canal opens

On August 14, 1914, the first ship passed completely through the man-made Panama Canal. **Eliminating** roughly 8,000 miles from the only **alternate** route around Cape Horn at the southern tip of South America, the 50-mile canal created a direct shipping route from the Atlantic to the Pacific Ocean through the Isthmus of Panama in Central America.

Between 1904 and 1914, engineers and workers excavated 211 million cubic yards of earth and rock from hills, dense jungles, and swamps; **constructed** the world's largest dam and man-made lake; and built three sets of double locks, the largest concrete pour in the world at that time. The largest American engineering **project** up to that date is designated one of the Seven Wonders of the Modern World by the American Society of Civil Engineers.

In the late 1800s, Colombia had sold the rights to build a canal across the province of Panama to a **succession** of French interests. The French began digging in 1882, but, lacking the technology and tools, the project **terminated** in bankruptcy. During the Spanish-American War in 1898, the U.S. Congress **sought*** a shorter route to move ships from the West Coast to Cuba and agreed to buy the Panamanian rights from the French in 1902. Colombia **rejected** the treaty in 1903, and a group of Panamanians, **anticipating** the loss of a lucrative **prospect**, declared their independence from Colombia. The United States hastily ratified the Hay–Bunau-Varilla Treaty, recognizing the independent Republic of Panama. In return the United States procured the use and control of the 10-mile-wide Panama Canal Zone in perpetuity.

Over the next 10 years, construction of the canal would cost $380 million and 5,600 lives. Just as water filled the canal during the final three weeks in preparation for the 1914 grand opening ceremonies, World War I broke out. The steamship *SS Ancon* made the first complete passage through the canal to little fanfare.

---

*Sought is the irregular past form and past participle of the verb *seek*.

EXERCISE 8-28

Choose the word that is closest in meaning to the word from Reading 10.

1. _____ **eliminate**   a. dispose of   b. remove   c. extinguish

2. _____ **alternate**   a. every second   b. different   c. possible

3. _____ **construct**   a. plan   b. formulate   c. build

4. _____ **project**   a. venture   b. assignment   c. design

5. _____ **succession**   a. sequence   b. combination   c. accession

6. _____ **terminate**   a. abort   b. discontinue   c. end

7. _____ **seek/sought**   a. locate   b. search for   c. request

8. _____ **reject**   a. repudiate   b. consider   c. decline

9. _____ **anticipate**   a. foreshadow   b. desire   c. predict

10. _____ **prospect**   a. possibility   b. project   c. notion

EXERCISE 8-29

Complete each of the following sentences with the appropriate choice from the words listed in Exercise 8-28. Be sure to use the correct form of each verb and to pluralize nouns if necessary.

1. Between the sixteenth and nineteenth centuries, many European explorers

   _____, but failed to discover, a Northwest Passage

   connecting the Atlantic with the Pacific.

2. When planning your essay, you need to _____ a solid,

   logical argument that is easy to follow.

3. In case you are not accepted into law school, it would be advisable to choose

   a/an _____ course of study.

4. The university is _____ a 15 percent increase in the enrollment of foreign students for next year.

5. You can find a list of job _____ for graduating students posted at the Student Union Building.

6. Our next _____ is to put together a business plan and prepare a PowerPoint presentation for the class.

7. The fall semester will _____ on December 15.

8. She has made the top of the class for the third year in _____.

9. Ashley will be devastated if her application to medical school is _____.

10. When taking a multiple-choice quiz, one strategy is to _____ the answers that you know for sure are wrong.

EXERCISE 8-30

Choose the word that corresponds to the best answer.

1. The word *designate* in the passage is closest in meaning to _____.

   Ⓐ denote

   Ⓑ know as

   Ⓒ design

   Ⓓ classify

2. The word *excavate* in the passage is closest in meaning to _____.

   Ⓐ dig up

   Ⓑ destroy

   Ⓒ bury

   Ⓓ investigate

3. The word *ratify* in the passage is closest in meaning to _____.

(A) sanction

(B) pass into law

(C) evaluate

(D) review

4. The word *procure* in the passage is closest in meaning to _____.

(A) petition

(B) acquire

(C) provide

(D) anticipate

CHAPTER 9

How to use advanced vocabulary in an academic context

Objective

To use advanced vocabulary in an academic context

In addition to academic words from the AWL, there are numerous **advanced** words that occur frequently in academic texts and readings. The words in the following ten academic-style readings (ranging from 250 to 425 words each) represent only a sample of words you should understand and be able to use. If you find others in the text that are new to you, include them in your records.

Note: Lists of advanced vocabulary can be found by searching for "academic and TOEFL® test vocabulary" on the Internet, or by checking out a variety of books that feature advanced vocabulary for academic purposes.

The academic words in the following readings are indicated in **bold type**. Do not consult a dictionary as you do the exercises; rather, try to use the strategies in Chapter 3 to determine the meaning from context or eliminate words that you know are wrong.

Reading 1: Sigmund Freud

Recognized as the founder of psychoanalysis, Sigmund Freud continues to have a **profound** and lasting influence on contemporary humanity and culture. During his lifetime his work was debated, as it still is, and often rejected in scientific and medical circles as selfish, **speculative,** and **flawed**. However, his central theories about sexuality, **repressed** emotions, the power of dreams, and the **autonomy** of the human mind have become tenets of the self in modern society.

Freud studied medicine at the University of Vienna during a period when Vienna was vibrant, romantic, and alive with political **intrigue** and opposing scientific thought. This **contentious** climate helped shape Freud's thought and contributed significantly to his life's work. Freud received his medical degree in 1881, and after studying in Paris under neurologist Jean-Martin Charcot, he returned to Vienna where he **collaborated** with Dr. Josef Breuer on a paper called *On the Physical Mechanism of Hysterical Phenomena* (1893). Their research promoted the treatment of hysteria by hypnosis, which would help patients **discharge** unresolved emotional energy. Poorly received by the scientific community, the paper signalled the first stirrings of modern psychoanalysis.

In 1902, Freud became an associate professor at the University of Vienna and published some of his most famous work. *Interpretation of Dreams* presented his views about repressed memories surfacing in the **volatile** subconscious. *Psychopathology of Everyday Life* introduced the now-famous concept of a Freudian slip, or the way in which menial events and occurrences can reveal the inner workings of our minds. Later, *Three Essays on the Theory of Sexuality* tied the development of the human sex drive to childhood.

EXERCISE 9-1

Match the vocabulary from Reading 1 with the word that is closest in meaning.

1. _____ profound	a. controversial
2. _____ speculative	b. cooperate
3. _____ flawed	c. hypothetical
4. _____ repress	d. subterfuge
5. _____ autonomy	e. release
6. _____ intrigue	f. restrain
7. _____ contentious	g. unstable
8. _____ collaborate	h. imperfect
9. _____ discharge	i. independence
10. _____ volatile	j. intense

EXERCISE 9-2

Complete each of the following sentences with the appropriate word in **bold type** from Reading 1. Be sure to use the correct form of each verb and to pluralize nouns if necessary.

1. After the tsunami struck Fukushima, high levels of radiation were

    _____ from the nuclear power plant into the

    environment.

2. In a dictatorship, the ruling power _____ its citizens

    and deprives them of human rights.

3. This argument is _____ and cannot be taken seriously.

4. The Industrial Revolution precipitated _____ changes in the structure of society.

5. Indigenous people around the world have been fighting for

    _____ and recognition of their aboriginal rights.

6. In a group project, all members are expected to share information and

    _____ .

7. The issue of gay marriage is very _____ and subject to a lot of heated debate.

8. John le Carré's novels deal with political _____ during and following the Cold War.

9. Relations between Israel and Palestine are extremely

    _____ and can erupt into violence at any time.

10. Descriptions of what Earth will look like in a hundred years are, to a large

    degree, _____ .

EXERCISE 9-3

Answer the following questions using the vocabulary in **bold type**. Remember: Your answer must contain the vocabulary, as shown in the example.

1. Who or what has had a **profound** influence on your life?

    Example: My grandfather encouraged me to get a good education, and this had
        a profound influence on my life. _____

    _____

    _____

2. Do you think that life exists on other planets, or would you say that assumption is purely **speculative**? Why?

    _____

    _____

3. Give an example of a **flawed** argument.

   _____

   _____

4. Is it healthy or unhealthy to **repress** your feelings? Why or why not?

   _____

   _____

5. How important is it to have **autonomy** when you are living in a group situation?

   _____

   _____

6. What kinds of stories deal with political **intrigue**?

   _____

   _____

7. Why is allowing women to drive a **contentious** issue in Saudi Arabia at the moment?

   _____

   _____

8. Why is it important to **collaborate** when doing a group assignment?

   _____

   _____

9. What happens when pollutants are **discharged** into the ocean?

   _____

   _____

10. What countries are in a **volatile** political situation?

   _____

   _____

Reading 2: The race for space

On October 4, 1957, the U.S.S.R. successfully **launched** *Sputnik 1* from the Baikonur Cosmodrome in Kazakhstan, making it the first country to orbit a man-made satellite around the Earth. Although the launch was the first of many milestones to **emanate** from the **burgeoning** space programs in the United States and Soviet Union, the event had a major impact on the political climate between the two countries.

At the time, the two superpowers were engaged in a "cold war" of competing political ideologies—communism in the Soviet Union, and democracy in the United States. The U.S.S.R. used its victory in space to **assert** communism's **supremacy** over the democratic system. Meanwhile, many Americans feared the Soviet Union could utilize its satellite technology to spy on the United States or its rockets to **spearhead** a nuclear attack. The possibility that tensions could **explode** into full-scale nuclear war became a major international concern.

The United States' first success after an embarrassing failure to launch its Vanguard rocket in December 1957 came on January 31, 1958, with the launch of its satellite, *Explorer 1*. In that same year, the United States **escalated** its space program with increased funding for the establishment of the National Aeronautics and Space Administration. In May 1961, President John F. Kennedy **upped the ante** with a challenge to land a man on the moon before the end of the decade. On July 20, 1969, *Apollo 11* landed American astronauts Neil Armstrong and Buzz Aldrin on the moon's surface.

Whether the lunar landing **signaled** the end of the space race is debatable. It's generally agreed, however, that the race which began with *Sputnik I* provided some brighter moments in an otherwise tense cold war climate, as both countries pushed each other's space programs to new heights.

EXERCISE 9-4

Match the vocabulary from Reading 2 with the word that is closest in meaning.

1. _____ launch		a.	declare
2. _____ emanate		b.	indicate
3. _____ burgeon		c.	lead
4. _____ assert		d.	blow up
5. _____ supremacy		e.	issue
6. _____ spearhead		f.	predominance
7. _____ explode		g.	intensify
8. _____ escalate		h.	increase the risk
9. _____ up the ante		i.	send into space
10. _____ signal		j.	grow

EXERCISE 9-5

Complete each of the following sentences with the appropriate word in **bold type** from Reading 2. Be sure to use the correct form of each verb and to pluralize nouns if necessary.

1. The environmental group is _____ a campaign against

   GMOs.

2. Currently, conflicts in the region threaten to _____

   into a full-scale war.

3. A good amount of heat _____ from a fireplace.

4. If you want others to believe what you say, you have to

   _____ your opinion with confidence and conviction.

5. The signing of the peace treaty _____ the end of

hostilities and the beginning of a new era of cooperation.

6. Within minutes of its launch, the space shuttle _____

and broke apart, killing all astronauts on board.

7. The United States and China are in competition for economic

_____.

8. In the late 1990s, investment in new Internet companies

_____, leading to a stock market bubble.

9. Toyota _____ its breakthrough hybrid gasoline-

electric automobile, the Prius, in 1997.

10. The two brothers have always been so competitive that when one buys

something new, the other _____ by buying a more

expensive, more prestigious model.

EXERCISE 9-6

Answer the following questions using the vocabulary in **bold type**. Your
answer must contain the same vocabulary.

1. When did Apple **launch** the iPhone 5?

_____

_____

2. What **emanates** from the Pyramids at Giza?

_____

_____

3. What are the signs of a **burgeoning** economy?

_____

_____

4. If a person cannot **assert** himself, what will others think of him?

_____

_____

5. What companies are competing for **supremacy** in the cell phone market?

_____

_____

6. Who **spearheaded** the Civil Rights Movement in the United States?

_____

_____

7. What do people use in excavation work to make something **explode**?

_____

_____

8. What kind of action can cause a demonstration to **escalate** into violence?

_____

_____

9. In a poker game, why does one player **up the ante**?

_____

_____

10. What events or behavior **signal** an economic recovery?

_____

_____

Reading 3:
The 1906 San Francisco earthquake and fire

AUDIO TRACK 13

Shortly before sunrise at 5:12 a.m. on April 18, 1906, a massive earthquake rocked San Francisco, California, for nearly a minute. For stunned San Franciscans, a 72-hour **ordeal** was just beginning.

As the shaking **subsided**, broken gas lines fueled thirty fires across the city. Blazes raged out of control for the next three days, **incinerating** the central business district and **reducing** five hundred city blocks—almost five square miles—to **smoldering** ruins. Troops were called in to help keep order and assist firefighters. Citizens were forced to evacuate at bayonet point, and looters were shot on sight.

Residents crowded into parks and military **installations**, where makeshift accommodations were set up. For months, soldiers and Red Cross workers distributed food and supplies to survivors. Remarkably, the enforcement of **sanitation** measures **averted** widespread outbreaks of disease amongst the population.

Altogether the earthquake and ensuing fires destroyed 28,000 buildings, killed 3,000 people, and left 250,000 homeless. At the time, property losses were assessed at $250 million. Outside of San Francisco, communities all along the San Andreas Fault suffered damage. Estimated at anywhere between 7.7 and 8.3 on the Richter Scale, the earthquake is notable for its **unprecedented** range, which stretched from southern Oregon all the way south to Los Angeles and as far east as central Nevada. The **rupture** extended roughly 290 miles with displacements as wide as twenty feet.

The 1906 earthquake marked the beginning of American seismic research and preparedness. A landmark state-sponsored study published in 1908 showed the importance of seismic observation and engineering construction standards.

EXERCISE 9-7

Match the vocabulary from Reading 3 with the word that is closest in meaning.

1. _____ ordeal   a. unparalleled

2. _____ subside   b. burn up

3. _____ incinerate   c. break

4. _____ reduce   d. public health

5. _____ smolder   e. trauma

6. _____ installation   f. burn slowly

7. _____ sanitation   g. prevent

8. _____ avert   j. recede

9. _____ unprecedented   h. facility

10. _____ rupture   i. decrease

EXERCISE 9-8

Complete each of the following sentences with the appropriate word in **bold type** from Reading 3. Be sure to use the correct form of each verb and to pluralize nouns if necessary.

1. During an earthquake, gas lines _____ and leak, or worse, explode, causing extensive damage.

2. After two weeks, the heat wave _____ and people were able to sleep normally again.

3. People with high blood pressure have to _____ their sodium intake and increase their exercise.

4. The hostages were relieved when they were finally rescued and their three-

day _____ was over.

5. Thanks to the watchman's quick thinking, we narrowly

_____ a disaster.

6. The army is building a new _____ in the north.

7. Due to cheap and readily available credit, housing prices reached a/an

_____ high in the mid-2000s.

8. Diseases, such as cholera and typhoid fever, are rampant in areas with

substandard _____.

9. For health reasons, animal carcasses should be _____,

not just buried or disposed of.

10. The accused woman was so angry that she sat there

_____ for the rest of the day.

EXERCISE 9-9

Answer the following questions using the vocabulary in **bold type**. Your
answer must contain the same vocabulary.

1. Give an example of an **ordeal** during which people had to suffer extreme
conditions for a number of days.

_____

_____

2. How long does it take for an attack of nervousness or anxiety to **subside**?

_____

_____

3. What substances have to be **incinerated** under carefully controlled conditions?

_____

_____

4. How can you **reduce** your intake of calories?

_____

_____

5. What can happen if a fire is left to **smolder** unattended?

_____

_____

6. Where is the nearest military **installation** located?

_____

_____

7. What will happen if the **sanitation** in a city does not meet health standards?

_____

_____

8. What's an example of an **unprecedented** natural disaster?

_____

_____

9. What will happen if your appendix **ruptures**?

_____

_____

10. How can people **avert** panic in the case of a fire?

_____

_____

Reading 4:
Don Quixote de la Mancha

AUDIO TRACK 14

"In a certain corner of La Mancha, the name of which I do not choose to remember, there lately lived one of those country gentlemen, who **adorn** their halls with a rusty lance and worm-eaten target, and ride forth on the skeleton of a horse, to course with a sort of a starved greyhound."

So begins the first modern novel, *Don Quixote de la Mancha,* by Miguel de Cervantes. Born near Madrid, Spain, in 1547, Cervantes was a courageous soldier, government clerk, and **literary** figure who **endured** five years of **incarceration** at the hands of Barbary pirates. At first glimpse the novel he wrote seems to **satirize** books of **chivalry,** but on deeper inspection, one comes to appreciate it as a comic masterpiece.

Don Quixote de la Mancha is a parody of the romances of the time that featured knights and damsels in distress and served as a platform for larger themes regarding the nature of art and reality and the tension between them. Published in two parts in 1605 and 1615, this massive text **chronicles** the **escapades** of Don Quixote, a scraggly lord of the manor so besotted with books of chivalry that he **ventures** out into the world to seek his own adventures. He **deludes** himself into thinking prostitutes are ladies in waiting, that seedy inns are noble castles, and that windmills are evil giants. Along the way, he picks up one of literature's first sidekicks, Sancho Panza, a simple soul who recognizes Quixote's delusions but tags along as his squire anyway. The lengthy novel became a worldwide success in Cervantes's time and paved the way for the picaresque novels of the eighteenth century, such as *Tom Jones.*

EXERCISE 9-10

Match the vocabulary from Reading 4 with the word that is closest in meaning.

1. _____ adorn   a. undergo

2. _____ endure   b. adventure

3. _____ incarceration   c. record

4. _____ satirize   d. poetic

5. _____ chivalry   e. imprisonment

6. _____ literary   f. set out

7. _____ chronicle   g. decorate

8. _____ escapade   h. deceive

9. _____ venture   i. parody

10. _____ delude   j. good manners

EXERCISE 9-11

Complete each of the following sentences with the appropriate word in **bold type** from Reading 4. Be sure to use the correct form of each verb and to pluralize nouns if necessary.

1. In the days of knights, _____ was an important value, and men were expected to follow a strict code of behavior toward ladies.

2. When under the influence of certain drugs, people can be

_____ into thinking they have superpowers.

3. On May 14, 1804, Meriwether Lewis and William Clark

_____ with a team of thirty-three on an expedition to

map the territory between the Mississippi River and the Pacific Ocean.

4. The murderer was sentenced to _____ for the rest of

his life.

5. During the time that they were trapped in the rubble, the survivors of the

   earthquake had to _____ hunger, thirst, pain, and

   terror for hours until they could be rescued.

6. At Christmastime, people _____ their homes with

   colored lights and all kinds of sparkling decorations.

7. Bruce Chatwin's *In Patagonia* _____ his six-month

   travel experiences in southern Argentina.

8. The _____ of Superman have fascinated readers of

   comic books for decades and continue to do so.

9. This semester we have to take a class in _____ criticism.

10. In the novel, *Gulliver's Travels*, seventeenth-century Anglo-Irish author

    Jonathan Swift _____ European government.

EXERCISE 9-12

Answer the following questions using the vocabulary in **bold type**. Your
answer must contain the same vocabulary.

1. Is **chivalry** dead, or do societies that place value on chivalry still exist? Give an
   example to support your answer.

   _____

   _____

2. How do people in your country **adorn** their houses for national celebrations?

   _____

   _____

3. What is the most challenging situation you've ever had to **endure**?

   _____

   _____

4. For which crimes do people face a long period of **incarceration**?

_____

_____

5. In your country are there any television programs that **satirize** politicians or famous people? What are they?

_____

_____

6. What are some popular **literary** figures in your country? Are they based on real people?

_____

_____

7. Name a book or television series that **chronicles** the lives of a family—for example, _The Forsyte Saga_ by John Galsworthy.

_____

_____

8. Do you like to read stories about romantic or dangerous **escapades**? Why or why not?

_____

_____

9. If you had an opportunity, what country or place would you like to **venture** to? Why?

_____

_____

10. Have you ever **deluded** yourself into thinking that studying at a foreign university was easier than it is?

_____

_____

Reading 5:
Haiti's independence

During the eighteenth century, Haiti—or Saint-Domingue as it was known at the time—was France's most **lucrative** colony. More than 500,000 slaves were imported from western Africa to work thousands of coffee, sugar, cocoa, and tobacco plantations.

The French Revolution of 1789 spurred revolutionary fever in Haiti as well. Slaves outnumbered wealthy plantation owners ten to one, and the brutality they had been enduring at the hands of the white colonists set the stage for a violent conflict. In August 1791, a slave named Boukman led an uprising during which slaves burned plantations to the ground and used any weapon at their disposal to indiscriminately kill whites. After only three weeks, infighting between different slave **factions** weakened their position and enabled white slave owners to regroup and **retaliate**.

During the conflict, Pierre Toussaint, a savvy military leader, organized and strengthened 55,000 former slaves to defeat both France and Britain by 1798. In 1800 rebel forces liberated the entire island from French rule. Emperor Napoleon Bonaparte was not about to **relinquish** control over Saint-Domingue, however, and deployed 20,000 men to reestablish French rule. In January 1802 French soldiers arrived, and in May Toussaint surrendered. Although France assured Toussaint peaceful retirement after the war, he was betrayed, captured, and imprisoned. He died in April 1803.

Two of Toussaint's lieutenants—Jean-Jacques Dessalines and Henri Christophe—**resumed** the fight and defeated Napoleon's forces on November 18, 1803. On New Year's Day 1804, Dessalines declared the country's independence, making Haiti the first black-governed republic in the western hemisphere.

After a bloody twelve-year revolt, Haiti was in shambles. Most of the plantations had been destroyed, and the United States, Spain, and Britain, which still practiced slavery, did little to **foster** the young nation's development. In October 1804 Dessalines crowned himself Jacques I, Emperor of Haiti, but in October 1806 Haitians resisted Dessalines's **despotic** governing style, and he was assassinated in October 1806.

Despite its post-independence hardships, Haiti **inspired** uprisings abroad. In the United States, slave rebellions led in 1831 by Nat Turner and in 1859 by white **abolitionist** John Brown demonstrated that the struggle to end slavery was not **insurmountable**.

EXERCISE 9-13

Match the vocabulary from Reading 5 with the word that is closest in meaning.

1. _____ lucrative	a. crusader
2. _____ faction	b. tyrannical
3. _____ retaliate	c. unconquerable
4. _____ relinquish	d. group
5. _____ resume	e. stimulate
6. _____ foster	f. renounce
7. _____ despotic	g. fight back
8. _____ inspire	h. promote
9. _____ abolitionist	i. continue
10. _____ insurmountable	j. profitable

EXERCISE 9-14

Complete each of the following sentences with the appropriate word in **bold type** from Reading 5. Be sure to use the correct form of each verb and to pluralize nouns if necessary.

1. Nelson Mandela _____ black South Africans to

overcome their suffering during the apartheid regime.

2. When the army moved into the capital, the rebels

_____ control and fled into the mountains.

3. Ventures that carry high financial risk can be very

_____; on the other hand, they can end in ruin.

4. Peace talks will _____ as soon as there is a ceasefire.

5. The mediator invited representatives of the different warring

_____ to the peace talks.

6. All members of Ernest Shackleton's Antarctic expedition survived against

seemingly _____ odds.

7. Despite General Augusto Pinochet's _____ rule in

Chile, he was never tried for his regime's crimes against humanity.

8. United Nations programs _____ economic

development in poor countries.

9. After their leader was captured, the insurgents _____

by bombing the embassy.

10. The _____ movement to end slavery in the United

States began in the 1830s and contributed to the animosity between North

and South that culminated in the American Civil War.

EXERCISE 9-15

Answer the following questions using the vocabulary in **bold type**. Your
answer must contain the same vocabulary.

1. What is an example of a **lucrative** business?

_____

_____

2. How many different **factions** are fighting in Afghanistan?

_____

_____

3. If one person or group attacks another, is it better to **retaliate** or to resist peacefully?

_____

_____

4. How likely is China to **relinquish** control over Tibet?

_____

_____

5. Should Israel and Palestine **resume** peace talks?

_____

_____

6. What activity can **foster** positive intercultural relations among students at a university?

_____

_____

7. Which countries have **despotic** governments?

_____

_____

8. Who **inspires** you?

_____

_____

9. Name a famous **abolitionist** who sought to end slavery.

_____

_____

10. What would be an **insurmountable** difficulty?

_____

_____

Reading 6:
Booker T. Washington and the Tuskegee Institute

Booker T. Washington was an influential educator, thinker, orator, and civil rights crusader in a time of great change for the United States and tremendous hardship for black Americans. Born into a Virginia slave settlement in 1856, Washington moved with his family after **emancipation** to West Virginia, where they labored in the salt mines.

Longing for an education, Washington set out on foot at the age of sixteen for the Hampton Institute, a preparatory school for former slaves located hundreds of miles away in Virginia. The **resourceful** Washington funded his education with a janitor's wages and impressed his teachers with his curiosity and intellectual drive. After completing his studies in 1875, Washington worked briefly as a schoolteacher in West Virginia but soon returned to Hampton Institute as a **full-fledged** faculty member.

In 1881, Hampton founder Samuel Chapman Armstrong asked Washington to head up a newly founded black school with no staff, a ramshackle classroom building, and on a few thousand dollars in funding at Tuskegee, Alabama, for the practical training of blacks in trades and professions. The Tuskegee Institute benefited financially from Washington's skills as a speechmaker and energetic fund-raiser, and in addition to developing its curriculum, Washington established an agriculture school headed by George Washington Carver.

At Tuskegee students were **urged** to become educators themselves and spread knowledge to the **disenfranchised**. Vocational trades and farming were emphasized, and Washington insisted on physical and moral cleanliness. He believed the promotion and support of job skills and strong character would bring economic and social progress more rapidly than the push for higher education. Although his theories and opinions were at times **contentious**, Washington provided a role model to African Americans struggling against the racial **antagonism** of the era, and he remained a tireless advocate for economic progress and social equality.

Washington was president of Tuskegee Institute from 1881 until his death in 1915, when he was buried on its campus. "He lifted the veil of ignorance from his people," his **inscription** reads, "and pointed the way to progress through education and industry." Beginning as the greatest challenge of Booker T. Washington's remarkable life, Tuskegee became his **legacy** and an enduring tribute to his vision, **perseverance**, and passion for education.

EXERCISE 9-16

Match the vocabulary from Reading 6 with the word that is closest in meaning.

1. _____ emancipation   a. encourage

2. _____ resourceful   b. hostility

3. _____ full-fledged   c. liberation

4. _____ urge   d. inheritance

5. _____ disenfranchised   e. lettering

6. _____ contentious   f. ingenious

7. _____ antagonism   g. determination

8. _____ inscription   h. controversial

9. _____ legacy   i. complete

10. _____ perseverance   j. deprived of citizens' rights

EXERCISE 9-17

Complete each of the following sentences with the appropriate word in **bold type** from Reading 6. Be sure to use the correct form of each verb and to pluralize nouns if necessary.

1. The _____ on the tombstone reads, "But many that are first shall be last and the last shall be first."

2. The regional conflict has erupted into a/an _____ war.

3. A good teacher is _____ and can find a variety of ways to present material so that students understand.

4. The women's liberation movement advocated the _____ of women and equality of the sexes.

5. At this university, students are _____ to attend and participate in cultural events.

6. Banning the use of cell phones and electronic devices during class time has become a/an _____ issue among students.

7. In order to reach your goals, especially when the road is long and difficult, you need _____.

8. Poverty and despair are the plight of the _____.

9. Following 9/11 there was a lot of _____ toward people from the Middle East.

10. Abraham Lincoln is considered among American's greatest presidents, and the defense of the principles of democracy, liberty, and equality is his lasting _____.

EXERCISE 9-18

Answer the following questions using the vocabulary in **bold type**. Your answer must contain the same vocabulary.

1. Do women in your country enjoy full **emancipation**?

_____

_____

2. Why is it important to be a **resourceful** student?

_____

_____

3. How many years does it take to become a **full-fledged** lawyer?

_____

_____

4. Did your parents **urge** you to study at a university, or did you decide on your own?

_____

_____

5. Under which conditions are people **disenfranchised**, and what are the consequences?

_____

_____

6. What is a **contentious** issue in your country?

_____

_____

7. What is one reason for **antagonism** between groups of people?

_____

_____

8. Where can you find a lot of interesting **inscriptions**?

_____

_____

9. What is William Shakespeare's **legacy**?

_____

_____

10. Which goal requires **perseverance** to achieve?

_____

_____

Reading 7:
1964 and Beatlemania

1964 was the signature year for the Beatles—John Lennon, Paul McCartney, George Harrison, and Ringo Starr. The band had become a **sensation** in England the previous year, sending young pop fans into hysterics on the strength of **irresistible** early singles like "Twist and Shout" and "Please Please Me." On February 7, 1964, the band arrived at John F. Kennedy Airport in New York City and took America by storm during their now-**legendary** performance on television's popular "Ed Sullivan Show" two days later. A whirlwind American tour took them 22,000 miles in twenty-nine days. The Beatles propelled themselves to worldwide stardom and acted as **catalysts** for the eventual British Invasion.

Meet the Beatles!, the quartet's second U.S. album, was released January 20, 1964, and hit number one on the Billboard chart on February 15, where it remained for eleven weeks. In a music industry first, it was **supplanted** by *The Beatles' Second Album*. The Fab Four were suddenly everywhere, and the world would never be the same.

The Beatles also became movie stars in 1964. More than just an opportunistic marketing **gimmick**, *A Hard Day's Night* was a madcap comic spree that showcased the group's **quirky** sense of humor in addition to the musical segments. *A Hard Day's Night* and its accompanying soundtrack were an immediate hit. The band continued to cause a public relations stir throughout the year, becoming darlings of not only screaming teenage girls, but also the media. From newsreels to television appearances across America, the Beatles were fresh kids whose music drew equally from rock and roll and rhythm and blues, and added a **scintillating** layer of innovative songwriting that defined the look and feel of a new pop music form.

The Beatles went on to release "I Feel Fine" in 1964, plus EPs (extended plays) like *Four by the Beatles*, and they closed out the year with the release of *Beatles for Sale*, their fourth studio album. It featured the single "Eight Days a Week," ballads like the Paul McCartney composition "I'll Follow the Sun," and cover songs too, since the band barely had enough material of their own to keep the world **sated**. The world had never seen anything like the Beatles before 1964, and there's a good chance no other band will ever attain that level of success in one year again.

EXERCISE 9-19

Match the vocabulary from Reading 7 with the word that is closest in meaning.

1. _____ sensation   a. captivating

2. _____ mania   b. stimulant

3. _____ irresistible   c. eccentric

4. _____ legendary   d. uproar

5. _____ catalyst   e. sparkle

6. _____ supplant   f. madness

7. _____ gimmick   g. famous

8. _____ quirky   h. satisfy

9. _____ scintillate   i. displace

10. _____ sate   j. publicity device

EXERCISE 9-20

Complete each of the following sentences with the appropriate word in **bold type** from Reading 7. Be sure to use the correct form of each verb and to pluralize nouns if necessary.

1. Advertising attempts to make a company's products

   _____ to consumers, particularly children and youth.

2. The problem with junk food is that at first you feel

   _____, but after a short time you're still hungry.

3. J. K. Rowling's success with her Harry Potter series is

   _____ among writers of children's books.

4. If a company wants its products to become hugely popular, it has to

   create a/an _____ so that everyone knows about them

   and wants them.

5. The band wore sequin-covered costumes that _____

   in the spotlight.

6. A good question or outrageous example can act as a/an

   _____ in a discussion that lacks momentum.

7. Touch-tone phones have completely _____ the rotary

   dial phones.

8. With the help of the Internet, Harry Potter _____

   spread like wildfire.

9. Dave has a/an _____ style of dressing that not

   everyone can appreciate or understand.

10. Beware of _____ that entice you to buy something

    that turns out to be more expensive than you think.

EXERCISE 9-21

Answer the following questions using the vocabulary in **bold type**. Your answer must contain the same vocabulary.

1. What electronic device or musical group has created a **sensation** recently?

   _____

   _____

2. Why did Harry Potter become a **mania**?

   _____

   _____

3. What smells do you find **irresistible**?

   _____

   _____

4. Who is a **legendary** hero in your country?

_____

_____

5. What would be a **catalyst** for economic growth?

_____

_____

6. What energy source could **supplant** fossil fuels as the main source of energy in the future?

_____

_____

7. What **gimmicks** does advertising use to get your attention?

_____

_____

8. Name a **quirky** comic character or actor.

_____

_____

9. What materials **scintillate**?

_____

_____

10. What kind of food **sates** you very quickly?

_____

_____

Reading 8:
The storming of the Bastille

The storming of the Bastille prison on July 14, 1789, signaled the beginning of the French Revolution and the end of absolute monarchy in France. Originally built in the fourteenth century as a fortress to defend Paris, the Bastille evolved into a prison for enemies of state—real or imagined. Under Louis XIV, a *lettre de cachet* signed by the king was all that was required for someone to be sent to the Bastille, making it a potent symbol of royal **tyranny**. By 1789, the prison was already **slated** to be closed and housed only seven prisoners: four forgers, two **insanity** cases, and a **dissolute** aristocrat sent there by his family.

In June 1789, facing a financial crisis and food shortages, King Louis XVI had convened the Estates-General to raise taxes. As it splintered into warring factions, the Third Estate (the commoners, who were also France's taxpayers) formed a National Assembly and, on June 20, 1789, made its Tennis Court Oath, **pledging** to write a new constitution. While Louis XVI accepted the assembly, he also surrounded Paris with troops and dismissed Jacques Necker, his finance minister, who was sympathetic to reform. Many in Paris saw these actions as signs that Louis XVI was planning to impose his authority by force.

Looking for gunpowder to supply 28,000 muskets taken on July 13 from the Hôtel des Invalides, a mob of around 1,000 approached the Bastille on the morning of July 14 and demanded arms, gunpowder, and the release of its prisoners. The Bastille was guarded by only 84 pensioners and 30 Swiss guards, so its governor, the Marquis de Launay, began **negotiations** with the mob. But confusion ensued when part of the crowd in an interior courtyard was fired upon by the Bastille's defenders. The enraged mob escalated its attack, de Launay **capitulated**, and the **demolition** of the Bastille began. On August 26, 1789, the National Assembly **adopted** the *Declaration of the Rights of Man and of the Citizens*, which defined the principles of liberty that would inspire the French Revolution.

The anniversary of the storming of the Bastille is now a national holiday in France. Bastille Day is often celebrated with military parades, dances, **communal** meals, and fireworks.

EXERCISE 9-22

Match the vocabulary from Reading 8 with the word that is closest in meaning.

1. _____ tyranny   a. bargaining

2. _____ slate   b. surrender

3. _____ insanity   c. assume

4. _____ dissolute   d. madness

5. _____ pledge   e. totalitarianism

6. _____ negotiation   f. shared

7. _____ capitulate   g. decadent

8. _____ demolition   h. schedule

9. _____ adopt   i. promise

10. _____ communal   j. destruction

EXERCISE 9-23

Complete each of the following sentences with the appropriate word in **bold type** from Reading 8. Be sure to use the correct form of each verb and to pluralize nouns if necessary.

1. Some conservative critics consider the Summer of Love as a/an

   _____ period in which young people indulged in sex, drugs, and rock 'n' roll.

2. When becoming naturalized citizens of a country, individuals have to

   _____ an oath of allegiance to the flag or head of state.

3. The old bridge will undergo _____ before construction of the new one can begin.

4. Students can save a lot of money by choosing a/an

   _____ living situation in a larger group.

5. Although individual generals surrendered on separate dates, General Robert

   E. Lee _____ on April 9, 1865, signaling the end of the

   American Civil War.

6. _____ excludes all human rights and liberties.

7. _____ between the employer and the union will begin

   tomorrow morning to settle the labor dispute.

8. A defense lawyer can use _____ as grounds for

   acquittal in a murder trial.

9. The old city hall is _____ for demolition because it is

   not earthquake safe.

10. The Universal Declaration of Human Rights was _____

    by the United Nations General Assembly on December 10, 1948, in Paris, France.

EXERCISE 9-24

Answer the following questions using the vocabulary in **bold type**. Your answer must contain the same vocabulary.

1. Under a system of **tyranny,** what happens to human rights?

   _____

   _____

2. When and where are the next Olympic Games **slated** to be held?

   _____

   _____

3. Is unlimited growth possible, or is the idea an example of man's **insanity**?

_____

_____

4. What is an example of **dissolute** behavior?

_____

_____

5. If one of your friends wanted to participate in a marathon to raise money for a good cause, how much money would you **pledge**?

_____

_____

6. Is **negotiation** a better solution to a dispute than war? Why or why not?

_____

_____

7. What is the result when one army **capitulates** in a war?

_____

_____

8. Are any buildings or installations scheduled for **demolition** in your city?

_____

_____

9. Which countries have not **adopted** the Kyoto Protocol in order to reduce greenhouse gases?

_____

_____

10. What is an advantage or disadvantage of living in a **communal** situation?

_____

_____

Reading 9: The Civil Rights Act of 1964

On July 2, 1964, President Lyndon B. Johnson signed into law the Civil Rights Act of 1964. It was the most **rigorous** civil rights bill in U.S. history, providing for nondiscrimination in voting, the workplace, public schools, public accommodations, and federally funded programs. It ordered businesses that serve the general public, including hotels, restaurants, theaters, and stores, to serve everyone regardless of race, color, religion, or national origin.

The act **outlawed** discrimination by employers or unions based on the same criteria, with the addition of gender, and established the Equal Employment Opportunity Commission (EEOC) to enforce fair labor practices and to compensate victims. It authorized a cutoff of federal funds for any establishment that failed to **comply**. Most controversially, and most **potently**, Article III of the act authorized the Attorney General to file lawsuits on behalf of individuals **deprived** of rights secured by the Constitution or U.S. law, thereby protecting voters and peaceful protestors from police brutality.

In the wake of peaceful civil rights protests and violent retaliation in Birmingham, Alabama, President John F. Kennedy first called for a civil rights bill during his televised Civil Rights Address of June 11, 1963. The president **garnered** increasing support among the public and in Congress. Another **impetus** was the August 28, 1963, March on Washington for Jobs and Freedom—the largest civil rights rally ever held and one that featured Martin Luther King, Jr.'s "I Have a Dream" speech.

After Kennedy's assassination on November 22, 1963, President Johnson kept up Kennedy's momentum, telling Congress the best way to honor the late president would be through passage of the bill. With increased public support, the bill quickly passed the House of Representatives. But it took some legal **maneuvering** to navigate it through the Senate, despite the opposition of the "southern bloc" of eighteen southern senators—most vocally Strom Thurmond—who filibustered for more than fifty-four days. With a **compromise** bill that **diluted** the government's power to regulate private business, the Senate eventually got seventy-one supporters and for the first time in history had enough votes to cut off a filibuster on a civil rights bill.

EXERCISE 9-25

Match the vocabulary from Reading 9 with the word that is closest in meaning.

1. _____ rigorous
2. _____ outlaw
3. _____ comply
4. _____ potent
5. _____ deprive
6. _____ garner
7. _____ impetus
8. _____ maneuver
9. _____ compromise
10. _____ dilute

a. prohibit
b. dispossess
c. weaken
d. force
e. agreement
f. navigate
g. conform
h. gather
i. strict
j. powerful

EXERCISE 9-26

Complete each of the following sentences with the appropriate word in **bold type** from Reading 9. Be sure to use the correct form of each verb and to pluralize nouns if necessary.

1. We need more _____ laws to prevent people from using cell phones while driving.

2. Toys that contain dangerous chemical substances should be _____.

3. If this solution is too strong, you can _____ it by adding water.

4. This medication is very _____ and should be stored out of the reach of children.

5. A close brush with death can act as a/an _____ for change in a person's life.

6. Pixar Studios has _____ numerous prestigious awards for its computer-animated films.

7. Many children in poor countries are _____ of adequate nutrition and education.

8. After considerable _____, the driver finally succeeded in parking his car in a very small space.

9. Marriages succeed because when facing a problem, couples are able to reach a/an _____ that each partner can live with.

10. Failure to _____ with the university's rules and regulations can result in expulsion.

EXERCISE 9-27

Answer the following questions using the vocabulary in **bold type**. Your answer must contain the same vocabulary.

1. What is an example of a **rigorous** law or regulation?

   _____

   _____

2. What kind of substances or chemicals should the government **outlaw**?

   _____

   _____

3. What will happen if people do not **comply** with traffic laws?

   _____

   _____

4. What is an example of a **potent** alcoholic drink?

_____

_____

5. What happens when the human body is **deprived** of vitamins?

_____

_____

6. What is a recent event that has **garnered** a lot of attention in the press?

_____

_____

7. What kind of action can add **impetus** to an advertising campaign?

_____

_____

8. What kind of car is very easy to **maneuver**?

_____

_____

9. If you and a friend cannot agree on where to go on a trip, how can you come to a satisfactory **compromise?**

_____

_____

10. When mixing drinks, what do bartenders **dilute** alcohol with?

_____

_____

Reading 10:
"The Star-Spangled Banner"

The national **anthem** of the United States started as a poem, hastily scribbled by a lawyer and sung to the tune of a bawdy drinking song.

During the War of 1812, Georgetown lawyer Francis Scott Key was granted permission by President James Madison to negotiate the release of a **prominent** doctor captured by the British army. In September 1814, accompanied by U.S. Prisoner Exchange Officer John S. Skinner, Key **embarked** on the HMS *Minden*, an American vessel, to locate the British fleet in Chesapeake Bay. While dining aboard Britain's HMS *Tonnant*, they negotiated the American's release. They were not permitted, however, to return immediately to shore because they had learned of the fleet's **impending** attack on Baltimore.

While **detained** on HMS *Minden* at the back of the British fleet, Key witnessed the **bombarding** of Fort McHenry throughout the day of September 13 and all through the night, as British warship HMS *Erebus* provided the "rockets' red glare" and HMS *Meteor* launched "bombs bursting in air." In the darkness, Key had no idea of the fate of **vulnerable** Fort McHenry, but at daybreak on September 14, the smoke **dissipated** and Key was overjoyed to see the U.S. flag still there. Key feverishly scrawled a poem he titled "The Defense of Ft. McHenry." The poem was subsequently printed in Baltimore newspapers, and it was suggested that it be sung to the tune of a popular drinking song called "To Anacreon in Heaven," **composed** by British teenager John Stafford Smith in the 1760s.

Key's **patriotic** lyrics were first published under the title "The Star-Spangled Banner" by a Baltimore music store. In 1889 it was made the official tune of flag raisings by the secretary of the navy, and in 1916 President Woodrow Wilson ordered it to be played at military occasions. It was not until 1931, however, that Congress adopted it as the first official national anthem.

EXERCISE 9-28

Match the vocabulary from Reading 10 with the word that is closest in meaning.

1. _____ anthem   a. disappear

2. _____ prominent   b. exposed

3. _____ embark   c. imminent

4. _____ impending   d. song

5. _____ detain   e. board

6. _____ bombard   f. nationalistic

7. _____ vulnerable   g. hold

8. _____ dissipate   h. attack

9. _____ compose   i. eminent

10. _____ patriotic   j. write

EXERCISE 9-29

Complete each of the following sentences with the appropriate word in **bold type** from Reading 10. Be sure to use the correct form of each verb and to pluralize nouns if necessary.

1. Alex Colville's painting, *Horse and Train*, depicts a scene of

   _____ doom as a horse races toward an oncoming

   train.

2. An unarmed, unaccompanied woman is _____ to

   attack in dark, secluded environments.

3. A/An _____ guest speaker from the government will

   appear at the commencement ceremony.

4. Do you know the words to your country's national

_____ by heart?

5. The suspect was _____ by police until it could be

established that they had arrested the wrong man.

6. Remembrance Day in Canada and Memorial Day in the United States are

_____ holidays that celebrate the men and women

who served their countries in times of war.

7. Mozart _____ several masterpieces at a young age.

8. After the sun came out, the morning fog _____.

9. Every day we are _____ with television, Internet, print,

and billboard advertising.

10. The *Titanic* _____ on its fateful journey on April 14,

1915.

EXERCISE 9-30

Answer the following questions using the vocabulary in **bold type**. Your
answer must contain the same vocabulary.

1. Which national **anthem** do you know?

_____

_____

2. Who is a **prominent** entertainer in your country?

_____

_____

3. What are passengers required to show before they can **embark** on a cruise ship?

_____

_____

4. Do you think that a climate catastrophe is **impending**, or can it be avoided?

_____

_____

5. Why are travelers sometimes **detained** at customs when they enter a foreign country?

_____

_____

6. When are people **bombarded** by advertising?

_____

_____

7. Which people are most **vulnerable** when there is a health epidemic such as SARS?

_____

_____

8. What substances rapidly **dissipate** when exposed to air?

_____

_____

9. Who **composed** _All You Need Is Love_?

_____

_____

10. Do you consider yourself **patriotic**? Why or why not?

_____

_____

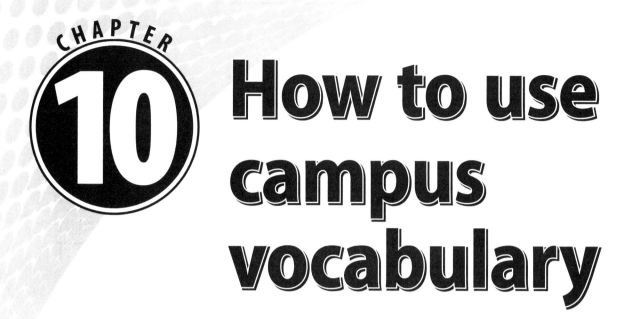

How to use campus vocabulary

Objectives

To understand and use vocabulary specific to academic study and campus life

To accustom yourself to the type of content found in the listening section of the TOEFL® test for campus-related topics

As part of your university experience, you will encounter new vocabulary that is specific to post-secondary education. You will need to be familiar with these words and terms in order to

- Understand written and verbal instructions
- Fill out forms
- Complete assignments and take examinations
- Find your way around campus

The listening, speaking, and writing sections of the TOEFL® test will examine students' ability to understand and use campus-related vocabulary.

The vocabulary in this chapter has been organized according to the following topics:

- Application and acceptance
- Orientation
- The first day of class
- Campus life

- A tour of the library
- The first major assignment
- Final exams

Dialogue 1:
Application and acceptance

Cara: Hi, Mom, I'm home.

Mom: A letter came for you this morning. From Regent Roads. Hi there, Hye-Jin. Nice to see you.

Hye-Jin: Hi, Mrs. Campbell.

Cara: I'm scared to open it. What if I didn't get accepted? (pause) Yes! I've been offered admission. I can't believe it!

Hye-Jin: Congratulations, Cara! That's awesome!

Cara: So it says here that I have to send an authorized **Notice of Acceptance** to the **Registrar's Office** and pay the **tuition fees** before the **deadline**. Once the tuition and acceptance have been processed, they'll send me an e-mail **confirmation**.

Hye-Jin: How exciting! Then you can start classes!

Cara: Well, first I need to **register** online and get a student ID. Then I'll have to see if there's still a seat in the classes I want to **enroll** in.

Hye-Jin: Can you choose your classes?

Cara: All first- and second-year Environmental Studies classes are **required**, but after that I can choose the **electives** that correspond to the area I want to **major in**.

Mom: What about you, Hye-Jin? Have you heard anything yet?

Hye-Jin: Actually I still haven't **applied**. I'm waiting for my TOEFL® test results, and to get accepted I need a score of 88 or better on the Internet test.

Cara: I bet you **aced** it.

Hye-Jin: Even if I did, I don't have a lot of time left. Besides, it's very hard to decide where to apply. All the really good colleges and universities have very strict **admission requirements**.

Mom: What are you thinking of studying?

Hye-Jin: Well, I'd like to get a **degree** in hotel management and tourism.

Cara: You should apply to Regent Roads, too. They have a great **undergraduate** program, and after getting your **B.A.** you can go on to graduate studies.

Hye-Jin: I heard that the **faculty** there is excellent, and it's a smaller **campus.**

Cara: So let's get going on this. After I write my reply, we can **fill out** your **application form**.

EXERCISE 10-1

Complete the sentences with the appropriate word in **bold type** from Dialogue 1.

If you want to attend a university, what steps do you have to take?

First you have to (1.) _____ to a university and

fill out a/an (2.) _____. Then you send everything,

including your documentation, to the (3.) _____. If you

meet the (4.) _____, the university will send you a/an

(5.) _____. When you accept, you have to pay the

(6.) _____ before the (7.) _____.

After the university processes your payment and acceptance, you will receive

a/an (8.) _____.

Before classes start, you have to (9.) _____

online in a/an (10.) _____ program and

(11.) _____ in the required classes. The classes you

have to take are called (12.) _____, and the classes you

can choose to take are (13.) _____.

After you have completed your three- or four-year university program, you

will receive a/an (14.) _____, also called a/an

(15.) _____. If you (16.) _____

your studies, you will have an excellent chance of landing a good job.

Each department has a/an (17.) _____ of professors

and assistant professors.

Regent Roads is a small but beautiful (18.) _____

with old historical buildings and lots of green space.

EXERCISE 10-2

Answer the following questions using the vocabulary in **bold type**, as shown in the example.

1. Which university or college do you want to **apply to** / have you already **applied to**?

Example: I've applied to Western University.

_____

_____

2. What documentation do you have to include with your **application**?

_____

_____

3. How much are the **tuition fees**?

_____

_____

4. What is the **deadline** for paying tuition?

_____

_____

5. What are the university's **admission requirements**?

_____

_____

6. If you are accepted, do you have to **register** online or in person?

_____

_____

7. Which courses do you plan to **enroll in**?

_____

_____

8. Are these courses **required** or **electives**?

_____

_____

9. What do you plan to **major in**?

_____

_____

10. When you complete your studies, what kind of **degree** will you receive?

_____

_____

Dialogue 2: Orientation

Sarah: Good morning, **freshmen**, and welcome to Regent Roads University. My name is Sarah, and I'm the Student Services Co-coordinator. Today I'm going to get you started on your first day of college. Now, as you can see on your program, today is Orientation Day. Anyone know what **orientation** is?

Student: Doesn't it have something to do with directions?

Sarah: Yes, you could say that. How many of you know your way around campus? Nobody? Well, this morning we're going to put you in groups and one of our **sophomores** will take you on a short tour of the most important sites and services on campus. These include the **Student Union building**, **transit exchange**, the library, the **administration building** (called "admin" for short), the **cafeteria**, the bookstore, the recreation center, and the Learning Technologies Center. Does anyone have any questions?

Student: What's the administration building?

Sarah: That's where you'll find the Registrar's and Records Offices, the Post Office and bank, **Campus Security** and first aid, **scholarships** and **bursaries**, and other business offices. All right? The last stop on our tour is the Learning Technologies Center where you can use the computer lab and business center to make photocopies, print, scan, and send documents. The LTC is also where you will be taking a language **placement test** so make sure you have your Student I.D. and password handy.

Student: I already have a TOEFL® test score, so do I have to take another test?

Sarah: Yes, it's **mandatory**. But don't worry, it's really just a formality so that we have something on record—especially for reading and writing, since you're all foreign students. OK? Now, just a short review of your academic schedule before we start the tour. As you know, the university runs on a two-**semester** academic year with a two-week Christmas break. Each semester runs fifteen weeks with one week of final exams. Since all of you registered online, you should have a **class schedule**, and if you don't, you should come and see me afterwards. You will also be organized into **cohorts**.

Student: Is that like a group?

Sarah: Yes, since there are so many of you, you will be divided up into cohorts of thirty students, and you will take all your classes together as one group. So, if there are no more questions, we can begin with the tour. Group 1 will stay here, and I ask you to have your passports and **student visas** ready. Also we will need to see your evidence of **medical insurance**. OK, is everyone ready? Then, let's go.

EXERCISE 10-3

Complete the dialogue using the appropriate vocabulary in **bold type** from Dialogue 2.

A: Excuse me, are you new to campus?

B: Actually, I'm a/an (1.) _____. This is my second year. How can I help you?

A: Well, I'm a/an (2.) _____ and this is my first time here. We had (3.) _____ this morning, but there was so much information that I feel a little lost.

B: What are you looking for?

A: Where can I get a bus pass?

B: You have to go to the (4.) _____. Anytime you need help that's the best place to go. It's right over there, behind the (5.) _____ where all the buses stop and leave from.

A: Thanks. And where can I find the (6.) _____? I have to go there to show someone proof of (7.) _____ in case I get sick, and I need to find out where I can get my (8.) _____. My government gives us money to study overseas.

B: That's cool! Hey, I'm going that way so you can come with me.

A: Thanks a lot. Do I need to show them my (9.) _____?

It's in my passport.

B: Most likely. Everyone here likes to see documents. At a university, documents

are (10.) _____.

A: What does that mean?

B: It's absolutely necessary, like a rule.

A: I see.

B: See that building over there? It's called the Heywood Building, and that's

where you can talk to someone from (11.) _____ in

case you lose something, or someone steals your bike.

A: I don't have a bike.

B: Right. You're getting a bus pass. So, are you ready to start classes?

Do you know your (12.) _____ or which

(13.) _____ you're in yet?

A: Yes, I have a copy, but it's just for the first (14.) _____.

What about you?

B: Mine's pretty full. Well, here we are. Look, I'm going to the

(15.) _____ for coffee. Want to join me when you're done?

A: Thanks, I'd love to, but I have to take a/an (16.) _____

in 30 minutes in the computer lab. I hope it's not too hard. The TOEFL® test

was challenging enough.

B: Don't worry. You'll pass with flying colors.

Dialogue 3:
The first day of class—Part 1

Pat: Good morning, class, and welcome to Introduction to Academic Writing 101. I'm Pat Duncan, your **instructor**. Now, before I introduce the **course outline**, course materials, and **syllabus**, which you will see on the **overhead**, I'd like to outline some basic rules which, if you follow them, will help you to succeed in this class. First, please turn your cell phones off and put them away. Cell phone use in class is prohibited. Yes?

Student: What if there's an important call?

Pat: Is this class not important?

Student: I guess so.

Pat: Then you know what to do. Now, if you have a laptop or tablet, you may use it to take notes or work on **assignments** in class, which doesn't include surfing the Internet, checking Facebook and e-mail, or watching videos on YouTube. Is that clear? Okay. **Attendance**. I expect your attendance to be regular and **punctual**, and you are to behave respectfully, attentively, professionally, and appropriately in class at all times. Yes?

Student: What if I get sick or there's an accident or **emergency**?

Pat: In the case of illness or emergencies, you are required to submit documentation to the Registrar's Office.

Student: Do you mean like a **doctor's note**?

Pat: That's correct, or an **official excuse** signed by a **person of authority**. In addition to regular, punctual attendance, you are asked not to walk in and out of class or be **disruptive** in any way. You are responsible for meeting the requirements of this class. That means you should know what work has been covered and assigned in class, and when assignments have to be submitted. Deadlines for papers and exam dates are **non-negotiable**, as are **grades**. Who can explain "non-negotiable"?

Student: You can't, like, make a deal, right?

Pat: Well put. With grades there are no deals. A D is a D and an F is an F. Remember, if you do the work, you will get the grades. If, however, you're having problems completing assignments on time or understanding course material, you can arrange to see me during **office hours**, which are 3:00 to 4:30 Monday to Thursday, but you cannot come crying that this **mark** is unfair and you deserve a better grade. Also don't expect me to give you an **extension** on deadlines because you cannot manage your time, and if you miss a test, you will not be allowed to write a **makeup test**. Another thing is **participation**. In this class I expect you to ask and answer questions, take part in discussions, work and interact with your classmates. Participation will count one third of your in-class work grade, which makes up 15 percent of your final grade. Now, if there are no questions, I'll proceed to the course outline.

EXERCISE 10-4

Using the information and vocabulary in **bold type** from Dialogue 3, write a summary of the course.

Introduction to Academic Writing 101

Instructor:_____

Office hours:_____

Basic rules:
- Cell phone use: _____
- Laptop/tablet use: _____
- Attendance: _____
- Behavior in class: _____

Students' responsibilities:

_____

_____

_____

Participation:

_____

_____

_____

Assignments:
- Deadlines: _____
- Extension: _____
- Emergency or illness: _____

Evaluation:
- Grades: _____
- Missed exams and assignments: _____

EXERCISE 10-5

Answer the following questions using the vocabulary in **bold type** from Dialogue 3.

1. Where can students find information about the contents of the course?

_____

2. Where can students see information presented during the class?

_____

3. Why can't students discuss their grades with their instructor if they are unhappy with them?

_____

_____

Dialogue 4:
The first day of class—Part 2

Pat: The course outline is here on the overhead and on the **handout**, which I will now circulate. Everyone please take a copy and pass the rest on. Please notice that my name, office number and hours, e-mail address, and phone number are listed at the top. Please use the last two with **discretion**. As the course title indicates, the central focus of this class is on academic or research writing. What's the difference between writing and academic writing?

Student: We have to use formal language, not slang or everyday English. And you can't just write your opinion about something. You have to back it up with evidence.

Pat: That's correct. What kind of evidence?

Student: Well, examples, facts, statistics. Stuff like that.

Pat: And where do you get the evidence?

Student: Off the Internet?

Pat: Although the Internet's very convenient, you'll need to find credible sources from books, journals, scholarly publications, academic papers, and so on. You will be required to include a number of **citations** in your work and provide a **reference list** of all sources.

Student: What's a citation?

Pat: A citation refers to any words that you quote, paraphrase, or summarize from external sources; in other words, anything that doesn't come from you. That's where the university library will be of use. Now, the course consists of fourteen weeks of instruction and one week of final exams, and the content is divided into six sections: grammar and syntax; APA formatting; **paraphrase** and **summary** writing; organizational structure including **thesis statement**, **counterarguments**, and **refutation**; **rhetorical devices**; and finally **critical thinking.** For the course there are two required textbooks: *Strategies for Academic Writing* and *Contemporary Issues*, plus a recommended dictionary, which you can buy at the campus bookstore. There will be two **term papers**, one major **research paper**, and all other assignments are listed, including how much they count toward your final mark.

Pat: This brings me to another point that differentiates academic writing. Academic writing conforms to what is called either APA or MLA style. At Regent Roads we use **APA style**, and that means papers must conform to specific **formatting** conventions; for instance they must be **double-spaced**, use a standard 12-point **font** with 1-inch **margins** on all sides of the document, **running heads**, and so on. You must include a **title page** with the title of your paper, the course name, your name and student I.D., and the due date.

Finally, I want to talk about two obstacles that will definitely stand in the way of your success: **plagiarism** and **procrastination**. First: plagiarism, for those of you who've never heard of it, is copying someone else's work and claiming it as your own. Plagiarism is a capital offense and will earn you an automatic **fail**, and it will go on your academic record. So don't even try it because, believe me, you will get caught. Anyone know what it means to procrastinate?

Student: Isn't it when you don't do your homework until tomorrow or the next day?

Pat: And the next, and the next. Any procrastinators in the room? Yes, I thought so. So, always make sure that you practice good **time management**, and hand in your **assignments** when they are **due**. Besides their being on the course schedule and on MOODLE* for all to see, I will always give assignments well ahead of the due date. The only time you won't be given **advance notice** is for **pop quizzes**, which will be short and related to lectures.

---

*MOODLE is a course-management system that can be used by universities and colleges to create and manage online learning sites.

EXERCISE 10-6

Complete the following assignment description with vocabulary in **bold** type from Dialogue 4. Pay careful attention to the hints.

Introduction to Academic Writing 101. Instructor: Pat Duncan

(1.) _____ #1: Summary

In this paper you are required to read and summarize the article "Feeding the World" from your textbook, *Contemporary Issues*, and to write a 500-word comment, stating your reflections on the author's argument.

Your paper should contain:

- A/An (2.) _____ stating your purpose and main argument

- At least two direct quotations, or (3.) _____, from the text

- A/An (4.) _____ or short

  (5.) _____ of the author's main arguments

  (in your own words, please!) according to (6.) _____

- A/An (7.) _____ at the end in APA style (even though you are using only one source). Your paper should also demonstrate

  (8.) _____, not just restate the author's ideas.

  (I want to know *your* thoughts!)

- A/An (9.) _____ with your name, date, etc.

Pay careful attention to the following (10.) _____ instructions:

- Spacing: (11.) _____

- (12.) _____: Times New Roman, 12 pt

- (13.) _____: 1 inch on all sides

- (14.) _____: title at top of page, left-hand margin

   Warning! Do not (15.) _____. This will result in an

   automatic (16.) _____.

   Deadline: All papers are (17.) _____ **at 4:00 p.m.
   on October 26**.

EXERCISE 10-7

Complete the following dialogue with vocabulary from the text.

A: Have you looked at the (1.) _____ for our writing

   assignment?

B: Yes, it's murder!

A: If this is just a/an (2.) _____, I'd hate to see what a

   major (3.) _____ looks like!

B: Me, too! He'll probably expect us to read twenty books.

A: And spend the rest of the semester in the library. And since the deadline's

   in three weeks, he's not giving us a lot of (4.) _____.

B: I understand that we have to present our arguments and back them up

   with supporting evidence, but I'm not really clear what he means by

   (5.) _____.

A: After we present our arguments, we have to come up with at least two

   opposing arguments.

B: What's the sense of shooting down our own arguments?

A: Well, I think the idea is to show that we can defend our arguments. That's

   where the (6.) _____ comes into play. Let's say you

   argue that capital punishment is wrong because innocent people are put to

   death.

B: So, I have to oppose that argument by stating that a much greater number of guilty people are executed than innocent people.

A: Right.

B: And then?

A: Your next step is to attack that argument and show that it's invalid.

B: How?

A: By proving, for instance, that executing an innocent person is the same as committing murder.

B: I see. I guess I should get started on it pretty soon, but I have a lot of other stuff to do.

A: Whatever you do, don't (7.) _____. I find it's better to set priorities and follow a study plan for each day, or you'll never get it done on time.

B: That sounds like good (8.) _____. That's something I need to learn.

A: And if you run into difficulty, you can always talk to Professor Duncan during office hours.

B: But he said to use our (9.) _____.

A: I think he means he doesn't want us running to him with every little problem.

B: Then maybe he should stop giving us unannounced (10.) _____, so we can focus on other things! This class is so stressful!

A: You tell him that!

Dialogue 5: Campus life

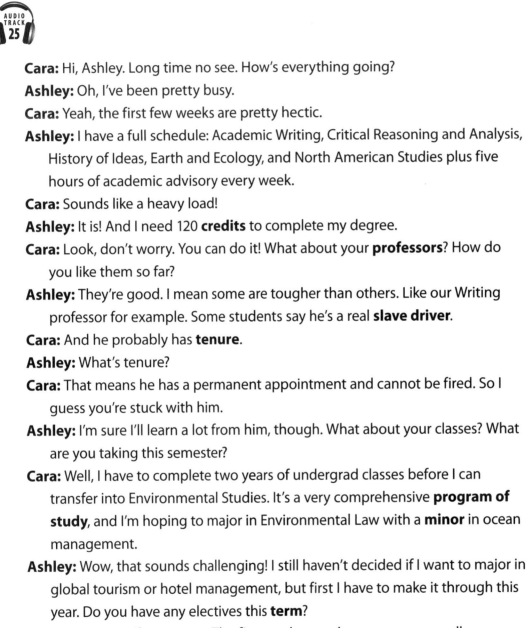

Cara: Hi, Ashley. Long time no see. How's everything going?

Ashley: Oh, I've been pretty busy.

Cara: Yeah, the first few weeks are pretty hectic.

Ashley: I have a full schedule: Academic Writing, Critical Reasoning and Analysis, History of Ideas, Earth and Ecology, and North American Studies plus five hours of academic advisory every week.

Cara: Sounds like a heavy load!

Ashley: It is! And I need 120 **credits** to complete my degree.

Cara: Look, don't worry. You can do it! What about your **professors**? How do you like them so far?

Ashley: They're good. I mean some are tougher than others. Like our Writing professor for example. Some students say he's a real **slave driver**.

Cara: And he probably has **tenure**.

Ashley: What's tenure?

Cara: That means he has a permanent appointment and cannot be fired. So I guess you're stuck with him.

Ashley: I'm sure I'll learn a lot from him, though. What about your classes? What are you taking this semester?

Cara: Well, I have to complete two years of undergrad classes before I can transfer into Environmental Studies. It's a very comprehensive **program of study**, and I'm hoping to major in Environmental Law with a **minor** in ocean management.

Ashley: Wow, that sounds challenging! I still haven't decided if I want to major in global tourism or hotel management, but first I have to make it through this year. Do you have any electives this **term**?

Cara: No, not until next term. The first- and second-year courses are all mandatory.

Ashley: I see.

Cara: Doing anything fun? Been to any **social functions** or joined any clubs?

Ashley: I really haven't had time. Besides, my **homestay family** lives across town so I have to get up early to catch the bus, and I don't get home until late, and then I have to **hit the books**.

Cara: I know what you mean. I have a big **group project** coming up, and at the end of next month we have **midterms** already. So much for social life!

Ashley: Do you know if there are any **sororities** or **fraternities** on this campus?

Cara: No, Regent Roads is too small and too young, but there are athletic clubs if you're into sports. You can also become a **class rep** and get involved in the student union.

Ashley: Right now I think I'd better concentrate on my studies.

Cara: Look, I've got some time before my next class, so why don't we grab a snack at the cafeteria and head over to one of the **study lounges** in the LTC. Maybe we'll run into some friends and I can introduce you.

Ashley: Sure, thanks. That'd be great!

EXERCISE 10-8

Answer the questions in complete sentences, using the vocabulary in **bold type**.

1. How many **credits** do you need to complete your program?

_____

_____

2. What kind of person makes a good **professor**?

_____

_____

3. Do students like teachers who are **slave drivers**? Why, or why not?

_____

_____

4. If a teacher has **tenure**, can he or she be fired? Why, or why not?

_____

_____

5. In what **program of study** do you want to enroll at your college or university?

_____

_____

6. What subject do you want to choose as a **minor**?

_____

_____

7. How many classes will you take this coming **term**?

_____

_____

8. What **social functions** do you think a university or college should provide for its students? What is the importance of social functions?

_____

_____

9. What are the advantages of living with a **homestay family**?

_____

_____

10. What time do you usually **hit the books**?

_____

_____

11. Have you ever been part of a **group project**? If so, what was the assignment?

_____

_____

12. When do students take **midterms**?

_____

_____

13. Are there any **sororities** or **fraternities** at the university or college you plan to attend? What are their names? If so, why do you want to join?

_____

_____

14. What are a **class rep**'s duties and responsibilities?

_____

_____

15. What can students do in the **study lounge**, and what facilities or equipment does it have?

_____

_____

Dialogue 6: A tour of the library

Brendan: Welcome to Regent Roads Library. My name is Brendan, and I'm one of the **librarians** here. Since this is where you will be spending a lot of time, I'm going to show you how to use the library resources.

We're open from 8:00 a.m. to 9:00 p.m. every day except holidays. When you come into the library, the first thing you see is the Help Desk over here, where you can **check out** books, **renew** or return them, **reserve a book**, pay a **fine**, and, of course, ask for assistance. You can also do all of this from any of the computer terminals at different locations or online from your home or your cell phone, Blackberry, etc. Now, your student I.D. card is also your library card, so make sure you have it with you when you come in.

In addition to books, e-books, reference books, scholarly journals, periodicals, CDs, DVDs, and videos, the library has a **collaborative study space** where you can work in groups as well as **carrels** and individual study rooms. These rooms can be booked online. There is a computer lab on each floor, and everyone has access to them at all times. There are also print/scan/copy machines located throughout the library.

Now, how do you locate and check out material? All materials are **catalogued** alphabetically according to author, title, or subject matter, and they are assigned a **call number,** which consists of a series of numbers that correspond to a subject area such as 303, for example, and the first letters of the author's last name in capitals. **In the stacks** materials are organized in sections according to subject matter and call numbers. So fiction is in one section, books about politics in another, and so on. For instance the call number for the book *The Limits to Growth* is HC59.L54 1972. **Electronic resources** have no call numbers.

To search for a title, you can use one of the terminals to do a basic, advanced, course reserve, or new books search. A **course reserve** is for materials that a professor has the library reserve for students in a particular class, but let's start with a basic search. Most of the time you will probably search by subject matter if you don't have a specific title. Let's say you're doing a paper on *racial discrimination* so we'll enter that in the search bar, and in the drop-down menu beside it, we'll click on subject. Under *Limit to* we can choose *all material, 2013 and after* if we want only recent material, English language materials, and videos, so let's select *all material.* When you see something you're interested in, jot down the call number and go to the stacks to **retrieve** it.

You can also refine your search according to content type, subject terms, and publication date, especially if you're looking for **abstracts, dissertations, archival information,** government documents, and academic research by using *Summon,* which is a search system that includes all records from our library and our **digital service,** so there's everything there at your disposal.

All right. Books can be **signed out** for 30 days at a time, but the only limit to how many you can take out is how many you can carry. If you still need the book after it's due, you can renew it as long as no one has **put a request on** the book. You can renew it at the Help Desk or online. All you have to do is go into My Library, click on the title, and renew. *Voilà!* If you forget to print out a receipt, don't worry. You will receive an e-mail reminder a couple of days before the material's due.

Speaking of due, we charge fines for **overdue** books, so it's good to keep track of what you have **on loan** because a fine of between $1 and $10 a day for reserve items can get expensive. If a book that you need is already out, you can put in a request again at the Help Desk or online.

EXERCISE 10-9

Complete the following dialogue with vocabulary in **bold type** from Dialogue 6.

Ashley: Hey, Cara. What're you up to?

Cara: I'm off to the library to do some research for my term paper. Want to join me?

Ashley: Actually, I have to (1.) _____ a book. It's due back

tomorrow and I don't want to have to pay another

(2.) _____ for a/an (3.) _____

book.

Cara: Yeah, that can get expensive. Did you know that you can renew books

online?

Ashley: Yes, but my problem is I always forget. Maybe I should just take out

(4.) _____ instead of the physical book.

Cara: The library has an awesome selection of e-books, and you can

(5.) _____ just about anything if you can't find it

(6.) _____.

Ashley: The (7.) _____ here are really helpful,

aren't they? The last time Brendan showed me how everything is

(8.) _____ by subject, author, date, and so on, and he

helped me do a search using the library's (9.) _____,

which is great if you want to do research from home or find stuff from other

libraries. Have you ever used it?

Cara: Not yet, but my boyfriend does a lot of research and he uses

academic sources like (10.) _____,

(11.) _____, and (12.) _____

all the time. Well, here we are. I'm going to find myself a vacant

(13.) _____ where I can study. What about you?

Ashley: First I have to go to the Help Desk to (14.) _____

a required book that my Ecology professor put on

(15.) _____ if one's still available. And then I have to

use the computer to find the (16.) _____ for another

book so that I can (17.) _____ it without having to

hunt all over. Right now all I have is the title.

Cara: You know that if you can't find a book or it's out

(18.) _____, you can (19.) _____.

Ashley: Yeah, Brendan showed me what to do. He also showed me how to book

the (20.) _____ for group projects.

Cara: Well, see you later. And don't get lost among the journals and periodicals.

Dialogue 7:
The first major assignment

Cara: Hey, you're looking a little **stressed out**? What's up?

Ashley: Well, we just got our first big assignment in North American Studies. A 1,500-word research paper on gay marriage, genetic databases, illegal immigration, women in the military, or the legalization of marijuana.

Cara: Wow, those are serious topics! When's it due?

Ashley: The final paper has to be **turned in** in six weeks, but first we have to put together a research plan by the end of the week. Then we have to write a detailed **outline**, including the sources we're using, and a **first draft**. And it's worth 15 percent of our final grade.

Cara: That's a lot!

Ashley: Yeah! And it's a lot of work. The prof gave us four pages of instructions and a research **worksheet** to fill out. Besides using our course material, we have to include three **citations** from the course material or external sources and present three arguments for or against, plus counterarguments and refutation. And a conclusion, of course, and **reference list** of all sources. And we have to use **rhetorical devices**.

Cara: It sounds like you'll be hanging out in the library.

Ashley: More like moving in. And on top of the research paper I have to **catch up on** my reading for Earth and Ecology, and in Writing we have to summarize a two-page article on world hunger and write a comment for Monday. How are your classes going?

Cara: They're just as **grueling**. We have a **group presentation** coming up next week—on some aspect of global warming. My group's going to talk about the impact on wild salmon stocks, so we've had to gather a lot of statistics. We're meeting this afternoon to start putting our PowerPoint together.

Ashley: Sounds interesting.

Cara: We also have to lead a **class discussion** after the presentation. Say, have you heard anything yet about your midterms?

Ashley: As if I didn't have enough on my plate already without midterms!

EXERCISE 10-10

Complete each sentence with the appropriate word in **bold type** from Dialogue 7.

1. The class had to _____ their finished essays by yesterday at 4:00.

2. Every Friday in our North American Studies class, we have stimulating _____ about current affairs, and almost everyone participates.

3. A detailed _____ in point form is like a map. Without it, when you sit down to write your essay, you won't know where you're going.

4. A/An _____ will help you gather and organize information and keep track of the sources you use for your _____ and _____.

5. Remember, your _____ is not your final essay. You need to edit it carefully and rewrite.

6. You shouldn't use more than a couple of _____ in your essay. In oral presentations and speeches, they are particularly effective if you want to command your audience's attention.

7. Whenever I'm _____ about school, I can't sleep very well.

8. My roommate loves Math 101, but I find it _____.

9. I'd much rather do a/an _____ than prepare one alone. That way we can share the responsibility and I don't have to do all the talking.

10. If you miss too many classes, you will have a lot of work to _____.

EXERCISE 10-11

Answer the questions in complete sentences, using the vocabulary in **bold type** from Dialogue 7.

1. What is an effective **rhetorical device** that you can use in an introduction?

_____

_____

2. What do you like most about **class discussions**? What do you like least?

_____

_____

3. When do you feel **stressed out**?

_____

_____

4. Why is it important to write an **outline** for an essay or paper?

_____

_____

5. If you miss classes because of illness, what do you do **to catch up on** what you've missed?

_____

_____

6. Why is it a good idea to have someone else read your **first draft**?

_____

_____

7. What is a good topic or subject for a **group presentation**? If there were three people in your group, how would you organize it?

_____

_____

8. If you have to do a major assignment, how can a **worksheet** help you?

_____

_____

9. What assignments have you **turned in** recently?

_____

_____

10. What is your most **grueling** subject? Why?

_____

_____

Dialogue 8: Final exams

Cara: I can't believe we'll be writing finals next week.

Ashley: Me either. Are you ready?

Cara: As ready as I'll ever be, I guess. This week we've been having mostly review sessions and finishing up projects, so I haven't had time to study yet. I'll probably end up **burning the midnight oil** or **pulling a couple of all-nighters**.

Ashley: I hate **cramming**, but sometimes you can't help it.

Cara: Have you seen the university **exam protocol**?

Ashley: Yes, it's pretty strict. No cell phones or electronic devices. You can't even wear a hat.

Cara: And you can't bring any personal belongings into the room, either. I guess they want to eliminate every opportunity for students to **cheat**, but there are still those who think they can get away with it. Regardless, academic **misconduct** just doesn't pay.

Ashley: What happens if the **invigilator** catches you cheating?

Cara: It's an automatic zero for the course and it stays on your record. No one would want that on their **transcript** when an employer asks to see one, would they?

Ashley: That's for sure. It'd be a disaster.

Cara: Of course there's a **hearing** before a **disciplinary committee** to determine a **penalty** or **punitive measures**.

Ashley: Like what?

Cara: They could have to rewrite the exam, or worse, you could face **expulsion**. Last year a couple of students got kicked out and that was the end of their academic careers.

Ashley: What happens if you miss the final for some reason?

Cara: Because you slept in?

Ashley: For instance.

Cara: You need a more legitimate reason than that. If you miss an exam, you get an incomplete on your record. However, there are **special provisions**. Last year a friend of mine got a **deferral** because of a death in the family.

Ashley: That's too bad. Say, how soon do we get our final grades?

Cara: Results are released and **posted** outside the Registrar's Office two weeks later.

Ashley: You mean everybody gets to see your grades!

Cara: No, they just post *Pass* or *Fail*. You can access your actual marks on MOODLE.

Ashley: I hope my marks will be good enough to **apply for a scholarship**.

Cara: I bet you'll make the **honor roll**.

Ashley: I don't know about that. All I want is 120 credits and a grade point average above 3.0 so that I can graduate in three years and qualify to apply to grad school!

Cara: Speaking of **graduation,** you'll have to come with me to the **commencement ceremonies**. My boyfriend's **convocating**.

Ashley: Wow! Then what's he going to do? Look for a job?

Cara: No, he's applied to **graduate studies**. He wants to get his **master's.**

Ashley: Graduate school! Wow! That means he'll have to write a **thesis**.

Cara: I'll be glad when I have my bachelor's degree in my hands, but who knows how I'll feel by then?

EXERCISE 10-12

Complete the following document with vocabulary in **bold type** from Dialogue 8.

(1.) _____ student responsibilities:

- The exam schedule is (2.) _____ on notice boards. Students are responsible for knowing the time, date, and locations of final examinations.

- Students are required to produce official photo identification (student I.D. cards) when requested. This I.D. is to be placed on the desk in full view for the duration of the examination.

- The examination will be supervised by a/an (3.) _____ who will not admit anyone 30 minutes after the exam has commenced. All students must remained seated for a minimum of 30 minutes, after which time they may leave in a quiet manner.

- Cellular phones, laptops, and electronic devices are not allowed in the examination room without the prior permission of the instructor.

- Books, bags, and jackets must be left in the designated area and cannot be claimed until the student has handed in his or her exam paper.

- Food and drink, other than water, are not be consumed during the examination.

- Any oral, written, or other forms of communication between students during the examination will be considered (4.) _____ and subject to a/an (5.) _____.

- Students may communicate with the invigilator by raising their hands, but they must remain in their seats.

- When they have finished, students are asked to bring all of their papers to the invigilator and leave the room quietly.

- All students shall stop writing at the conclusion of the exam. If they have not finished, the invigilator may seize their papers.

- Students who miss the examination will receive a/an

  (6.) _____, which will appear on their

  (7.) _____ unless they have obtained a/an

  (8.) _____ to take the exam at a later date.

Failure to adhere to the protocol during the examination will result in

(9.) _____, which will be determined by a/an

(10.) _____.

EXERCISE 10-13

Answer the following questions using the vocabulary in **bold type** from Dialogue 8.

1. Have you ever **pulled an all-nighter**? When?

   _____

   _____

2. How often do you **burn the midnight oil**?

   _____

   _____

3. Does **cramming** for an exam help? Why, or why not?

   _____

   _____

4. What are the consequences of **expulsion** from a college or university?

_____

_____

5. What would be some **special provisions** for retaking an examination or receiving a deferral?

_____

_____

6. What requirements do you have to meet in order to **apply for a scholarship**?

_____

_____

7. What do students have to do in order to make the **honor roll**?

_____

_____

8. When do schools and colleges hold **graduation**?

_____

_____

9. What happens at **commencement ceremonies?**

_____

_____

10. When do you hope to **convocate**?

_____

11. After completing **graduate studies**, what kind of degree does a graduate receive?

_____

12. In order to get your **master's**, what do you have to write?

_____

APPENDIX A

Checklist of academic, nonacademic, and campus vocabulary

To measure your progress in building vocabulary, put a check (√) in the column that applies to you.

AWL VOCABULARY

	I RECOGNIZE THIS WORD	I UNDERSTAND THIS WORD	I CAN USE THIS WORD
abandon			
abstract			
access			
accommodate			
accumulate			
accurate			
achieve			
acknowledge			
acquire			
adapt			
adaptation			
adequate			
adjust			
adjustment			
administration			
advocate			
affect			
aid			
albeit			
allocate			
alter			
alternate			
alternative			

(continued)

	I RECOGNIZE THIS WORD	I UNDERSTAND THIS WORD	I CAN USE THIS WORD
ambiguous			
amendment			
analogy			
analysis			
analyze			
annual			
anticipate			
anticipation			
apparent			
append			
appreciate			
approach			
appropriate			
approximate			
arbitrate			
assume			
attach			
attainable			
attitude			
attribute			
authority			
automate			
available			
aware			
benefit			
bias			
biased			
brief			
capacity			
category			
challenge			
cite			
civil			
clarify			
classify			
code			
coherent			
coincide			
collapse			

	I RECOGNIZE THIS WORD	I UNDERSTAND THIS WORD	I CAN USE THIS WORD
commence			
comment			
commit			
committee			
commodity			
compatible			
compile			
complement			
comprehensive			
comprise			
compute			
conceive			
concentrate			
concept			
conclude			
conclusion			
conduct			
confine			
confirm			
conflict			
conform			
conscious			
consequent(ly)			
consent			
considerable			
consist			
constitute			
construct			
consume			
consumer			
contemporary			
context			
contract			
contradict			
contrast			
contribute			
contributor			
controversy			
conventional			

(continued)

	I RECOGNIZE THIS WORD	I UNDERSTAND THIS WORD	I CAN USE THIS WORD
converse			
convert			
convince			
coordinate			
corporate			
correspond			
create			
credit			
criterion			
critical			
crucial			
debate			
decline			
deduce			
define			
demonstrate			
deny			
depress			
depression			
design			
despite			
detect			
deviate			
device			
differentiate			
dimension			
diminish			
discrete			
discrimination			
display			
dispute			
distinct			
distort			
distribution			
diverse			
diversify			
domestic			
dominance			
draft			

	I RECOGNIZE THIS WORD	I UNDERSTAND THIS WORD	I CAN USE THIS WORD
dramatic			
dynamic			
economic			
economical			
economy			
edit			
element			
eliminate			
emerge			
emphasize			
empirical			
enable			
encounter			
enforce			
enhance			
ensure			
environment			
environmental			
equivalent			
erode			
establish			
estimate			
ethical			
evaluate			
evidence			
evident			
evolve			
evolution			
exceed			
excess			
exclusion			
exclusive			
exhibit			
expand			
explicit			
exploit			
expose			
external			
extract			

(continued)

	I RECOGNIZE THIS WORD	I UNDERSTAND THIS WORD	I CAN USE THIS WORD
facilitator			
factor			
feature			
fee			
file			
financial			
finite			
flexible			
fluctuate			
focus			
foul			
foundation			
framework			
fuel			
fundamental			
funds			
generate			
goal			
grant			
hence			
hierarchy			
hypothesis			
identity			
ideology			
image			
immigration			
impact			
impairment			
implementation			
implicate			
implicit			
imply			
incentive			
incidence			
inclined			
income			
incorporate			
index			
indicate			

	I RECOGNIZE THIS WORD	I UNDERSTAND THIS WORD	I CAN USE THIS WORD
individual			
induce			
inevitable			
infer			
infrastructure			
inherent			
inhibit			
initial(ly)			
injure			
innovative			
input			
insight			
institute			
instruction			
integral			
integrate			
intense			
interact			
interpret			
interpretation			
intervention			
intrinsic			
invalid			
invest			
investigate			
invoke			
irrational			
irreversible			
issue			
justify			
legislate			
levy			
liberal			
link			
locate			
logic			
maintain			
majority			
margin			

(continued)

	I RECOGNIZE THIS WORD	I UNDERSTAND THIS WORD	I CAN USE THIS WORD
mature			
mechanical			
mechanism			
media			
metaphor			
migrate			
migration			
modify			
monitor			
motivate			
motive			
mutual			
network			
negate			
nuclear			
objective			
obtain			
obtainable			
obvious			
occur			
occupy			
offset			
option			
orient			
overall			
overseas			
panel			
paradigm			
parallel			
participate			
partner			
passive			
perceive			
period			
perspective			
phenomenon			
portion			
pose			
potential			

	I RECOGNIZE THIS WORD	I UNDERSTAND THIS WORD	I CAN USE THIS WORD
practitioner			
precede			
precedence			
precedent			
precise			
precision			
predict			
predominant			
preliminary			
presumably			
previous			
primary			
principal			
principle			
priority			
proceed			
prohibit			
project			
promote			
promotion			
prospect			
psychological			
psychology			
publish			
purchase			
pursue			
quote			
radical			
random			
range			
ratio			
rational			
reconstruction			
recover			
refine			
register			
regulate			
reinforce			
reject			

(continued)

	I RECOGNIZE THIS WORD	I UNDERSTAND THIS WORD	I CAN USE THIS WORD
release			
reluctance			
rely			
require			
research			
reside			
resident			
resolution			
resource			
respond			
restore			
restrain			
restrict			
reveal			
revenue			
revise			
revolution			
revolutionary			
rigid			
satire			
schedule			
scheme			
secure			
seek			
sequence			
shift			
significant			
simulate			
site			
sole			
sophisticated			
specific			
spontaneous			
stabilize			
statistics			
subordinate			
subsidy			
succession			
sufficient			
supplement			

	I RECOGNIZE THIS WORD	I UNDERSTAND THIS WORD	I CAN USE THIS WORD
survival			
suspend			
sustainable			
symbol			
target			
technical			
temporary			
tension			
terminate			
theme			
theory			
trace			
trade			
tradition			
transfer			
transform			
transmit			
transport			
trend			
trigger			
ultimate			
undergo			
undertaking			
uniform			
unique			
valid			
validity			
vary			
vast			
vehicle			
violate			
virtual			
visible			
visual			
visualization			
volume			
voluntary			
welfare			
widespread			

(continued)

NON-AWL VOCABULARY

	I RECOGNIZE THIS WORD	I UNDERSTAND THIS WORD	I CAN USE THIS WORD
abolitionist			
absorb			
accomplishment			
accuse			
adopt			
adorn			
advent			
adverse			
advice			
advise			
afflict			
affordable			
aggravate			
allude			
allusion			
amoral			
anatomical			
antagonism			
anthem			
antipathy			
appraise			
apprise			
approval			
arbitrate			
artificial			
ascend			
ascertain			
assent			
assert			
assimilate			
aural			
autonomy			
averse			
avert			
boost			
bombard			
bureaucratic			

	I RECOGNIZE THIS WORD	I UNDERSTAND THIS WORD	I CAN USE THIS WORD
burgeon			
canvas			
canvass			
capital			
capitol			
capitulate			
catalyst			
catastrophic			
cede			
ceremony			
chronicle			
chivalry			
climactic			
climatic			
clutter			
coerce			
collaborate			
collide			
communal			
competition			
complacent			
complaisant			
compliment			
comply			
compose			
compromise			
concern			
condolence			
confidential			
conquest			
conscientious			
conscious			
consider			
considerate			
contaminate			
contamination			
contemplate			
contempt			
contentious			

(continued)

	I RECOGNIZE THIS WORD	I UNDERSTAND THIS WORD	I CAN USE THIS WORD
contest			
continual			
continuous			
conventional			
convict			
conviction			
cumbersome			
cure			
damage			
decrepit			
deduct			
defect			
deficiency			
defuse			
degrade			
deliberate			
delude			
demolition			
deprive			
descendant			
designate			
describe			
despise			
despotic			
destination			
detain			
deteriorate			
determine			
devastate			
develop			
development			
deviate			
devolve			
diagnose			
diagnosis			
diffuse			
dilemma			
dilute			
discharge			

	I RECOGNIZE THIS WORD	I UNDERSTAND THIS WORD	I CAN USE THIS WORD
discreet			
discipline			
disenfranchised			
disgust			
dispute			
dissipate			
dissolute			
divination			
ecotourism			
effect			
elaborate			
elect			
elicit			
elite			
elude			
emanate			
emancipation			
embark			
emigration			
eminent			
emission			
emit			
encompass			
endure			
engender			
enormous			
entrance			
epidemic			
equality			
eradication			
err			
escalate			
escapade			
essential			
evacuate			
evade			
evoke			
excavate			
existence			

(continued)

	I RECOGNIZE THIS WORD	I UNDERSTAND THIS WORD	I CAN USE THIS WORD
exotic			
expedition			
experience			
explode			
explore			
explosion			
external			
extinction			
exuberance			
faction			
fake			
famous			
far-reaching			
fascination			
fertilize			
fiction			
fictional			
fictitious			
flawed			
flourish			
fortify			
foster			
frustrate			
full-fledged			
garner			
gimmick			
graphic			
grotesque			
harm			
harmony			
heir			
horticulture			
hygiene			
illegal			
illicit			
illusion			
imagination			
immaculate			
immanent			

	I RECOGNIZE THIS WORD	I UNDERSTAND THIS WORD	I CAN USE THIS WORD
imminent			
immobile			
immoral			
immune			
impending			
impetus			
impoverish			
impulse			
incarceration			
incense			
incinerate			
incite			
incompetent			
incorrigible			
increase			
indigenous			
infallible			
inflation			
insanity			
inscription			
insist			
inspire			
installation			
insure			
insurmountable			
intentional			
interrogator			
intrigue			
invalid			
intimate			
irresistible			
knowledge			
launch			
legacy			
legendary			
legitimate			
lessen			
lethal			
limb			

(continued)

	I RECOGNIZE THIS WORD	I UNDERSTAND THIS WORD	I CAN USE THIS WORD
literary			
longitude			
loyalty			
lucrative			
luxurious			
magnify			
malicious			
malignant			
maneuver			
mania			
manifest			
marshal			
martial			
measure			
mediocre			
merchant			
mimic			
minute			
navigate			
nausea			
negotiation			
nutrient			
nutrition			
oblige			
observe			
omit			
omnipotent			
operate			
oppress			
oral			
ordeal			
originate			
outlaw			
pariah			
pastoral			
patriotic			
pattern			
peddle			
perform			

	I RECOGNIZE THIS WORD	I UNDERSTAND THIS WORD	I CAN USE THIS WORD
perilous			
permission			
permit			
perpetual			
perseverance			
pledge			
plummet			
potent			
precipitate			
preclude			
preconceived			
predicament			
preeminent			
prescribe			
prestige			
prevent			
priceless			
priority			
probable			
procure			
produce			
profile			
profitable			
profound			
project			
proliferate			
prominent			
propaganda			
propel			
prosaic			
proscribe			
prospective			
provide			
quirky			
rate			
ratify			
rebel			
reciprocal			
recognizable			

(continued)

	I RECOGNIZE THIS WORD	I UNDERSTAND THIS WORD	I CAN USE THIS WORD
recreation			
reduce			
refuse			
relative			
religious			
relinquish			
renewable			
repercussion			
replicate			
repress			
repulse			
request			
resourceful			
respectable			
respectful			
respective			
responsible			
resume			
retaliate			
retrieve			
revolve			
reward			
rigorous			
romance			
rupture			
sacrifice			
safeguard			
sample			
sanitation			
sate			
satirize			
scale			
scintillate			
scrutinize			
secede			
sensation			
sequel			
sewer			
sibling			

	I RECOGNIZE THIS WORD	I UNDERSTAND THIS WORD	I CAN USE THIS WORD
signal			
slate			
slope			
smolder			
sophisticated			
spearhead			
speculative			
spontaneous			
stigma			
stimulate			
stipulate			
subside			
substance			
substantial			
substantiate			
subjective			
succeed			
sundry			
supplant			
supremacy			
susceptibility			
surveillance			
tally			
tangible			
testify			
therapeutic			
toxic			
treat			
tumor			
tyranny			
unconscious			
unintentional			
unit			
unleash			
unprecedented			
up the ante			
urge			
utilize			
venerable			

(continued)

	I RECOGNIZE THIS WORD	I UNDERSTAND THIS WORD	I CAN USE THIS WORD
venture			
verdict			
verify			
versatility			
vessel			
vicarious			
volatile			
vulnerable			
worthless			
yield			

CAMPUS VOCABULARY

	I RECOGNIZE THIS TERM	I UNDERSTAND THIS TERM	I CAN USE THIS TERM
abstract			
academic advisor			
academic record			
academic year			
ace something			
administration building			
admission			
admissions requirements			
advance notice			
APA style			
application			
apply for a scholarship			
apply to college/university			
archival information			
assignment			
attendance			
bachelor's degree (B.A./B.SC.)			
be behind in a class			
bring up grades			
burn the midnight oil			
bursary			
cafeteria			
call number			

	I RECOGNIZE THIS TERM	I UNDERSTAND THIS TERM	I CAN USE THIS TERM
campus			
campus security			
carrel			
catalog			
catch up on an assignment			
cheat			
check out books			
citation			
class discussion			
class rep			
class schedule			
cohort			
collaborative study space			
commencement ceremony			
confirmation			
convocate			
counterargument			
course outline			
course reserve			
cram			
credit			
critical thinking			
cut class			
deadline			
deferral			
degree			
digital service			
disciplinary committee			
discretion			
disruptive			
dissertation			
doctor's note			
double-spaced			
drop a class			
drop out			
due			
elective			
electronic resources			
emergency			

(continued)

	I RECOGNIZE THIS TERM	I UNDERSTAND THIS TERM	I CAN USE THIS TERM
enroll			
exam protocol			
expel			
expulsion			
extension			
faculty			
fail			
fill out an application			
fine			
first draft			
font			
formatting			
fraternity			
freshman			
grade			
graduate			
graduate studies			
graduation			
group presentation			
group project			
grueling			
handout			
health center			
hearing			
hit the books			
homestay family			
honor roll			
incomplete			
instruction			
instructor			
in the stacks			
invigilator			
leave of absence			
librarian			
library resources			
margin			
major			
makeup test			
mandatory			
margin			

	I RECOGNIZE THIS TERM	I UNDERSTAND THIS TERM	I CAN USE THIS TERM
mark			
master's degree (M.A.)			
medical insurance			
midterm			
minor			
misconduct			
nonnegotiable			
notice of acceptance			
office hours			
official excuse			
on loan			
orientation			
outline			
overdue			
overhead			
paraphrase			
penalty			
periodical			
personal issues			
person of authority			
placement test			
plagiarism			
pop quiz			
post a grade			
procrastinate			
procrastination			
professor			
program of study			
pull an all-nighter			
punctual			
punitive measures			
put a request on a book			
put on probation			
recreation center			
reference			
reference book			
reference list			
refutation			
register			

(continued)

	I RECOGNIZE THIS TERM	I UNDERSTAND THIS TERM	I CAN USE THIS TERM
Registrar's Office			
renew a book			
required classes			
research paper			
reserve a book			
retrieve			
rhetorical device			
running head			
scholarly journal			
scholarship			
section			
semester			
show up for class			
sign out a book			
slave driver			
social function			
sophomore			
sorority			
special provision			
stressed out			
Student Union			
student visa			
study lounge			
summary			
suspend			
syllabus			
tenure			
term			
term paper			
thesis			
thesis statement			
time management			
title page			
transcript			
transit exchange			
tuition fees			
turn in an assignment			
tutor			
typewritten			
undergraduate			
worksheet			

APPENDIX B

Vocabulary journal and flashcard templates

Journal entry #1: Full-page entry

1. Word: _____ (_____)

2. Word family:

Noun	Adjective/adverb	Verb
_____	_____	_____
_____	_____	_____

3. Definition: _____

_____

4. Synonyms: _____

Antonyms: _____

5. Examples: _____

_____

6. Collocations: _____

_____

_____

7. Sentences: _____

_____

_____

_____

8. Picture, clue, or personal association:

Journal entry #2: Short form

Word: _____ (_____)

Noun: _____

Adjective/adverb: _____

Verb: _____

1. Definition: _____

_____

2. Synonyms/antonyms: _____

3. Sentences: _____

_____

_____

_____

4. Collocations: _____

_____

_____

Word: _____ (_____)

Noun: _____

Adjective/adverb: _____

Verb: _____

1. Definition: _____

_____

2. Synonyms/antonyms: _____

3. Sentences: _____

_____

_____

_____

4. Collocations: _____

_____

_____

Word: _____ (_____)

Noun: _____

Adjective/adverb: _____

Verb: _____

1. Definition: _____

_____

2. Synonyms/antonyms: _____

_____

3. Sentences: _____

_____

_____

_____

4. Collocations: _____

_____

_____

Word: _____ (_____)

Noun: _____

Adjective/adverb: _____

Verb: _____

1. Definition: _____

_____

2. Synonyms/antonyms: _____

_____

3. Sentences: _____

_____

_____

_____

4. Collocations: _____

_____

_____

Journal entry # 3: Flashcard template

Card front

word

Card back

1. Part of speech: _____

2. Word family: _____

3. Definition: _____

4. Synonyms: _____

Antonyms: _____

5. Examples: _____

6. Collocations: _____

7. Sentences: _____

8. Picture, clue, or personal association: _____

Journal entry # 4: Word families

Noun	Adjective/adverb	Verb

APPENDIX C

Common suffixes and prefixes

The following lists contain the most useful prefixes and suffixes for your purposes. For more, refer to the resource list following the Bibliography. Unfortunately, you will find that no one list contains *all* the prefixes, suffixes, and roots and that you will have to carry out your own investigations from different sources

NOUN-FORMING SUFFIXES

SUFFIX	MEANING	EXAMPLES
acy	quality or state	literacy, supremacy
age	action or result	suffrage, advantage
ance / ence	quality, action, state, process	appearance, permanence
ant / ent	agent, indication	servant, resident
ary / ory	place	library, dormitory
ate	state, office, function	advocate, particulate
dom	domain, collection, rank, condition	kingdom, freedom
er / or	person or thing that does	singer, orator
hood	state, condition, character	childhood, neighborhood
ia	medical condition, place	insomnia, East Anglia
ic	quality, relation	topic, magic
	related to science	arithmetic, physics
ion	action, condition	union, nation
ism	doctrine, belief, action, conduct	nationalism, communism
ist	person who practices	realist, materialist
itis	inflammation, abnormal condition	tendonitis
ity	state, condition	purity, unity
ive	condition, having the quality of	sedative, missive
le / ole	diminutive	muscle, oracle
ment	condition, result	firmament, testament
ness	quality, state, condition	cleanliness, happiness
ology	study of	biology, geology

SUFFIX	MEANING	EXAMPLES
ship	condition, status	friendship, kinship
tude	abstract nouns	platitude, altitude
ure	action, condition, process, function	feature, nature
y	state, condition, result of an activity	baby, society

VERB SUFFIXES

SUFFIX	MEANING	EXAMPLES
ate	cause to be	liberate, substantiate, activate
en	cause to become	strengthen, harden
er / or	action	wonder, clamor
esce	become or change	coalesce, convalesce
ify	make, form	purify, simplify
ise / ize	cause	revolutionize, sterilize
le	having a frequent force	dazzle, twinkle

ADJECTIVE SUFFIXES

SUFFIX	MEANING	EXAMPLES
able / ible	worth, ability	capable, flexible
al / ial / ical	quality, relation	nasal, territorial, cylindrical
ant / ent / ient	kind of agent, indication	arrogant, latent, transient
ar / ary / ory	resembling, related to	spectacular, stationary
ate	state	irate
ed	condition, quality	inflated, elated
en	made of	wooden, golden
er	comparative	hotter, bigger
est	superlative	hottest, biggest
ful	marked by, full of, tending to	sorrowful, helpful
ic	quality, in the style of	poetic, archaic
ile	capability, aptitude	fragile, volatile
ing	activity	refreshing, fascinating
ish	having the character of	selfish, oldish
itive / ative / itive	tendency, disposition	pensive, active
less	without, missing	penniless, worthless
ly	like	daily, saintly
ose	full of, abounding in	verbose, comatose
ous / eous / ious	having the quality of	porous, dangerous
y	marked by, having	crazy, naughty

ADVERB SUFFIXES

SUFFIX	MEANING	EXAMPLES
fold	in a manner of, marked by	manifold, tenfold
ly	in the manner of	quietly, carefully
ward	in the direction or manner	toward, downward
wise	in the manner of, with regard to	likewise, clockwise

BIBLIOGRAPHY AND ONLINE RESOURCES

Dictionaries

Oxford Advanced Learner's Dictionary

Dictionary.com (http://dictionary.reference.com)

Word use in English

Bauman, John, and Brent Culligan. General Service List (updated, 1995) (http://jbauman .com/gsl.html).

Coxhead, Averil. Academic Word List. 1998.

Global Language Monitor (www.languagemonitor.com).

Ogden, Charles K. *Basic English: A General Introduction with Rules and Grammar.* 1932.

West, Michael. *A General Service List of English Words.* 1953.

TOEFL® test resources

McGraw-Hill Education: TOEFL iBT by Tim Collins (0-07-179622-3).

Online practice vocabulary tests and exercises for the TOEFL® test

http://www.examenglish.com/index.html

http://www.english-test.net/toefl

http://www.quiz-tree.com/TOEFL_main.html

http://www.vocaboly.com/vocabulary-test/toefl40.php

http://www.englishdaily626.com/tfvocab.php

http://www.edmantra.com/ivocab/index.php

Specialist sites

Roots, prefixes, and suffixes

The most common roots, prefixes, and suffixes: http://www.docstoc.com/docs/120694040
/The-most-common-roots_-prefixes_-and-suffixes

Prefixes and suffixes: http://www.prefixes-suffixes.com/common-prefixes.html

Prefixes and suffixes, English-language roots reference: http://www.prefixsuffix.com
/rootchart.php

A list of common prefixes and suffixes used in the AWL can be found at http://www
.englishcompanion.com/pdfDocs/acvocabulary2.pdf.

Academic Word List

Burke, Jim, *Academic Vocabulary List*: http://personales.mundivia.es/emca/english4u
/wordfor.html

English Club: http://www.englishclub.com/vocabulary/prefixes.htm

Learn that word: http://www.learnthat.org/pages/view/roots.html

Commonly confused words

http://grammarist.com/easily-confused-words

Homonyms, homophones, and heteronyms

http://www.cooper.com/alan/homonym_list.html

http://richard.tangle-wood.co.uk/heteronym.html

Collocations and mnemonics

Online collocation dictionaries: http://www.ozdic.com or http://collocations
.longmandictionariesonline.com

Online mnemonic dictionary: http://www.mnemonicdictionary.com

ANSWER KEY

Note: All listed definitions can be found in the *Oxford Advanced Learner's Dictionary*.

Exercise 1-1

1. The <u>report</u> unleashed a <u>controversy</u> concerning the <u>future</u> of the <u>planet</u>.
2. Even identical <u>twins</u> with the same genetic <u>makeup</u> are distinct in their <u>thoughts</u>, <u>feelings</u>, and <u>behavior</u>.
3. The <u>majority</u> of <u>people</u> have always lived simply, and most of <u>humanity</u> still struggles on a daily <u>basis</u> to eke out a meager <u>existence</u> under dire <u>circumstances</u>.

4. Remote-controlled <u>robots</u> are indispensable in <u>space</u> and <u>underwater exploration</u>, military <u>reconnaissance</u>, and <u>search</u>-and-<u>rescue operations</u>.
5. At the <u>Stanford Research Institute</u> in <u>California</u>, a <u>team</u> of <u>researchers</u> programmed a small adult-sized <u>robot</u> named <u>Shakey</u> to sense colored <u>blocks</u> and <u>wedges</u> with an onboard <u>camera</u>, and to push them around a carefully constructed <u>set</u> of <u>rooms</u>.

Exercise 1-2

Answers will vary, but some example responses follow.

1. The <u>professor</u> read an <u>analysis</u> about <u>deforestation</u>.
2. A <u>team</u> of <u>scientists</u> conducted <u>research</u> into <u>climate change</u>.
3. According to the <u>survey</u>, several <u>generations</u> of <u>citizens</u> originated in the <u>coastal</u> <u>area</u> of <u>Ireland</u> around the <u>turn of the century</u>.

4. Many <u>engineers</u> have made precise <u>calculations</u> designed to test the <u>strength</u> of <u>metals</u> and <u>fibers</u>.
5. In <u>Renaissance England</u> one of the most important <u>concerns</u> of <u>the monarchy</u> was the <u>threat</u> posed by <u>Spain</u>.

Exercise 1-3

Answers will vary, but many of the following suggestions are in the AWL and advanced word lists in Appendix A.

	Prefix	Meaning	Example
1.	an	not, in the process of	analgesia
2.	ante	before, preceding	antecedent
3.	anti	against, opposition	antipathy
4.	auto	self	autonomy
5.	bi	two	biannual
6.	circum	around	circumnavigate
7.	co	together with	coordinate
8.	com	with, jointly, completely	comprehensive
9.	con	together with	conceive
10.	counter	against, opposition	counteract
11.	di	apart, through, across	dilute
12.	dis	apart, not, opposite	discrimination
13.	ex	out, previous	extract
14.	geo	of the earth	geothermal

(continued)

	Prefix	Meaning	Example
15.	hyper	extreme, more than normal	hyperextend
16.	hypo	below normal	hypotension
17.	in	the converse of, inside	invalid
18.	inter	between, among	intervention
19.	kilo	thousand	kilogram
20.	mal	bad, wrong	malignant
21.	mega	million, large, great	megabyte
22.	mini	small	miniseries
23.	mis	bad, wrong	misapply
24.	mono	one	monotone
25.	multi	many	multifaceted
26.	neo	new	neoclassical
27.	non	not connected with	non-aligned
28.	out	exceeding, external	outlaw
29.	over	outer, too much	overall
30.	photo	related to light	photosynthesis
31.	poly	many	polyester
32.	post	after	post-war
33.	pro	forward, in advance, favoring	project
34.	pseudo	false	pseudoscience
35.	re	again, back, down	renewable
36.	semi	half, partly	semitone
37.	sub	under, low, nearly	subordinate
38.	super	more than, above	superhuman
39.	sur	over and above	surveillance
40.	tele	distant	television
41.	trans	across, beyond	transform
42.	tri	three	tricycle
43.	ultra	beyond, extreme	ultraviolet
44.	under	too little, below	underground
45.	uni	one	uniform

Exercise 1-4

1. counteraction, interaction, overreaction, reaction, transaction
2. intercommunication, miscommunication
3. conflation, deflation, inflation, hyperinflation, overinflation, underinflation
4. malfunction, subfunction
5. kilogram, polygram, telegram
6. counterculture, monoculture, pseudoculture, subculture, superculture
7. disinformation, information, misinformation, transformation
8. excess, process, recess
9. autograph, monograph, photograph, polygraph, telegraph
10. induction, production, reduction

Exercise 1-5

Examples will vary, but many of the following suggestions are in the word lists in Appendix A.

	Suffix	Meaning	Example
1.	age	action, condition	suffrage
2.	al	having, pertaining to, like	visual
3.	acy / cy	state, quality	supremacy
4.	an	agent or performer	publican
5.	ance / ence	state of being	transcendance
6.	ant / ent	agent or performer	resident

Suffix	Meaning	Example
7. er / or	agent or performer	advisor
8. ary / ery / ory / ry	place where	library, laboratory
9. dom	domain, condition	fiefdom
10. ian	pertaining to	librarian
11. ic / ics	pertaining to	specific, politics
12. ism	condition of, belief/practice	ecotourism
13. ist / yst	person who	analyst, elitist
14. ite	product, part	meteorite
15. itis	inflammation (*med.*)	tonsilitis
16. ity / ty / y	state, quality	authority
17. ive	quality, result, relating to	passive
18. ment	action, state of being	accomplishment, impairment
19. ness	state of being, condition	awareness
20. ology	study of	biology
21. oma	growth (*med.*)	hematoma
22. ship	state of being, condition	internship
23. sis	action, result	analysis
24. sion / tion / ation	the act of	administration
25. ure	pertaining to	tenure

Exercise 1-6

1. artist
2. commencement
3. revolution
4. Christianity
5. restriction
6. constituent, constitution
7. individuality, individualism, individualist
8. environmentalist, environmentalism
9. interpretation
10. illegality
11. election, elective
12. occurrence
13. computer, computation
14. availability
15. wisdom
16. appendicitis
17. consequence
18. injury
19. participant, participation
20. slavery
21. goodness
22. kinship
23. closure
24. obstetrician
25. resident, residence
26. security
27. emphasis
28. publisher, publication
29. adequacy
30. commitment

Exercise 1-7

1. The report <u>unleashed</u> a controversy concerning the future of the planet.
2. Even identical twins with the same genetic makeup <u>are</u> distinct in their thoughts, feelings, and behavior.
3. The majority of people <u>have</u> always <u>lived</u> simply, and most of humanity still <u>struggles</u> on a daily basis <u>to eke out</u> a meager existence under dire circumstances.
4. Remote-controlled robots <u>are</u> indispensable in space and underwater exploration, military reconnaissance, and search-and-rescue operations.
5. At the Stanford Research Institute in California, a team of researchers <u>programmed</u> a small adult-sized robot named Shakey <u>to sense</u> colored blocks and wedges with an onboard camera, and <u>to push</u> them around a carefully constructed set of rooms.

Exercise 1-8

Answers will vary, but some suggestions follow.

1. delivered
2. registered / conferred
3. found / graduated
4. concerned
5. indicates / is absorbed / determines / divide

Exercise 1-9

Examples will vary, but many of the following suggestions are in the word lists in Appendix A.

	Prefix	Meaning	Examples
1.	be	having, covered with, cause	bedevil
2.	co	together with	cohabit
3.	con	together with	conform
4.	de	do the opposite of	depress
5.	dis	reverse, reduce, remove	disenfranchise
6.	e / ex	away, out	emit, expose
7.	fore	earlier, before	forecast
8.	in	into, on, near, toward	induce
9.	inter	between, among	intervene
10.	mis	bad, wrong	misbehave
11.	out	surpassing, exceeding, external	outlaw
12.	over	too much	overbear
13.	pre	before	precede
14.	pro	before, forward, for	promote
15.	re	again, back	recover
16.	sub	under, lower	subordinate
17.	trans	across, beyond	transmit
18.	under	too little	undervalue

Exercise 1-10

1. interact, overact, react, transact
2. concur, incur, recur
3. deduce, induce, produce, reduce
4. conduct, deduct, induct
5. conform, deform, inform, reform, transform
6. confer, defer, infer, prefer, refer
7. confuse, defuse, infuse, refuse
8. describe, inscribe, proscribe, transcribe
9. consist, desist, insist, resist
10. construct, instruct

Exercise 1-11

Examples will vary, but many of the following suggestions are in the word lists in Appendix A.

	Suffix	Meaning	Examples
1.	ate	cause, make	allocate
2.	en	make	lessen
3.	er / or	action	encounter, factor
4.	esce	change, become	coalesce
5.	ify / fy	cause, make	diversify
6.	ise / ize	cause, make	stabilize

Exercise 1-12

1. revolutionize
2. shorten
3. publicize
4. simplify
5. unionize
6. violate
7. minimalize
8. visualize
9. anticipate
10. moisten

Exercise 1-13

1. The <u>recent</u> report unleashed a <u>major</u> controversy concerning the future of the planet.
2. Even <u>identical</u> twins with the <u>same genetic</u> makeup are <u>distinct</u> in their thoughts, feelings, and behavior.
3. The <u>vast</u> majority of people have <u>always</u> lived <u>simply</u>, and most of humanity <u>still</u> struggles on a <u>daily</u> basis to eke out a <u>meager</u> existence under <u>dire</u> circumstances.
4. <u>Remote-controlled</u> robots are <u>indispensable</u> in space and underwater exploration, <u>military</u> reconnaissance, and search-and-rescue operations.
5. At the Stanford Research Institute in California, a <u>reputable</u> team of researchers programmed a <u>small adult-sized</u> robot named Shakey to sense <u>colored</u> blocks and wedges with an <u>onboard</u> camera, and to push them around a <u>carefully constructed</u> set of rooms.

Exercise 1-14

Answers will vary, but some suggestions follow.

1. tired, nervously, recorded
2. dire, mindless, environmentally conscious, excessive, harmful, nonrenewable, overall
3. free, renewable, available, plentiful, closest
4. efficient, basic, significant
5. light, compact, fuel-efficient, automatically

Exercise 1-15

Examples will vary, but many of the following suggestions come from the word lists in Appendix A.

Suffix	Meaning	Examples
1. able / ible	worth, ability	compatible
2. al / ial / ical	quality, relation	conventional
3. ant / ent / ient	kind of agent, indication	inherent
4. ar / ary / ory	resembling, related to	preliminary
5. ate	state	illiterate
6. ed	—	tired
7. en	made of	leaden
8. er	comparative	colder
9. est	superlative	largest
10. ful	marked by, full of, tending to	remorseful
11. ic	quality, in the style of	satiric
12. ile	capability, susceptibility, liability, aptitude	mobile
13. ish	having the character of, almost	peckish
14. ive / ative / itive	having the quality of, relating to	qualitative
15. less	without, missing	penniless
16. ose	having the quality of, relating to	morose
17. ous / eous / ose / ious	having the quality of, relating to	obvious
18. y	marked by, having	temporary

Exercise 1-16

1. horrible
2. revolutionary
3. illusory
4. imaginary, imaginative
5. ceremonious, ceremonial
6. boorish
7. penniless
8. contemptuous, contemptible
9. greedy
10. fictitious, fictional
11. sensual, sensuous
12. comical
13. dramatic
14. creative
15. spatial, spacious
16. identifiable
17. economic, economical
18. nauseous
19. romantic
20. infantile

Exercise 1-17

Examples will vary, but some suggestions follow.

	Suffix	Meaning	Examples
1.	fold	in the manner of, marked by	ninefold
2.	ly	in the manner of	initially
3.	ward	in the manner of	backward
4.	wise	in the manner of	healthwise

Exercise 1-18

1. luxurious (adj.)
2. destinations (n.)
3. has shrunk (v.)
4. exotic (adj.)
5. dramatically (adv.)
6. to travel (v.)
7. affordable (adj.)
8. immersion (n.)
9. to dream (v.)
10. globetrotters (n.)
11. possible (adj.)
12. experiences (n.)
13. travel agency (n.)
14. fastest (adv.)
15. cheaper (adv.).

Exercise 1-19

		Noun	Verb	Adjective/adverb
1.	achieve (v.)	achievement, achiever	achieve	achievable
2.	incorrigible (adj.)	incorrigibility	—	incorrigibly
3.	innovation (n.)	innovation, innovator	innovate	innovative/ly
4.	acquire (v.)	acquisition	acquire	acquisitive/ly
5.	perceive (v.)	perception	perceive	perceptive/ly, perceptual/ly, perceptible/ly
6.	research (n./v.)	research	research	—
7.	rigid (adj.)	rigidity	rigidify	rigid, rigidly
8.	secure (adj./v.)	security	secure	secure, securely
9.	induce (v.)	inducement	induce	inducible
10.	conversion (n.)	conversion	convert	convertible
11.	consent (n./v.)	consent	consent	consensual
12.	utilize (v.)	utilization, utility	utilize	utilitarian, utility
13.	deviate (v.)	deviation, deviance, deviancy	deviate	deviant
14.	stimulate (v.)	stimulation, stimulant, stimulus	stimulate	stimulating
15.	proliferate (v.)	proliferation	proliferate	prolific
16.	venerable (adj.)	veneration	venerate	venerable
17.	procrastinate (v.)	procrastination, procrastinator	procrastinate	—
18.	mediocre (adj.)	mediocrity	—	mediocre
19.	aggression (n.)	aggression, aggressor	—	aggressive/ly
20.	hypothesis (n.)	hypothesis	hypothesize	hypothetical
21.	devious (adj.)	deviousness	—	deviously
22.	arbitrate (v.)	arbitration, arbitrator, arbiter, arbitrage	arbitrate	arbitrary
23.	condolence (n.)	condolence	condole	—
24.	exploit (n./v.)	exploit, exploitation, exploiter	exploit	exploitable, exploitive, exploitative
25.	justifiable (adj.)	justification, justifiability, justifier	justify	justifiable/ly

Exercise 1-20

1. c		**16.** c	
2. b		**17.** b	
3. a		**18.** c	
4. b		**19.** b	
5. c		**20.** c	
6. a		**21.** c	
7. c		**22.** a	
8. a		**23.** a	
9. a		**24.** c	
10. b		**25.** b	
11. c		**26.** c	
12. a		**27.** c	
13. b		**28.** b	
14. a		**29.** a	
15. b		**30.** c	

Exercise 2-2

		Part of speech	**Definition**
1.	vast	adj.	of very great extent or quantity
	Word family:	vastness (n.), vastly (adv.),	
2.	reconstruction	noun	something that has been constructed again
	Word family:	reconstruct (v.), reconstructive (adj.)	
3.	anatomical	adj.	referring to the structure of the body
	Word family:	anatomy (n.), anatomist (n.), anatomize (v.)	
4.	resolution	noun	degree of detail visible in a photographic image
	Word family:	resolve (v.)	
5.	detect	verb	notice a slight detail
	Word family:	detection (n.), detectable (adj.)	
6.	precision	noun	the quality or fact of being exact
	Word family:	precise (adj.)	
7.	intervention	noun	action taken to improve a medical disorder
	Word family:	intervene (v.), intervener (n.), interventional (adj.)	
8.	sophisticated	adj.	highly developed and complex
	Word family:	sophisticate (n.), sophistication (n.)	
9.	display	noun	an electronic device for showing data
	Word family:	display (v.)	
10.	monitor	noun	a display screen
	Word family:	monitor (v.)	
11.	analyze	verb	examine something in detail to explain it
	Word family:	analysis (n.), analyst (n.), analytical (adj.)	
12.	visualization	noun	process of forming an image in the mind
	Word family:	visualize (v.), visual (adj.)	
13.	integrate	verb	combine to form a whole
	Word family:	integration (n.), integral (adj.), integrative (adj.)	
14.	enable	verb	make possible
	Word family:	enablement (n.), enabler (n.), enabled (adj.)	
15.	critical	adj.	at a point of danger or crisis
	Word family:	none	
16.	ultimate	adj.	final
	Word family:	ultimate (n.), ultimatum (n.), ultimately (adv.)	
17.	fundamental	adj.	of central importance
	Word family:	fundamental (n.), fundamentalism (n.)	

(continued)

	Part of speech	Definition
18. eradication	noun	complete removal or destruction
Word family:	eradicator (n.), eradicate (v.)	
19. defect	noun	fault or imperfection
Word family:	defectiveness (n.), defective (n.)	
20. afflict	verb	cause pain or trouble to
Word family:	affliction (n.)	
21. available	adj.	able to be used or obtained
Word family:	availability (n.)	
22. profile	noun	an outline of something
Word family:	profiling (n.), profile (v.)	
23. determine	verb	establish something by calculation
Word family:	determinant (n.), determinable (adj.)	
24. diagnosis	noun	the identification of the nature of an illness
Word family:	diagnose (v.), diagnostic (adj.)	
25. focus	noun	center of interest or attention
Word family:	focus (v.), focal (adj.), focused (adj.)	
26. prevent	verb	stop something from happening
Word family:	prevention (n.), preventable (adj.) , preventative (adj.), preventive (adj.)	
27. sample	noun	a specimen taken for testing or analysis
Word family:	sample (v.)	
28. transfer	verb	move from one place to another
Word family:	transfer (n.), transference (n.), transferral (n.), transferable (adj.)	
29. predict	verb	state that an event will happen
Word family:	prediction (n.), predictor (n.), predictable (adj.), predictive (adj.)	
30. factor	noun	a circumstance that contributes to a result
Word family:	factorial (n), factorize (n.), factor (v.)	

Exercise 2-3

1. a
2. c
3. b
4. b
5. a

6. a
7. d
8. b
9. a
10. a

Exercise 2-4

1. accommodate (v.); **lodge**: house, put up, billet, board; **hold**: take, have room for, sleep, seat; **help**: assist, oblige, cater for, fit in with, satisfy

2. bias (n.); **prejudice**: partiality, partisanship, favoritism, unfairness, one-sidedness, bigotry, intolerance, discrimination, a jaundiced eye, leaning, tendency, inclination, predilection; **diagonal**: cross, slant, angle

3. mutual (adj.); **reciprocal**: reciprocated, requited, returned, common, joint, shared

4. enhance (v.); **increase**: add to, intensify, heighten, amplify, magnify, inflate, strengthen, build up, supplement, augment, boot, raise, lift, elevate, exalt, improve, enrich, complement

5. predominant (adj.); **main**: chief, principal, most important, primary, prime, central, leading, foremost, key, paramount, number one; **controlling**: dominant, predominating, more/most powerful, preeminent

6. voluntary (adj.); **optional**: discretionary, elective, noncompulsory, volitional; **unpaid**: unsalaried, for free, without charge, for nothing, honorary

7. subsidy (n.); **grant**: allowance, contribution, handout, backing, support, sponsorship, finance, funding

8. offset (v.); **counterbalance**: balance (out), cancel (out), even up/out, counteract, countervail, neutralize, compensate for, make up for

9. discriminate (v.); **differentiate**: distinguish, draw a distinction, tell the difference, tell apart, separate; **be biased**: be prejudiced, treat differently/unfairly, put at a disadvantage, pick on

10. radical (adj.); **thorough**; complete, total, comprehensive, exhaustive, sweeping, far-reaching, wide-ranging, extensive, profound, major, stringent, rigorous; **fundamental**: basic, organic, constitutive; **revolutionary**: progressive, reformist, revisionist, extreme, fanatical, militant, diehard

Exercise 2-5

1. c (n.)
2. e (v.)
3. i (v.)
4. f (adj.)
5. h (v.)
6. a (adj.)
7. j (v.)
8. d (adj.)
9. g (adj.)
10. b (n.)
11. o (n.)
12. k (adj.)
13. t (v.)
14. m (n.)
15. r (v.)
16. s (n.)
17. l (adj.)
18. p (v.)
19. q (v.)
20. n (n.)

Exercise 2-6

1. c (v.)
2. a (adj.)
3. a (v.)
4. c (v.)
5. b (v.)
6. c (n.)
7. b (n.)
8. a (v.)
9. b (n.)
10. c (adj.)
11. a (adj.)
12. a (v.)
13. b (n.)
14. c (v.)
15. a (v.)

Exercise 2-7

1. a
2. d
3. c
4. a
5. b
6. c
7. b
8. d
9. a
10. b
11. c
12. b
13. a
14. c
15. a
16. d
17. a
18. b
19. d
20. c

Exercise 2-8

1. approximately
2. profitable
3. attracted
4. famous
5. ran into
6. prospective
7. embarked on
8. voyages
9. sign
10. stimulates
11. resistance
12. sustenance
13. vital
14. adaptability
15. total
16. came from
17. set up
18. bought and sold
19. help
20. shipping

Exercise 2-9

1. d		**11.** j	
2. i		**12.** h	
3. j		**13.** d	
4. b		**14.** a	
5. f		**15.** c	
6. a		**16.** g	
7. c		**17.** b	
8. e		**18.** f	
9. g		**19.** i	
10. h		**20.** e	

Exercise 2-10

1. S, A		**16.** S, A	
2. A, S		**17.** S, A	
3. A, S		**18.** A, S	
4. S, A		**19.** S, A	
5. S, A		**20.** S, A	
6. A, S		**21.** A, S	
7. A, S		**22.** A, S	
8. A, S		**23.** S, A	
9. A, S		**24.** S, A	
10. S, A		**25.** A, S	
11. S, A		**26.** S, A	
12. A, S		**27.** A, S	
13. S, A		**28.** A, S	
14. A, S		**29.** S, A	
15. S, A		**30.** A, S	

Exercise 3-1

TEXT A

The responsibility for <u>city management</u> lies with municipal governments that derive <u>revenue</u> from <u>service fees and property taxes</u>. To build and maintain infrastructure, cities also depend on federal and state or provincial government <u>payment transfers</u>. / For several years now federal and state governments with <u>high debt loads</u> have offloaded more responsibilities onto already <u>cash-strapped</u> municipalities without providing the <u>necessary financial support</u>. / In addition to <u>funding</u>, city governments need a <u>clear vision</u> for the future and innovative public administrators who can see that vision through. Unfortunately elected public officials are more often bogged down in <u>crisis management</u> and Band-Aid solutions that they hope will get them reelected. / In the end, demands on <u>failing services</u> increase, an <u>outdated infrastructure</u> deteriorates, and <u>poverty</u> spirals downward into <u>crime and despair</u>.

1. Main idea: the financial problems of cities
2. Words related to main idea: city management, revenue, fees, taxes, payment, debt, cash, financial, funding, clear vision, crisis management, failing services, outdated infrastructure, poverty, crime and despair
3. Purpose of text: to explain the cause and effect of the problem

TEXT B

From summer to fall, <u>hurricanes</u>—also called <u>typhoons</u> or tropical <u>cyclones</u>—form when hot air, often from the Sahara Desert, races over the Atlantic Ocean. As these <u>columns of hot air</u> spin, they <u>pick up moisture</u> and <u>attract strong winds</u> that bend as <u>the storm travels.</u> / At the center of the <u>rotating storm</u> is <u>the eye</u>, a deceptively calm area of low pressure that can stretch from 2 miles to 200 miles in diameter. Encircling the eye is the <u>eye wall</u>, the most intense part of the storm. Most hurricanes die at sea, but if they are sufficiently fueled with moisture and <u>driven by tremendous winds</u>, <u>all hell breaks loose</u> when they hit land. / In August 2005, <u>Hurricane Katrina</u>, the <u>worst Atlantic</u> <u>hurricane on record</u>, <u>roared</u> from the Bahamas toward Louisiana with winds up to 175 miles per hour and <u>laid waste to the city of New Orleans</u>. More than 1,800 <u>people were killed</u> and <u>property damage</u> was estimated at more than $81 billion.

1. Main idea: the destructive power of hurricanes
2. Words related to main idea: typhoons, cyclones, columns of hot air, moisture, strong winds, storm, eye, tremendous winds, hell, worst on record, roared, laid waste, killed, property damage
3. Purpose of text: to describe hurricanes and their destructive effects

Exercise 3-2

Consult a dictionary for the definitions and compare your answers.

1. Clue: the speaker nodded. People generally nod to let someone know that they have heard or seen them.
2. Clue: paper clip. Papers clips are used to hold two pieces of paper together.
3. Clue: 9:00. If a class finishes at 11:10, it must begin at 9:00.
4. Clue: 4,250 athletes from 164 countries. Athletes take part in the Olympics.
5. Clue: to build vocabulary and to increase your chances of achieving a high score in the TOEFL® test. These are the reasons you use this book.
6. Clue: three policemen and handcuffs. No one can put handcuffs on someone who is free to move around or fight back.
7. Clue: Monster Mash theme. Monsters are extremely ugly.
8. Clue: high income, prestigious profession. Only a select few belong to this category.
9. Clue: $25,000. People who help the police find a dangerous criminal generally receive money for the information.
10. Clue: older. Beside the father, the only other people in the family are brothers and sisters.

Exercise 3-3

Consult a dictionary to check your definition.

1. Clue: "meets the needs of the present without compromising the ability of future generations to meet their needs."
2. Clue: keeper, who ensures that participants show respect for each other and follow the guidelines.
3. Clue: all those nonessential things, patterns, habits, and ideas that take control of our lives and distract us from what is really important.
4. Clue: money would go to developing cures for genetic diseases. The government decides what to do with its money and who gets how much.
5. Clue: a free and conscious choice. A voluntary choice is one that a person makes on his or her own without influence or pressure.

Exercise 3-4

Consult a dictionary to check your definition.

1. Synonym: environmental tourism
   Clue: "green" and environmental protection
2. Synonym: go beyond
   Clue: 70 percent
3. Synonym: worsen
   Clue: not expected to survive
4. Synonym: wounded
   Clue: bomb attack
5. Synonym: important
   Clue: key component

Exercise 3-5

Consult a dictionary to check your definition.

1. Examples: fighting crime syndicates, defeating evil megalomaniacs. challenging alien forces
2. Examples: an eagle's feather, a stone or crystal, a figure
3. Examples: getting a well-paid job
4. Examples: racial, sexual, religious, economic
5. Examples: collection of books, newspapers, magazines, journals, e-resources, a staff of research librarians

Exercise 3-6

Consult a dictionary to check your definition.

1. Clue: contrast / flexible
2. Clue: comparison / suitable
3. Clue: comparison / huge
4. Clue: contrast / limited
5. Clue: comparison / alter

Exercise 3-7

Consult a dictionary to check your definition.

1. Context clue: examples / fingerprints, hair, fibers, blood, and other DNA samples
2. Context clue: synonym / copied
3. Context clue: restatement / no one can come back to life to tell their tale
4. Context clue: definition / harm or kill birds, insects, butterflies, bees, and other animals, and threaten biodiversity
5. Context clue: contrast / women are emotional
6. Context clue: general knowledge / only maps and a compass
7. Context clue: example / *Toy Story 2* and *Toy Story 3*
8. Context clue: synonym / young athlete's achievements
9. Context clue: general knowledge / the story of the *Titanic* is common knowledge
10. Context clue: example / service fees and property taxes
11. Context clue: comparison / requirements
12. Context clue: contrast / allowed
13. Context clue: general knowledge / without academic records an application will not be accepted
14. Context clue: example / such as vitamins and minerals
15. Context clue: definition / very small amounts

Exercise 3-8

1. a; clue: urban dwellers
2. c; clue: limited
3. b; clue: such as repetition, pauses, and increased volume
4. a; clue: historical reports, experiments, and extensive interviews and surveys
5. d; clue: higher yields and prevent hunger
6. d; clue: was still raging in the media
7. c; clue: death, war, loss
8. c; clue: global financial crisis
9. b; clue: the volatility of oil prices
10. d; clue: human error and negligence

Exercise 4-1

Bananas <u>do not grow on a tree</u>, as most people would imagine, <u>but on a</u> sturdy <u>plant that can</u> reach 6 to 7.6 meters in height <u>with</u> large <u>leaves up to a</u> 0.6 meter <u>wide and</u> 2.75 meters <u>long</u>. In <u>fact the</u> banana <u>plant</u>, *Musa acuminata*, <u>is the</u> world's largest perennial herb. Cultivation <u>is</u> best suited <u>to</u> tropical and subtropical areas <u>with</u> ample <u>water</u>, rich soil, <u>and good</u> drainage. <u>Because</u> bananas <u>have</u> been cultivated <u>to</u> become <u>seedless</u>, commercially grown bananas <u>are</u> propagated <u>through</u> division, <u>a process of</u> separating offshoots <u>or</u> "pups" <u>from the mother plant</u>.

Exercise 4-2

Consult a dictionary for the definitions.

1. adjustment: n.
2. approval: n.
3. committee: n.
4. competition: n.
5. conscious: adj.
6. damage: n./v.
7. development: n.
8. existence: n.
9. harmony: n.
10. impulse: n.
11. measure: n./v.
12. probable: adj.
13. request: n./v.
14. responsible: adj.
15. substance: n.
16. unit: n.
17. vessel: n.

Exercise 4-3

1. measure
2. existence
3. committee
4. approval
5. development
6. conscious
7. substance
8. harmony
9. vessels
10. request
11. probable
12. responsible
13. damage
14. adjustment
15. competition
16. units
17. impulse

Exercise 4-4

TEXT A

<u>Although</u> Superman started out as an evil character, the second version was a savior in the tradition of Moses, Samson, or Hercules. <u>This time</u> he used his superpowers to fight for truth, justice, <u>and</u> the American way of life. <u>In addition</u> he wore his trademark bright blue costume with a red cape and a diamond-shaped **S** emblazoned on his chest. <u>Because</u> Superman's birth father, Jor-El, had sent his infant son, Kal-El, from the doomed planet of Krypton to the safety of Earth in a rocket, he was raised in an orphanage. <u>Later</u> the story changed <u>and</u> Superman was raised by a kind elderly couple, Jonathan <u>and</u> Martha Kent, from Smallville, Kansas. Unaware of his powers until the age of eighteen, the boy grew up as Clark Kent <u>and</u> became a newspaper reporter for the *Daily Planet*. <u>Unlike</u> Superman, Clark Kent was myopic, socially awkward, <u>and</u> meek, <u>but</u> he was also intelligent, hard-working, <u>and</u> decent to the core—the kind of guy no one, including his pretty, feisty, and disdainful co-reporter, Lois Lane, would ever suspect of having superhuman powers.

TEXT B

<u>First of all</u>, a Pixar movie begins with an idea for a story. <u>If</u> the employee with the idea can sell it to the development team, different versions of the story, called treatments, are written in summary form. <u>From there</u> artists draw storyboards that resemble comic book sequences <u>and</u> develop the storyline <u>and</u> its characters. <u>On condition that</u> the story meets the director's approval, the script is written <u>and</u> <u>then</u> employees record the first voices. <u>After that</u> the dialogue is perfected <u>and</u> professional actors are hired to read the parts. <u>Next</u>, the best versions are made into a videotape, <u>or</u> reel, which goes to editing for cleanup. <u>Afterward</u> the art department creates the visuals: characters, set, props, lighting—everything that appears on the movie screen.

Exercise 4-5

1. Nahuatl
2. Middle English
3. Arabic
4. Old English
5. Greek
6. Greek
7. German
8. Greek
9. Italian
10. French
11. Russian
12. Japanese
13. Finnish
14. New Latin
15. Latin American Spanish
16. Swedish
17. Tamil
18. Spanish
19. Persian
20. Hindi

Exercise 4-6

In 1990, the United States National Institutes of Health and the Department of Energy, in collaboration with partners from eighteen countries, embarked on the most ambitious venture to be undertaken since the Manhattan Project to develop the atom bomb or the Apollo project to put a man on the moon: the Human Genome Project. At an estimated cost of $3 billion to complete the task by 2005, leading scientists and researchers in the field of molecular biology set out to identify all 30,000 to 40,000 genes belonging to the human genome and to map the location of three billion bases of DNA; in other words, to write the Book of Life. This definitive resource was meant to lead to the understanding of genetic diseases, the creation of effective pharmaceuticals and medical treatments and the alleviation and prevention of human suffering due to genetically transmitted diseases. In order to serve all mankind and to prevent control by any scientific, corporate, or national interests, all information was to be stored in public electronic databases and made freely and readily accessible to anyone who required it.

Exercise 4-7

BASIC	SIGNAL	INTERNATIONAL	ACADEMIC	USEFUL
death	as	anesthesia	elements	experiences
cases	because	evidence	verified	provide
children	furthermore		(pre)conceived	knowledge
adult	although		notions	fake
color	while		visual	described
roof	later		accurately	observed
hospital	after		located	immobile
short			unconscious	profound
event			confirmed	effect
			validity	testifies
			individuals	religious
			aware	determined
			affected	increased
				concern
				sacrifices
				previous

Exercise 4-8

1. a. affect, b. effect
2. a. heir, b. air, c. err
3. a. aloud, b. allowed
4. a. oral, b. aural
5. a. basis, b. bases
6. a. brake, b. break
7. a. canvas, b. canvass
8. a. capitol, b. capital
9. a. cede, b. seeds
10. a. sent, b. scent, c. cent
11. a. sensor, b. censor
12. a. cite, b. sight, c. site
13. a. cereal, b. serial
14. a. coarse, b. course
15. a. complacent, b. complaisant
16. a. compliments, b. complement
17. a. council, b. counsel
18. a. discreet, b. discrete
19. a. disgust, b. discussed
20. a. draft, b. draught
21. a. earn, b. urn
22. a. illicit, b. elicit
23. a. elude, b. allude
24. a. insight, b. incite
25. a. lesson, b. lessen
26. a. martial, b. marshal
27. a. patience, b. patients
28. a. peddle, b. pedal
29. a. precedents, b. precedence
30. a. principal, b. principle

Exercise 4-9

1. a, b
2. b, a
3. b, a
4. a, b
5. a, b
6. b, a
7. a, b
8. a, b
9. a, b
10. b, a
11. a, b
12. b, a
13. a, b
14. a, b
15. b, a

Exercise 4-10

1. a. activity, b. action
2. a. adverse, b. averse
3. a. advice, b. advise
4. a. alternately, b. alternatively
5. a. amoral, b. immoral
6. a. apprise, b. appraise
7. a. ascend, b. assent
8. a. presumed, b. assume
9. a. avoid, b. prevent
10. a. climatic, b. climactic
11. a. conscientious, b. conscious
12. a. considerate, b. considerable
13. a. continuous, b. continual
14. a. injury, damage, b. harm
15. a. deduct, b. deduce
16. a. defuse, b. diffused
17. a. disinterested, b. uninterested
18. a. extinct, b. distinct
19. a. economic, b. economical
20. a. immigration, b. emigration
21. a. omit, b. emit
22. a. insure, b. ensure
23. a. invoke, b. evokes
24. a. fictitious, b. fictional
25. a. illusion, b. allusion
26. a. immanent, b. imminent, c. eminent
27. a. implying, b. infer
28. a. permission, b. permit
29. a. proceed, b. precedes
30. a. prescribed, b. proscribed
31. priceless, worthless
32. a. respectful, b. respectable, c. respective
33. a. seceded, b. succeed
34. a. subjective, b. objective
35. treats, curing

Exercise 4-11

1. b, c, a
2. c, a, b
3. c, a, b
4. a, c, b
5. c, b, a
6. c, a, b

7. a, c, b	**19.** a, b, c
8. b, c, a	**20.** c, b, a
9. a, c, b	**21.** b, c, a
10. b, c, a	**22.** b, a, c
11. b, a, c	**23.** a, c, b
12. a, b, c	**24.** b, a, c
13. c, a, b	**25.** c, a, b
14. c, a, b	**26.** c, b, a
15. b, a, c	**27.** a, c, b
16. b, a, c	**28.** b, a, c
17. a, c, b	**29.** a, b, c
18. b, c, a	**30.** c, a, b

Exercise 5-1

Consult a dictionary for the answers.

Exercise 5-2

Consult a dictionary for the definition, word families, and synonyms/antonyms. Collocations are listed here. Suggested answers follow.

1. passive (adj.)
   nouns: role, attitude
   adverbs: extremely, very, fairly, relatively
   verbs: be, seem, become, remain
2. principle (n.)
   adjectives: high, guiding, moral, basic, fundamental, essential
   verbs: establish, formulate, lay down, adhere to, stick to
   phrases: a matter of principle, against my principles
3. incorporate (v.)
   nouns: data, facts, business, conditions
   adverbs: fully, largely, properly, gradually, eventually
4. maximize (v.)
   adverbs: fully, completely
   phrases: to the full extent, to one's advantage
5. enhance (v.)
   adverbs: considerably, dramatically, enormously, significantly, substantially
   verbs: can, be able to, help to, serve to, be designed, seek to
6. absorb (v.)
   adverbs: quickly, easily, readily, completely, gradually
   phrase: be absorbed into
7. consider (v.)
   adverbs: carefully, thoroughly, seriously
   preposition: for
8. sloping (adj.)
   adverbs: steeply, gently, gradually, upward, downward
   prepositions: toward, to

Exercise 5-3

Consult a dictionary for the answers.

Exercise 5-4

	Noun	Adjective/adverb	Verb
1.	**objective**/objectivity	objective	objectify
2.	radical/radicalism	**radical**	radicalize
3.	violation/violator	violent	**violate**
4.	**margin**	marginal	marginalize
5.	externals/externalization	**external**	externalize
6.	exploitation/exploit/exploiter	exploitable	**exploit**
7.	**insight**	insightful	—
8.	approximation	**approximate**	approximate
9.	conception	conceivable	**conceive**
10.	**contamination**/contaminant	—	contaminate

Noun	Adjective/adverb	Verb
11. spontaneity	**spontaneous**	—
12. dispute/disputant	disputable	**dispute**
13. **explosion**/explosive	explosive	explode
14. relation/relativity	**relative**	relate
15. endurance	endurable	**endure**

Exercise 5-5

Suggested answers follow.

1. Mr. and Mrs. Brockhurst belong to an	**elite**	golf and country club.
Harvard is considered an	**elite**	university.
2. The protesters	**are occupying**	the executive offices.
Furniture	**occupies**	most of the space in a bedroom.
3. This year three first-year classes are scheduled to run	**parallel**	to each other.
Only	**parallel**	parking is allowed on this street.
4. I don't know how to get myself out of this	**predicament.**	
Sergio forgot to renew his student visa. What a	**predicament!**	
5. At university you have to learn how to set your	**priorities.**	
My first	**priority**	is to be happy and healthy.

Exercise 6-1

Sentences will vary according to what works for you. For example, a sentence for 1. could be, "In golf, the **goal** is to put the ball in the **hole**." For 2. it could be, "How funny to pose with a rose clenched in your teeth."

1. goal, (h) hole
2. pose, (d) rose
3. brief, (f) chief
4. code, (c) toad
5. core, (j) bore
6. grant, (i) ant
7. foul, (a) towel
8. quote, (g) goat
9. levy, (b) heavy
10. feature, (e) teacher

Exercise 6-2

Consult a dictionary for definitions. Images will vary, but some suggestions follow.

1. terminate: a guillotine.
2. category: a movie review or magazine.
3. rigid: a steel bar
4. investigate: a magnifying glass
5. migrate: a flock of birds flying south
6. virtual: a scene from a video game
7. malicious: an evil face
8. speculate: the stock market
9. responsible: a parent with small children
10. pattern: wallpaper

Exercise 6-3

Images will vary, but some suggestions follow.

1. compatible: a married couple
2. reluctance: someone being arrested
3. voluntary: a class of children with their hands up
4. precise: a surgeon with a scalpel
5. comprise: a list of ingredients on a package of food
6. prohibit: a no-smoking sign
7. deny: a boy trying to kiss a girl who's turning her head away with a look of disgust
8. lethal: a nuclear mushroom cloud
9. immaculate: the Virgin Mary
10. explore: Christopher Columbus
11. surveillance: video cameras in the street
12. assimilate: a melting pot
13. catastrophic: the aftermath of a tsunami
14. despise: an evil villain
15. potent: a flask with a chemical mixture

Exercise 6-4

Possible answers follow.

1. crime: murder, police, robbers, theft, prison, guilty, victim, innocent, trial, judge, lawyer, punishment, jail, arrest, break-in, assault, prevention
2. genetics: chromosomes, traits, inherited, modification, personality, children, parents, disease, biology, evolution, manipulation, DNA fingerprinting
3. advertising: money, television spots, creative, Coca-Cola, newspapers, billboards, slogans, catchy music, selling, promotion, annoying
4. jobs: professions, trades, menial, wages, promotion, demanding, teacher, income, training, employment, employer
5. money: dollars, investment, spend, credit cards, coins, currency, evil, banks, debt, cash, lottery, rich, poor, stock market, savings account, checks, loans, greed

Exercise 6-5

Suggested subcategories:

1. Government: Federal, Provincial/state, Municipal
2. Personality: Introvert, Extrovert, Optimist, Pessimist, Active, Passive
3. Human rights: Political, Social, Personal, Sexual, Employment
4. Communications: Spoken, Written, Electronic, Telecommunications

Exercise 6-6

Answers will vary.

Exercise 6-7

Suggested answers:

1. attitude (n.)
    adj.: favorable, positive, wrong
    verb: have, adopt, change
    prep.: about, to
2. civil (adj.)
    adv.: extremely, remarkably, very
    verb: be, become
    prep.: to
3. confirm (v.)
    adv.: merely, only, officially
    verb: be able to/can/could, appear to, seem to, tend to
4. define (v.)
    adv.: accurately, carefully, correctly, exactly, precisely, legally
    adj. + infinitive: easy to, difficult/impossible to
    prep.: in terms of
5. erode (v.)
    adv.: badly, deeply, seriously, gradually, slowly, steadily
6. fee (n.)
    noun: user, admission, entrance, tuition, handling
    adj.: exorbitant, high, substantial, flat, set, standard, hourly
    verb: charge, impose, cover, include
    prep.: for
7. implement (n./v.)
    adv.: fully, properly, widely, successfully
    verb: agree to, decide to, try to, fail to
8. index (n./v.)
    adj.: complete, general, alphabetical, cost-of-living, Dow Jones
    verb: use, compile, create, calculate, publish
9. mechanism (n.)
    noun: defense, avoidance, control, escape, survival
    adj.: firing, locking, steering, trigger, effective, underlying
    verb: operate, work
10. network (n./v.)
    noun: communications, computer, transportation, television
    adj.: extensive, large, complex, elaborate, global
    verb: build up, create, establish, form
11. option (n./v.)
    adj.: available, possible, viable, attractive
    verb: choose, exercise, take, look at
    phrase: keep/leave options open
12. phenomenon (n.)
    adj.: common, isolated, natural, strange, cultural, historical
    verb: emerge, occur

13. range (n./v.)
    adj.: broad, wide, whole, complete
    verb: cover, encompass, feature, include
    prep.: across a/the, in a/the, outside/within a, of
14. schedule (n./v.)
    noun: business, production, work, travel, flight
    adj.: daily, weekly, heavy, hectic, tight, strict
    verb: work out, set, arrange, run, stick to, meet
    prep.: on, behind

15. target (n./v.)
    noun: group, audience, market, date, figure, price
    adj.: likely, possible, potential, prime, military
    verb: aim at, attack, reach, hit, miss
    prep.: off

Exercise 6-8

1. annual
2. pursue
3. release
4. uniform
5. portion
6. predict
7. deny
8. challenge
9. compromise
10. conclusion

11 rate
12. deteriorate
13. nutrition
14. pattern
15. approval
16. bureaucratic
17. essential
18. evade
19. accomplishment
20. sacrifice

Exercise 8-1

1. b
2. a
3. a
4. c
5. b

6. c
7. b
8. a
9. b
10. a

Exercise 8-2

1. distinct
2. revise
3. confirmed
4. concept
5. inherent

6. convert
7. conduct
8. contradict
9. demonstrate
10. consider

Exercise 8-3

1. c
2. a

Exercise 8-4

1. a
2. c
3. b
4. a
5. b

6. c
7. c
8. a
9. a
10. b

Exercise 8-5

1. impact
2. attributed
3. significant
4. estimated, excess
5. poses

6. criterion
7. perspective
8. alter
9. evolution

Exercise 8-6

1. d
2. b
3. a

Exercise 8-7

1. c
2. a
3. b
4. b
5. c

6. a
7. b
8. a
9. b
10. c

Exercise 8-8

1. maintain
2. rely
3. indicates
4. conventional
5. consume

6. incidence
7. detect
8. implementation
9. inevitable
10. contrast

Exercise 8-9

1. c
2. a
3. b

Exercise 8-10

1. b
2. c
3. c
4. b
5. a

6. a
7. b
8. c
9. a
10. b

Exercise 8-11

1. prohibited
2. exceeding
3. exclusion, enforced
4. occur
5. established

6. trigger
7. Initially
8 Despite
9. release

Exercise 8-12

1. d
2. a

3. c
4. a

Exercise 8-13

1. a
2. c
3. a
4. b
5. a
6. c
7. b
8. a
9. c
10. b

Exercise 8-14

1. stabilize
2. consumers
3. dramatic
4. credit
5. purchase
6. depression
7. collapses
8. decline
9. obtainable
10. irrational

Exercise 8-15

1. c
2. b
3. a
4. b

Exercise 8-16

1. c
2. b
3. b
4. a
5. c
6. b
7. a
8. b
9. c
10. a

Exercise 8-17

1. priority
2. require
3. amendment
4. assume
5. primary
6. biased
7. promotes
8. linked
9. exhibited
10. transmitted

Exercise 8-18

1. a
2. d
3. b

Exercise 8-19

1. c
2. a
3. b
4. b
5. c
6. a
7. c
8. b
9. a
10. a

Exercise 8-20

1. acquire
2. confined
3. interpret
4. survival

5. funds
6 expand
7. ideology

8. instructions
9. migration
10. undertaking

Exercise 8-21

1. b
2. a

3. b
4. d

Exercise 8-22

1. b
2. a
3. c
4. a
5. c

6. b
7. a
8. b
9. c
10. b

Exercise 8-23

1. empirical
2. abstract
3. adaptation
4. design
5. pursue

6. evidence
7. conceived
8. differentiate
9. conclude
10. logic

Exercise 8-24

1. d
2. c

3. a
4. b

Exercise 8-25

1. c
2. b
3. a
4. b
5. c

6. a
7. b
8. a
9. c
10. b

Exercise 8-26

1. foundation
2. consists
3. Psychological
4. publish
5. coincides

6. contribute
7. comprised
8. hence
9. reinforce
10. Presumably

Exercise 8-27

1. b
2. a

3. d
4. a

Exercise 8-28

1. b
2. b

3. c
4. a

5. a

6. c

7. b

8. c

9. c

10. a

Exercise 8-29

1. sought

2. construct

3. alternate

4. anticipating

5. prospects

6. project

7. terminate

8. succession

9. rejected

10. eliminate

Exercise 8-30

1. d

2. a

3. b

4. b

Exercise 9-1

1. j

2. c

3. h

4. f

5. i

6. d

7. a

8. b

9. e

10. g

Exercise 9-2

1. discharged

2. represses

3. flawed

4. profound

5. autonomy

6. collaborate

7. contentious

8. intrigue

9. volatile

10. speculative

Exercise 9-3

Answers will vary.

Exercise 9-4

1. i

2. e

3. j

4. a

5. f

6. c

7. d

8. g

9. h

10. b

Exercise 9-5

1. spearheading

2. escalate

3. emanates

4. assert

5. signaled

6. exploded

7. supremacy

8. burgeoned

9. launched

10. ups the ante

Exercise 9-6

Answers will vary.

Exercise 9-7

1. e
2. j
3. b
4. i
5. f

6. h
7. d
8. g
9. a
10. c

Exercise 9-8

1. rupture
2. subsided
3. reduce
4. ordeal
5. averted

6. installation
7. unprecedented
8. sanitation
9. incinerated
10. smoldering

Exercise 9-9

Answers will vary.

Exercise 9-10

1. g
2. a
3. e
4. i
5. j

6. d
7. c
8. b
9. f
10. h

Exercise 9-11

1. chivalry
2. deluded
3. ventured
4. incarceration
5. endure

6. adorn
7. chronicles
8. escapades
9. literary
10. satirizes

Exercise 9-12

Answers will vary.

Exercise 9-13

1. j
2. d
3. g
4. f
5. i

6. h
7. b
8. e
9. a
10. c

Exercise 9-14

1. inspired
2. relinquished
3. lucrative
4. resume
5. factions

6. insurmountable
7. despotic
8. foster
9. retaliated
10. abolitionist

Exercise 9-15

Answers will vary.

Exercise 9-16

1. c
2. f
3. i
4. a
5. j

6. h
7. b
8. e
9. d
10. g

Exercise 9-17

1. inscription
2. full-fledged
3. resourceful
4. emancipation
5. urged

6. contentious
7. perseverance
8. disenfranchised
9. antagonism
10. legacy

Exercise 9-18

Answers will vary.

Exercise 9-19

1. d
2. f
3. a
4. g
5. b

6. i
7. j
8. c
9. e
10. h

Exercise 9-20

1. irresistible
2. sated
3. legendary
4. sensation
5. scintillated

6. catalyst
7. supplanted
8. mania
9. quirky
10. gimmicks

Exercise 9-21

Answers will vary.

Exercise 9-22

1. e
2. h
3. d
4. g
5. i

6. a
7. b
8. j
9. c
10. f

Exercise 9-23

1. dissolute
2. pledge
3. demolition
4. communal
5. capitulated

6. Tyranny
7. Negotiations
8. insanity
9. slated
10. adopted

Exercise 9-24

Answers will vary.

Exercise 9-25

1. i
2. a
3. g
4. j
5. b

6. h
7. d
8. f
9. e
10. c

Exercise 9-26

1. rigorous
2. outlawed
3. dilute
4. potent
5. impetus

6. garnered
7. deprived
8. maneuvering
9. compromise
10. comply

Exercise 9-27

Answers will vary.

Exercise 9-28

1. d
2. i
3. e
4. c
5. g

6. h
7. b
8. a
9. j
10. f

Exercise 9-29

1. impending
2. vulnerable
3. prominent
4. anthem
5. detained

6. patriotic
7. composed
8. dissipated
9. bombarded
10. embarked

Exercise 9-30

Answers will vary.

Exercise 10-1

1. apply
2. application form

3 Registrar's Office
4. admission requirements

5. Notice of Acceptance, or offer of admission
6. tuition fees
7. deadline
8. confirmation
9. register
10. undergraduate
11. enroll

12. required
13. electives
14. degree
15. B.A
16. ace
17. faculty
18. campus

Exercise 10-2

Answers will vary.

Exercise 10-3

1. sophomore
2. freshman
3. orientation
4. Student Union building
5. transit exchange
6. administration building
7. medical insurance
8. scholarship or bursary

9. student visa
10. mandatory
11. Campus Security
12. class schedule
13. cohort
14. semester
15. cafeteria
16. placement test

Exercise 10-4

Instructor: Pat Duncan
Office hours: 3:00–4:30, Monday to Thursday
Basic rules:
- Cell phone use: prohibited in class
- Laptop/tablet use: restricted to note taking and assignments only
- Attendance: regular and punctual
- Behavior in class: respectful, attentive, professional, and appropriate; nondisruptive at all times

Students' responsibilities:
- Must meet the requirements of the course
- Should know what has been covered and assigned
- Should know when assignments are due

Participation:
- Active
- Ask and answer questions during discussions
- Counts one third of 15 percent

Assignments:
- Deadlines: nonnegotiable
- Extension: no extension without documentation
- Emergency or illness: doctor's note or official excuse signed by person of authority

Evaluation:
- Grades: nonnegotiable
- Missed exams and assignments: no extensions or makeup exams

Exercise 10-5

1. in the course syllabus
2. on the overhead
3. Grades and marks are non-negotiable.

Exercise 10-6

1. Assignment
2. thesis statement
3. citations
4. paraphrase
5. summary
6. APA style

7. reference list
8. critical thinking
9. title page
10. formatting
11. double-spaced
12. Font

13. Margins
14. Running head
15. plagiarize

16. fail
17. due

Exercise 10-7

1. handout
2. term paper
3. research paper
4. advance notice
5. counterargument

6. refutation
7. procrastinate
8. time management
9. discretion
10. pop quizzes

Exercise 10-8

Answers will vary.

Exercise 10-9

1. renew
2. fine
3. overdue
4. electronic resources
5. put a request on/reserve
6. in the stacks
7. librarians
8. catalogued
9. digital service
10. abstracts

11. dissertations
12. archival information
13. carrel
14. sign out/check out
15. course reserve
16. call number
17. retrieve
18. on loan
19. reserve it (put it on reserve or hold)
20. collaborative study space

Exercise 10-10

1. turn in
2. class discussions
3. outline
4. worksheet, citations, reference list
5. first draft

6. rhetorical devices
7. stressed out
8. grueling
9. group presentation
10. catch up on

Exercise 10-11

Answers will vary.

Exercise 10-12

1. Examination protocol
2. posted
3. invigilator
4. cheating
5. penalty

6. incomplete
7. transcript
8. deferral
9. punitive measures
10. disciplinary committee

Exercise 10-13

Answers will vary.